THE TECHNIQUE
of
FILM ANIMATION

THE LIBRARY OF
COMMUNICATION TECHNIQUES

THE TECHNIQUE OF

FILM
ANIMATION

Written and compiled by
JOHN HALAS *and* **ROGER MANVELL**

Focal Press · London

Focal/Hastings House · New York

ISBN (excl. USA) 0 240 50900 5
ISBN (USA only) 0 8038 7024 8

First Edition 1959
Second Impression 1963
Third Impression 1966
Second Edition 1968
Fifth Impression 1969
Third Edition 1971
Seventh Impression 1973
Fourth Edition 1976
Ninth Impression 1978

Japanese Edition published by
DAVID PUBLISHING CO. LTD., TOKYO

Spanish Edition published by
EDICIONES OMEGA, S.A., BARCELONA

Reproduced and printed by photolithography and bound in Great Britain at The Pitman Press, Bath

CONTENTS

CONTENTS OF ILLUSTRATIVE SECTIONS

FILMS FOR PUBLIC RELATIONS 173–180

Because cartoon can convey an argument with wit and clarity, it has been extensively used for public relations and propaganda. Some of the best examples of animation come into this category, such as the work of the National Film Board in Canada and John Sutherland in Hollywood. In Britain some of the earliest films of this kind were sponsored by the Government during the War.

THE STORYBOARD 197–208

The technique of the storyboard which shows the visual conception of the future film is variously illustrated by the detailed work of Walt Disney, the bold starkness of John Hubley, and the meticulous elegance of other American and European animators.

INSTRUCTIONAL ANIMATION 241–248

Britain was the main centre for the early development of instructional animation in the pioneer work of Brian Salt, Robert Fairthorne and that of Gaumont-British Instructional. Since the War, animation has been widely used in the technological film, and particularly in films about advanced science in the Soviet Union. The Shell Film Unit in Great Britain has consistently used animation in its technical films for over twenty years.

THE PUPPET FILM 265–272

Puppet animation is almost as old as the animation of the flat figure. A number of different structural materials such as wood, wire, cloth, paper and plastics have been commonly used by various pioneers such as Starevitch, Pal and Alexeieff. The most permanent of the units specializing in this work are to be found in Eastern Europe, and in particular in the Czech studios of the late Trnka, and of Zeman and Pojar.

FILMS OF STILL PAINTINGS AND DRAWINGS 281–284

This is a comparatively new form of animated art, which aims to highlight the artists' original work and to achieve movement through camera mobility. The pioneers in this field include Luciano Emmer of Italy, who has filmed the work of painters of the Renaissance, and Joan and Peter Foldes, whose paintings have been specially created for the camera. This filming alike of established art, such as the drawings of Leonardo da Vinci, and of drawings and paintings originally designed by recognized artists for filming, presents limitless possibilities for the future.

SPECIALIZED FORMS OF ANIMATION 293–300

Much exciting artistic experiment in animation has been of a specialized nature, such as the abstract films of Oscar Fischinger, Len Lye and Norman McLaren, the silhouette films of Lotte Reiniger using cutout figures, and the films of Alexandre Alexeieff using various three-dimensional figures and objects. The impact of computerised animation is shown by several examples of Peter Foldes' latest film, as well as some of Stan Hayward's and Lilian Schwartz's computer graphic experiments.

9

This volume in the Library of Communication Techniques sponsored by the British Film Academy and published by the Focal Press in association with Hastings House, Publishers, New York, is devoted to animation—a specialized technique which has been rapidly expanding in recent years all over the world.

In common with the other books which have so far been published in this series this one does not set out to instruct artists and technicians in the job of animation. This is not a text-book on "how to do it" but an account of "how it is done".

It describes how animation is carried out in Europe and America, and attempts to give some idea of the great scope that this special medium undoubtedly possesses, potentialities which are only just in process of discovery and extend much more widely than the entertainment film. It is part of the purpose of this book to show how cartoon film can serve in almost every normal branch of film-making—entertainment, instruction, advertising, research—as well as develop special arts and functions of its own. Television also has opened up a new and permanent field for the animator, whose work is needed not only for advertising but for entertainment.

The book has been written primarily for all those working or intending to work in animation—both professionals and amateurs—and for those who are concerned in the sponsorship of animated films, either for advertising, entertainment or important specialized uses, such as education.

Finally, this book is addressed to anyone who is interested in the film as an art. For we have tried to show that animation is not the side-show or cul-de-sac in film-making that some people tend to think it.

The challenge to the imagination of the artist presented by film technique, which can give movement to his pictures and add the full range of sound to their impact on an audience, is a considerable one, and painters of the eminence of Picasso have begun to recognize that the artist who is prepared to understand the virtuosities of the film and work closely with the film-maker can reach a public that never enters a picture gallery.

We hope, therefore, that this book will be of use to artists, film-makers (professional and amateur), advertising experts, teachers and instructors, scientists and industrialists, as well as to the general reader who has a special interest in the art and technique of the film.

We would like to acknowledge the advice, help and co-operation we have received from many colleagues, especially those whose contributions are specified in the book. We have also received innumerable drawings and photographs, and the selection we have made from them shows (for the first time, we believe, in any book on the subject), the astonishing range of work that the animated film now represents in the world's studios. We would like to thank all those who have taken so much trouble in response to our requests for illustrations.

INTRODUCTION

EVERYTHING that moves is animated. In particular, everything that moves because it possesses life. All films show movement, so it is true to say that all films are in fact animated; but when a film-maker uses the word "animation" he intends you to understand it in a very specialized sense.

Every film is by its nature a break-down of movement into a series of arrested phases. When Marey "shot" the flight of a bird with his photographic gun in the eighteen-eighties he was in fact producing a pictorial analysis of the bird's movements in a sequence of closely related still pictures. A movie film exposed at normal speed can therefore be said to analyse every second of live action in terms of a given number of successive phases of movement. Project the film at normal speed and the sequence of still photographs reintegrate themselves into the illusion of natural and continuous movement on the screen.

From the earliest days of the cinema it was obvious that the film offered the draughtsman a medium through which he could turn a series of still drawings into what seemed on the screen to be a picture possessing the great quality of motion in time. But it has been left so far almost entirely to the cartoonists to develop, to a sensational degree, the challenging opportunities which the invention of the motion picture has created for the graphic artist. When the film-maker uses the term "animated film" he uses it in the narrow sense of the work of a graphic artist recreating on paper or celluloid separate phases of movement which give the illusion of continuous action when they are projected in sequence on to a screen.

When a painter wants to create the illusion of life and movement in the still picture on his easel, he may try to do so by isolating some momentary attitude which suggests that his subject has been caught in the act of motion. With hand turned, with eye raised, with hair

11

blown and lifted, the still image seems to rest poised on the edge of movement. The *Discobolus* is caught in an act of balance which can only be held for one fraction of a second—it is a momentary phase in the swing of his body. The artist—sculptor or painter—isolates that movement and suggests powerfully through it the before and after of motion. Life stirs in the hovering limbs, in the lips on the point of a smile.

To the film animator such a moment is perhaps but one phase in a series of phases which recreate a second's motion on the screen. He must see all movement in terms of its continuity. As the least imaginative of his exercises, he might take a strip of live-action film and trace from it on to paper the successive phases of its pictorial action, frame by frame. He could then recreate these phases in the series of outlines he requires for a drawn figure; thus, to take an example, the photographed movements of a live ballet dancer can be transferred to the drawn movements of a cartoon fairy.

Though the draughtsman can learn how the movements of real life take place from such an exercise as this, he will in fact be trying to fuse together two wholly divergent worlds—the worlds of actuality and the drawing-board. Though there is still, no doubt, some useful place in normal draughtsmanship and painting for the exactly representational illustration as against a good photograph, there would seem to us to be no argument in favour of an exactly representational animated picture. The process of the artificial recreation of actuality in terms of animated film is so technically laborious that a normal film of a living Sugar Plum Fairy is always to be preferred to an animated replica minutely reconstructed from life.

Animation on the screen has therefore almost always meant some degree of graphic stylization. This has, in fact, been the essence of its challenge as well as part of the fun. The draughtsman who turns to the animated film as his profession will soon realize that he is adopting a difficult and exacting art. He must not only understand the art and technique of the film itself, but he must understand and appreciate the characteristics of movement in the world of nature. He must, in fact, become a specialist in movement. He must appreciate what is characteristic in the motion of men and mice, air and water, machines and dragons.

The animator is continuously studying the vast background of movement with which life surrounds him. This is his blueprint. He is as interested in the motion of an automobile as he is in the movements of a cat. He builds up in his memory a dictionary of motion which is at his disposal whenever he calls upon it. This instinct for motion he combines with his other knowledge, that of film technique itself, for animation is, of course, a branch of film-making, and it must, if it is to be successful, accept and exploit the powers of the motion picture. The essential art of animation, its particular magic in fact, transforms what is essentially static into something essentially alive.

The requirements and the economics of contemporary television "commercials" (some twenty-five per cent of which take the form of animated films) have led since 1950 to the greatest expansion that cartoon film production has ever experienced. They have also brought the technique of animation round full circle, and forced animators to think once again of their art in elementary and even primitive terms.

The development of the animated film has depended almost entirely on the enterprise of a few individual artist-producers who have managed to combine a characteristic style of work with adequate business organization. Although a few outstanding films have been made by solitary pioneers, the animated film has reached its position in both theatrical and specialized production largely through the continuous output of a few studios which have been built up over the years, and which have established with the public their own tradition of work. Only recently, since the advent of commercial television, have they been joined by large numbers of newcomers who seem ready to use every standard of technique imaginable in their often hurried efforts to fulfil the demands of the advertisers.

The animated film has not, of course, been confined to the cartoon alone. Another branch of animation is the puppet film and somewhere between the puppet film and the drawn film comes the cut-out and silhouette animation, using jointed figures.

Broadly speaking, the history of the animated film has passed through four main phases: *1*, the initial period of trick-work and magic; *2*, the period of the establishment of the cartoon as a side-line to commercial entertainment (mainly during the nineteen-twenties); *3*, the period of technical experiment and of the development of animation in the form of full-length feature entertainment (during the nineteen-thirties and forties), and *4*, the contemporary period during which we are seeing a considerable expansion of the animated film into every kind of use from the television commercial to the highly specialized instructional film.

For the early audiences the drawing that moved was part of the new magic in the cinema. In France, Emile Cohl began to make his

13

little white match-stick figures jump about against a black background as early as 1908. A year later, the American Winsor McCay produced *Gertie the Trained Dinosaur* (for which he is said to have used some 10,000 drawings) and introduced audiences to the idea of the short cartoon as part of the normal theatrical programme. The period 1913 to 1917 saw the foundation of various American cartoon series—John R. Bray's *Colonel Heezaliar*, Ben Harrison and Manny Gould's *Krazy Kat* films, Pat Sullivan's *Felix the Cat* and Max Fleischer's *Koko the Clown*.

In ten years, 1908-1917, animation developed from something that audiences wondered at as a technical feat to something that they accepted and clamoured for as comic entertainment. The hand of the artist with accelerated speed sketched the beginnings of the cartoon figure, which then parted from the pen and assumed an independent life of its own. This seemed to belong to the new magic of the screen. The drawings were as crude and simple as the rough outlines of the contemporary comic strips; the rudimentary dialogue floated in balloons strung to the lips of the characters. But the cartoons were so successful as entertainment that their animal characters eventually became as famous as live stars, and had their regular strip adventures syndicated in the popular journals of the period. Felix the Cat had his own signature tune and theme song.

But animated films did not really come into their own until after the arrival of the sound track. Walt Disney, who had made *Little Red Riding Hood* after founding his own studio in 1923, had the foresight to hold back his first Mickey Mouse shorts in 1928, in order to take advantage of fully synchronized sound. The phenomenal development of cartoons as theatre entertainment came in the ten years 1928-1938, which was the richest period of achievement in the Mickey Mouse, Donald Duck and Silly Symphony Series, and ended with the production and release of the first full-length commercial animated cartoon, *Snow White and the Seven Dwarfs*. Colour, music and sound effects were combined to bring the cartoon film to a new level of maturity as theatre entertainment.

Experiment, however, also lay in certain simpler forms of animation which were eventually to set a pattern of stylization from which post-war animators were to take their cue, in particular the company known as United Productions of America (U.P.A., founded in 1943).

The famous cartoon *Joie de Vivre* completed as early as 1934 in France by Anthony Gross and Hector Hoppin used a much freer and simpler graphic line than that normally used by Walt Disney's

14

animators, who have too often been prepared to sacrifice imaginative caricature for naturalism of style and movement in their human characters. Before this, however, artists such as Viking Eggerling, Walter Ruttmann, Fernand Leger, Francis Picabia and Moholy-Nagy, who believed in the cinema as yet another artistic medium suitable for experiments in the abstract, all attempted to make films. Oscar Fischinger began to make his abstract mobile patterns to music in 1931, which were followed by the experimental colour abstract films that Len Lye initiated in Britain in 1933—the first models for Norman McLaren's films for the National Film Board of Canada.

During the period 1930 to 1934, Berthold Bartosch worked on the film *L'Idée* (for which he animated cut-out figures derived from woodcuts and introduced a special score composed by Honegger), and Alex Alexcieff and Claire Parker made their remarkable pin-head shadow film *Night on a Bare Mountain* in synchronization with Moussorgsky's music. These pioneer films in various ways helped to widen the conception of what the animated film could achieve in certain more advanced forms of graphic style.

Meanwhile other pioneers were developing the puppet film. In 1934 Ptushko made *The New Gulliver* and Starevitch, working in France, *The Mascot*, while the Hungarian George Pal started his famous puppet advertising films in Holland in the same year. After the War, the most prolific practitioner in motion picture puppetry, the Czech artist Jiri Trnka, was to have his own studio in Prague under state sponsorship.

Few of those who boldly experimented in animation were able to make more than the occasional film, but it is true to say that their work has survived the quarter of a century better than any but the very best live-action films of the period. Their styles differed sharply, and most of them derived their strength from the various contemporary styles in modern art. Thus their origins lay in the art world and not in the comic strips and popular illustrations which formed the background to the normal cartoon of the commercial cinema.

In the post-war period, parallel with the widening use of the animated film, came a revolution in the popular style as well. In this battle of the styles, other factors than films played their part. In Britain, America and France posters using advanced forms of design, the better kind of commercial art associated with advertising, the highly individual styles of the more sophisticated cartoonists in the press and in weekly journals helped to make possible the introduction into the theatrical cartoon of a less representational

15

graphic style. The modelling of figures to give them roundness and solidity, the careful reproduction of the details of human and animal movement, the expensive development of naturalism in animation gave ground to cartoons that took their style from the free, vivid and essentially simple lines of drawings by Matisse or Picasso. Given the wit and imagination, cartoon films could adopt the basic contemporary styles associated, for example, with "still" cartoonists such as Steinberg and Arno.

When U.P.A. developed their studio resources after breaking into successful commercial distribution with *Gerald McBoing-Boing*, they demonstrated clearly that the public was now quite ready to accept and enjoy cartoon entertainment in graphic styles derived from the many traditions of contemporary art. The Halas and Batchelor and the Larkins Units in Britain had also introduced similar advanced styles of line and colour, and so did André Sarrut in France. The abstract films of Norman McLaren won every kind of award, including an Oscar from Hollywood.

After thirty years of domination by a single tradition represented, at its best, by the work of Walt Disney, the success of these units and especially of U.P.A. in the commercial field, encouraged the film cartoonist to discover and develop his own personal style of animation. It also took him back to the origins of animation itself, to the match-stick figures of Emile Cohl, the simple unmodelled figure in bare outline with the potential humour in action reduced to its basic form of straight line and curve. Instead of the exactly human movements of Prince Charming in *Snow White and the Seven Dwarfs*, we had now the geometric characters of *Rooty-Toot-Toot*, and stylized legs that rotate like a little cog-wheel.

Such simplified animation, once imagined creatively, also offered the incidental advantage of permitting production on the restricted budgets available from advertisers on commercial television.

*   *   *   *   *

Animation is now rapidly developing in many of the main film-producing countries.

In Russia, Czechoslovakia and China, this form of film-making, like the rest, is state-subsidized, and normally has its own specialized units and studios. The graphic form it takes is traditional and representational in character, and the subjects favoured are usually old tales and legends. The use of advanced non-repre-

16

sentational styles of drawing seems to be unknown, or at least undeveloped, as these are not favoured in normal graphic art either.

In the West, although the hazards of the animator are much greater, the range and quality of his work are much broader. In the field of pure entertainment, animation has to repay its production costs either through the theatre or through television. In the field of sponsorship, it must serve promoters who want films to meet their many different needs. The advertiser requires the constant provision of animated films both for the theatre and for television. Industry wants animated films for public relations or for technical instruction. National and international organizations and Government departments all need animated films for explanation and publicity. Furthermore, there is the small field of the experimental and art film, for which money may sometimes be made available through various cultural organizations.

Television is now the main motivator of the increased output of animation. Employment figures show that in 1956, in comparison with ten years earlier, the number of artists and technicians employed had risen by four times in Britain and by three times in the United States. In the Far East, the ten years have seen entirely new animation centres set up in China and Japan.

While television has brought so much new work for the animator, there has been a drastic reduction in the number of animated films produced for theatrical entertainment. Disney has turned increasingly to the production of live-action films; his short cartoons are now designed for television, and he will make only feature-length films now and then for the theatres. The big studios which formerly had animation units have virtually ceased production. In the case of U.P.A., only a small proportion of their output is normally designed for the theatres. In Britain, which is gradually becoming one of the more productive centres for the animated film, there is very little production for theatrical distribution.

It has to be recognized that the television commercial is of necessity a very restricted form of film-making. None the less, imagination and a free graphic style can bring taste and artistry to the handling of this brief form. Although the commercial is the bread and butter of the animator, it may well provide him also with the resources to develop his own independent production side by side with his work for the advertisers.

The outstanding success of animation on television has also led to the promotion of the animated entertainment short or insert for the general television programmes. Here the scope for the artist will

17

obviously be far greater than in the commercial which counts its running-time in seconds. But the free style of animation established in the better class of commercial will stand the animator in very good stead when he comes to develop his original work for the general television programme.

The sponsored film, apart from television, has also proved to be a very important part of the animator's work. In Britain alone, sponsored animated films have been made on such subjects as geography, language-teaching, electronics, mathematics, science, agriculture and industry. This class of production for the non-theatrical screen is also expanding.

In theatrical production, the entertainment short must command international distribution to cover even a minimum budget. In the nineteen-thirties, Disney entered the field of the full-length feature mainly in order to obtain an adequate return for the costly technical process of animation. Only with maximum international distribution can short animated films pay their way. During the early seventies a sudden expansion of full length features opened the way for other than Disney features. Among these were Uderzo and Goscinny's *Asterix* made in Belgium and France, Tezuka's *Thousand and One Arabian Nights* made in Japan, Steve Krantz and Ralph Bakshy's *Fritz the Cat* made in the U.S.A. and the *Glorious Musketeers* made in Britain and Italy.

It seems that the present pattern of animated film production in the western world could be described as follows:

Feature-length films are produced occasionally that are designed for exhibition in the theatres.

A limited number of short entertainment films are made which are also intended for theatrical exhibition.

A fair number of animated advertising films are still made in colour for the theatres.

Many animated films are sponsored to promote public relations and for use in instruction connected with industry, science, technology and sales promotion.

A certain number of animated films are produced for national governments and for international organizations.

Entertainment cartoons and puppet films specifically designed for children are produced mainly for television.

Computer-generated films are made in an increasing number to teach sciences in high schools and universities.

Experimental films are being made by students and artists in the form of self-expression and study in motion.

Animation is, therefore, a relatively new art form for which there is at present an expanding demand from widely different sources. Each offers its own type and degree of challenge to the imagination and to the technical skill of the animator.

The animator, as it will be gathered by now, must have certain qualifications both as artist and technician if he is to become successful in this form of film-making. He must have the cartoonist's flair for getting the essentials of character firmly established with the minimum graphic effort. He must have an eye for movement so that he can visualize how his characters should move and at the same time retain in movement the essentials of their being. He must have a strong dramatic sense so that he can develop a movement to its own graphic climax within a given shot or sequence, making it part of the larger action as it has been planned on the storyboard for the complete film. He must have a sense of mobile composition, so that he can unfold and place movement within the limits of the screen-frame, and he must also have a musician's sense of timing, for much of his work will have to be animated in close synchronization with music.

It is not the purpose of this book to show how all this may be learnt. Much of it can, in fact, never be taught at all. Our purpose is to show, as clearly as we may, how the infinitely complex process of animation can be carried through; in short, to describe and analyse the various techniques of film animation, and to outline in some detail the organization of the studio for this work.

The principal process to be dealt with is that of the drawn film. The technique of the puppet film will also be described, and the more specialized work of the silhouette and other marginal forms of animated film is mentioned where techniques are divergent.

Broadly speaking, the drawn film consists of photographing frame by frame a combination of painted celluloid sheets and backings which, set by set, make up each phase of movement occupied by one twenty-fourth part of a second. (In the case of animation for television, one twenty-fifth part of a second.)

The puppet film consists of photographing frame by frame the slightly adjusted poses of a movable puppet placed against a background or in a three-dimensional set, the poses being altered so that each phase of the adjustment occupies one twenty-fourth (or twenty-fifth) part of a second.

In the silhouette film, flat cut-out figures which are jointed are laid out on a series of glass plates beneath the lens of the camera and adjusted fractionally for each successive frame on the film.

What is common to all normal animation is the frame by frame exposure of the film. This makes its fundamental distinction from live-action filming, where whatever moves is filmed in continuity as it moves. If the Special Effects Department in a live-action studio uses model ships for a sequence, these ships will be filmed in motion. If model ships are used in an animation studio their movements will normally be adjusted in between the exposure of each frame of the film. The result is, of course, totally different in its effect on the screen.

There is practically no other form of art in which the artist's idea and the technique he must use to express it are so closely inter-related. A painter may express himself directly by using his brush on canvas, a sculptor by shaping a block of stone with his tools. These are direct creative processes. But in the case of film animation, there is a complex technical operation to be undertaken before the artist's conception of what he wants to see actively put on the screen can achieve its realization. Every stage in this operation affects the nature of his work and requires his skilful foreknowledge if it is to be turned to advantage. For all art thrives on the subtle exploitation of technique.

As the film animator puts pencil to paper he must have in mind what will happen to his graphic ideas before they reach the screen—painting, tracing, the combination of cells with backgrounds, photography, music scoring, sound effects, narration and dialogue. He has to visualize planned movements and dramatic continuity to be achieved through the edited shot and sequence leading up to the final mobile structure of the film. At every stage of their reconstruction through these processes his original drawings will be vitally affected; their nature will expand, idea and technique will amalgamate as the cartoon is created. All these possibilities must occupy the animator's mind as his first sketches pile up on the paper.

He is working in terms of space towards creating effects in terms of time and sound as well.

PART ONE

FACTORS GOVERNING ANIMATION

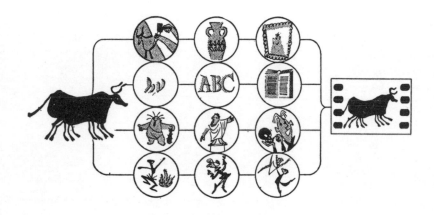

The earliest work of an artist is the cave drawing. From this evolved many arts including sculpture and pictorial art, the abbreviated pictures which were the basis of lettered script, story-telling through the mime of a performer, and the dance itself. All these separate arts were brought together once more in modern animated film.

1

THE NATURE OF ANIMATION

IT is obvious that movement is the essence of animation. Movement is one of the essential characteristics of life itself. Both animals and human beings express themselves continuously through movement, and have strong emotional reactions to creatures and things that move—especially things that move fast. As Puck says to impress Oberon, "I'll put a girdle round about the earth in forty minutes". Racing cars, aircraft and rockets followed.

To judge from the earliest forms of graphic art known to us, it seems that man has always sought to animate his pictures. If only he could breathe the stir of life into his creatures he would share the grand mystery with the gods. The great artists of pre-history, crouching with their rush-lights by the cave walls of Altamira, Lascaux and the hundreds of other caverns either known to the archaeologists or still to be discovered, were, as far as we can see, urged by some undefined instinct to try to animate their pictures.

Entering Lascaux is like entering a living zoo. Movement seems to dominate these bodies with their splayed legs and heads bent with the muscular effort of motion. The wonderful figures of the beautiful rearing horse, or those of the dark horse following the mare in foal, the jumping cow, the running and falling hares, the great aurochs, the charging bull, the charging bisons and the disembowelled bison with his head twisted in death all show the success of artists working over 20,000 years ago in the most difficult physical conditions to suggest life caught in arrested motion.

In Altamira the boars and bisons are poised with equal vitality, and curious cinematographic effects are achieved by the super-imposition of later paintings on older ones which have been partly worn away. These compound figures with six or eight legs in different positions achieve an additional suggestion of movement.

Keats's imagination was stirred by the arrested motions of the scene pictured on a Greek vase:

> What men or gods are these? What maidens loth?
> What mad pursuit? What struggle to escape?
> What pipes and timbrels? What wild ecstasy?

The athletic figures of Greek painting and sculpture achieve the suggestion of life through the excellence of their balanced poise and through the revelation of a sense of being which emanates from within the faces and bodies themselves.

The creation of vitality through the visual arts is one of the supreme imaginative achievements of mankind. It can be seen alike in the grotesque activities of Bosch's demons, in the tigers of Delacroix and in the multi-faceted portraits of Picasso.

In all the great formulations of art of which these are examples the artists seem to be pressing against the impassable barrier of achieving movement itself. The varied resolutions of this basic problem adopted by great artists have, of course, given "still" art some of its highest qualities. The triumph over limitations by observing them and staying within them is a necessary part of all disciplined artistic expression. If the statue of the Discobolus *really* began to move, he would cease to be the Discobolus with the particular virtues of a statue. He would enter a new phase of art. He would pass through the barriers of stillness into a new world of motion, into another artificial world with its own necessary limitations and its own necessary techniques which recognize these limitations and make use of them—the world of the art of the film.

With animation through film each drawing surrenders its independence as a separate picture and becomes a tributary to the mainstream of a continuously moving image. Only this moving image matters. The fact that an individual drawing representing one fraction of a second's motion happens to have artistic qualities when it is isolated from the series is as incidental to its main purpose as is the beauty of a still photograph derived from one of the frames of a motion picture shot. It is only a useful reminder of what moves pictorially in the film, a momentarily arrested scene.

In animation each successive drawing is part of a pictorial sequence, a movement which has a beginning and an end which is an essential part of its artistic form. The animator thinks of this movement first before he draws any phase of it as a sketch or a finished picture. For him composition within the frame has not only height, width and the suggestions of depth in perspective; it has a timed movement as well. It has mobile composition.

This movement may begin by being as completely representational as possible, copying in time and rhythm what is to be observed

24

and measured in the world of nature. The human figure, for example, may be made to move like the characters of Snow White and the Prince in Disney's *Snow White and the Seven Dwarfs*. But since a drawn figure is not the same thing as a real figure such superimposed naturalism mostly defeats its own purpose and can only look embarrassingly unnatural. It only serves to emphasize the differences between live-action and animated action. A drawn figure should possess the free qualities of drawing, like the richly caricatured dwarfs and the horrific witch in the same film. In fact, the essential qualities of animation start at the point where live-action film-making stops.

This is one of the reasons why animation is a separate art within an art, an extension of the main principles of film-making to the wholly specialized world of the graphic arts. The attempts to marry these two worlds in such a film as *Invitation to the Dance*, where animated figures are made to dance in synchronization with human dancers, may represent the achievements of remarkable technical skill but they have also the peculiar ugliness which comes when wholly disparate forms of art are forced to come together. They can merge no more easily than oil and water.

2

THE DISCOVERY OF THE BASIC TECHNIQUE

ANIMATION had to evolve its own laws and techniques in the same way as the normal film. This resulted from the combined efforts of pioneers working in several countries.

The French pioneer Emile Cohl put a series of black-line drawings on sheets of white paper and photographed them. On the screen he used the negative film and so achieved an action performed by white figures moving against a black background. It might be claimed in his case that he was less concerned with developing any particular technical skill in animation than with showing the simple charm possessed by his little match-stick creatures. Even at this primitive stage the emphasis was artistic rather than technical. Similarly the earliest German silhouette films were motivated by artistic rather than technical considerations.

In the early films of the American Winsor McCay the emphasis turned in the other direction. In the few years between *Gertie the Trained Dinosaur* (1909) and the first really memorable cartoon character, *Felix the Cat*, created by Pat Sullivan (an Australian immigrant to the U.S.A.), the technique of animation was pressed rapidly and competitively forward. The figures were drawn and screened as black outlines on a white background, and the emphasis was on the showman-draughtsman who could present the miracle of a mobile cartoon rather than on the artistry of the drawings themselves.

The technical phases through which animation passed in this pioneer period from Cohl to Sullivan were as follows:

1. Outline drawings photographed in series on successive sheets of white paper.

2. The reversal of this on the screen through retaining the negative for projection, thus producing animated white figures against a black background.

3. The development of the simplest form of silhouette film—

black cut-out figures placed against a plain white background.

4. The development of the background as a more important part of the picture. As a first stage, the backgrounds were drawn, like the foreground figures, on the same sheet of paper for each frame of the film.

5. The silhouette films revealed the economy in drawing which could be effected by using a constant background executed on a separate sheet of paper.

6. The invention of phase animation. This was the first stage in a technique involving the superimposition of the sketches one on top of another to save the repeated drawing of the background for each different phase in the movement of the foreground figures. This was a great economy. The activities of the foreground figures were confined to an area within the picture which could be left entirely free from the outlines required for the background. The sheet containing the animation drawings for the foreground figures was then trimmed down so that the background drawings, whether static or animated in their own right, were fully visible when the trimmed sheets of paper were placed successively over them during the process of photography.

7. The introduction of cell animation. This completely did away with the need for phase animation technique. While the backgrounds to the film remained as independent drawings on white paper, the successive phases of the animation of the foreground figures were traced on thin sheets of transparent celluloid and superimposed at the photographic stage. The introduction of cell animation has been attributed to the American film-maker Earl Hurd, who first patented the process in June 1915. Its use was later perfected by Raoul Barré for Edison and by another animator, Bill Nolan, who introduced the moving panoramic background to the cartoon film.

Cell animation is fundamental to all advanced cartoon film technique. The idea of using these transparencies may seem simple enough, but it was in fact a revolutionary one. From it stemmed the possibility of introducing division of work and specialization into animation, and thus effecting improvements in the whole character of cartoon drawing. It also made possible the introduction of certain relative forms of perspective, and released the artist from the primitive, two-dimensional quality of the early cartoon films.

The first stages of specialization were gradually introduced during the nineteen-twenties.

The work of drawing backgrounds became separated from the

27

more exacting task of animation itself, the task of developing the detailed phases of movement required for the active figures.

Further specialization came when the work of inking in the outlines of the figures was made distinct from that of "opaquing", or filling in the figures with opaque paint.

By the time the first notable films of Walt Disney were being produced after 1928, such specialization as this was normal in the more advanced animation units. It is obvious that the more the chief animators could be freed from the sheer, soul-destroying labour of repetitive drawing, the more they could concentrate on improving the imaginative and technical quality of their work.

Nowadays the Key Animators are concerned only with the broad aspects of all the movements of the characters allocated to them. Their assistants in turn fill in the intermediate stages of movement, and further assistants are concerned to polish their combined work and examine it in every detail in order to eradicate imperfections. The stage in production known as the pencil-test enables the animator to see his characters in motion at a comparatively early stage in the work.

Similarly the artist whose skill lies in the creation of backgrounds has his own department and his own assistants.

A further quite separate department is that of the camera specialist. In the early days of the cartoon, the artist carried out his own photography frame by frame, using a reliable old-style studio camera. Now the animation studios have their own specialized cameras mounted on rostra and capable of photographing multiplane images with back lighting.

In the full-scale modern studio each of these main aspects of the work—animation, backgrounds, photography—together with that of sound creation and recording demand trained staffs of artist-technicians all working in their own specialized categories.

Since the mid-nineteen sixties, computer generated animation has been developed by many organisations in the U.S.A. and Britain. Early pioneers of this technique are Dr Kenneth Knowlton and Dr Edward Zajac, who have made a number of computer animated films on scientific topics (See pages 314–322).

The employment of the computer driven cathode ray tube is still undergoing constant development. Among other systems available today are the Computer Image Corporation's SCANIMATE and ANIMAC which are based on the analog computer. The operation of their machines may be more direct and suitable for the animator than the digital computer.

28

3

EVOLUTION OF STYLE AND TIMING

ALTHOUGH the early cartoons and silhouette films made in Europe may have been primitive in technical execution, they tended to be artistic in their conception.

The subjects of these films mostly found their roots in fantasy and folklore and their styles stemmed from the conventional graphic art of the period.

In America, however, the roots of the cartoon film lay in the comic strip, which blew a blast of crude but fresh air through the cobwebs of European fantasy. In America, the newspaper comic strip and film cartoon have developed side by side since the days of the first World War. Often they shared in the creation of characters which became established and famous alike through their constant appearance in the press and on the screen, and the money earned from the syndication of comic strips based on the adventures of these characters helped substantially to cover the more extensive costs of film production, printing and distribution. The incisive, economical drawing used in these cartoons surrounded the figures with the absolute minimum of outlines to contain their bursting vitality.

Another important step taken by the American cartoonists was a new development in the timing of action. Paul Klee speaks of "taking a line for a gentle walk". Although this refers to his own particular form of lineal fantasy it could equally well describe the attitude of the early European artists to the animation of action for the screen.

The films of Cohl amble along towards their little visual jokes at an even tempo, and the German silhouette films ducked about at the normal tempo of stage marionettes.

Max Fleischer, a German artist who emigrated to the United States and became the creator of Koko the Clown in the *Out of the Inkwell* series, realized that the animator could originate his own special forms of timing suitable to the unreal world of the crude little figures of cartoon. When this happened the animated film took another step forward in the evolution of its natural form. The new timing gave a wholly comic punctuation to the story and substantially helped to dramatize it.

The comic or climactic application of speed to the action, or the sudden arresting of movement altogether, became characteristic of the free treatment of the timing of movement in the cartoon film.

A similar freedom was given to what comic creations like Felix the Cat could do. He was, after all, a super-cat. It was quite right for him to be able to take off his tail, use it as a handle and then put it back on his body. This free and imaginative approach to visual gags, as well as the new freedom of tempo, made the American cartoon a totally different popular art form from the animated folklore of Europe.

It is interesting to note that the beautifully-made cartoon films produced to-day in Soviet Russia adopt a normal, life-like tempo in their dramatizations of subjects derived from folk stories. The Western style seems to have no parallel in Russian studios. Yet it was evolved by artists like Sullivan, Lantz, Fleischer and Disney between thirty and forty years ago.

The application of cell animation in production technique assisted this development in dramatic treatment. The use of cells allowed for greater flexibility of graphic execution. A new world of quick timing was rapidly evolved, taking popular audiences of the day along with it stage by stage. Some old people might voice their objection to the speed of the action developed by the cartoonists of the 'twenties. But the young generation of cinema-goers thrived on it, and complete freedom of tempo soon became a traditional part of what an audience expected as soon as the familiar cartoon credits appeared on the screen.

4

ANIMATION: THE PHYSICAL LAWS

THE behaviour of every object in the natural world is controlled by elementary physical laws. Its movement depends on how it is affected by the forces of gravity and of friction. The behaviour of living bodies is similarly affected by these forces, but in their case there is the additional factor that living matter has a will of its own. Living bodies may therefore put up a fight against these basic forces, or in some other way modify their behaviour in relation to them.

In addition to the basic forces of gravity and friction, other natural powers can affect the behaviour of both objects and living bodies. The winds and tempests, the waves and tides, heat and cold all produce conditions which affect physical behaviour. The weight and the size of objects and living bodies are additional factors that govern their behaviour.

Before the animator begins the task of designing drawings that are to move, he must recognize the fundamental forces which create the laws of movement.

He must recognize that the laws of gravity and friction are absolute; they cannot be modified, they must always be accounted for.

The forces of nature (winds, waves, tides, temperatures) can to some extent be resisted; they are less than absolute.

As to weight and size, further checks and controls can be exercised by the long-suffering objects and living bodies existing in the natural world.

In live action these forces and their relative powers are taken for granted on the basis of experience. If a man steps over the edge of a cliff you know that he must fall to the ground below. If an aeroplane rises from the ground, you know that it has been designed to achieve flight with full allowance for the force of gravity, and not as a result of the suspension of that force.

The animator, however, creates a new world of his own on paper, and he has to decide the exact relationship of the creatures of his imagination to all the forces that govern behaviour in the world of nature. As soon as he draws a figure on paper and considers its potential movement, he cannot escape these other considerations, for his audience will anticipate that the figure will conform to whatever forces would affect it were it to exist in actuality. It may be part of his design to exploit this anticipation and give his figure a certain licence—for in the world of cartoon elephants fly and men walk up walls to wipe their feet on the ceiling.

But in order to exploit those natural forces effectively and with validity it is first of all necessary to understand them, and this the animator is obliged to do. Let us therefore examine these forces in greater detail.

First, there are the three principles or laws of motion established by Newton.

(i) A body that is still tends to remain still. In the same way, a body that is in motion tends to remain in motion.

(ii) The states of stillness and movement of a body can only be changed by the action of an outside force. The body will move in the direct line in which the force is applied, until another force acts to change its direction.

(iii) Every action causes an equal reaction in the opposite direction.

These three laws, which seem the simplest and the most obvious, are in fact the most important in animation. They give the cue to the animator's art, to the exaggerations and distortions which he must introduce but which in fact derive from natural behaviour.

For instance, a large soft ball rests quietly on the ground. A boy comes along and gives it a mighty kick. You can see the toe of his boot overcome the ball's inert tendency to remain quiet and still. The toe sinks into the ball and it immediately loses its roundness as the result of its initial resistance to any alteration in its position. Then, after the force of the kick has been transferred to all its parts, it regains its proper shape, although this may now be slightly affected by the forces of gravity and the friction of the air. Suddenly it collides with a brick wall. At once it loses its roundness; the part of its surface first receiving the impact squashes flat, because a ball in motion needs to retain its motion.

The cartoonist can take his cue from this real ball. He turns its round outline into a face, peaceful, static, contented. A toe violently intrudes; the face is squashed in almost flat. The expression assumes

Emile Cohl, originator of the cartoon film in 1904.

THE ENTERTAINMENT CARTOON

Drame chez les Fantoches (Emile Cohl; France, 1908).

Koko Chop Suey (Copyright Max Fleischer; U.S.A. 1917).

Felix the Cat (Copyright Pat Sullivan; U.S.A. 1917).

Skeleton Dance (Copyright Walt Disney Productions; U.S.A. 1929).

Sam and his Musket (Copyright Anson Dyer; Great Britain 1933).

Joie de Vivre (Copyright Gross and Hoppin; France 1933).

Popeye (Copyright Max Fleischer; U.S.A. 1933).

Mickey Mouse (Copyright Walt Disney Productions; U.S.A. 1928).

Three Little Pigs (Copyright Walt Disney Productions; U.S.A. 1931).

Snow White and the Seven Dwarfs (Copyright Walt Disney Productions; U.S.A. 1938).

Pinocchio (Copyright Walt Disney Productions; U.S.A. 1940).

The Reluctant Dragon (Copyright Walt Disney Productions; U.S.A. 1941).

Fantasia (Copyright Walt Disney Productions; U.S.A. 1941).

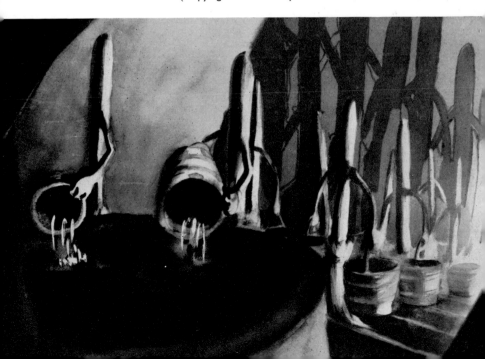

Dumbo (Copyright Walt Disney Productions; U.S.A. 1942).

Victory Through Airpower (Copyright Walt Disney Productions; U.S.A. 1943).

Mickey Mouse and Pluto (Copyright Walt Disney Productions; U.S.A.).

Donald Duck (Copyright Walt Disney Productions; U.S.A.).

Tom and Jerry (Copyright M.G.M.; U.S.A.).

Woody Woodpecker (Copyright W. Lantz; Universal-International Pictures; U.S.A.).

Kittens Scribbling (Copyright Toei Company; Japan).

The Owl and the Pussycat (Copyright Halas & Batchelor; Great Britain).

The Animals and The Brigands (Copyright State Film; Czechoslovakia 1946).

The Tell-Tale Heart (Copyright U.P.A.; U.S.A. 1953).

Toot Whistle Plunk and Boom (Copyright Walt Disney Productions; U.S.A. 1953).

Left: *Bugs Bunny* (Copyright 1968 Warner Brothers Pictures; U.S.A.).
Right: *Sylvester* (Copyright 1958 Warner Brothers Pictures; U.S.A.).

Madeline (Copyright U.P.A.; U.S.A. 1952).

Is it Always Right to be Right? (Lee Mishkin/Steve Bosustow Production; U.S.A.).

How Now Boing Boing (Copyright U.P.A.; U.S.A. 1953).

Unicorn in the Garden (Copyright U.P.A.; U.S.A. 1950).

Mr. Magoo Goes West (Copyright U.P.A.; U.S.A. 1956).

The Jaywalker (Copyright U.P.A.; U.S.A. 1956).

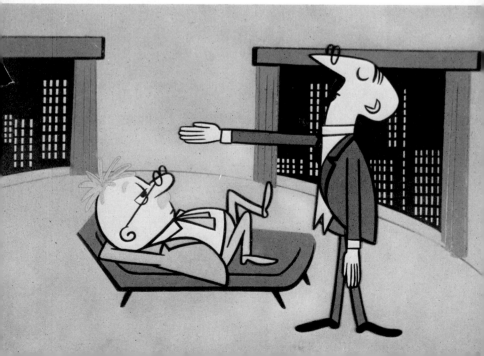

The Unusual Match (Copyright Mosfilm U.S.S.R. 1955).

The Golden Antelope (Copyright Mosfilm U.S.S.R. 1955).

La Bergère et le Ramoneur (Copyright Les Gémeau; France 1952).

The Red Flower (Copyright State Film; China).

Animal Farm (Halas & Batchelor; Great Britain 1953).

The Quartet (Copyright Film Polski; Poland).

The Creation of the World (Copyright State Film; Czechoslovakia 1956).

Who Am I? (Copyright Bulgaro Film; Bulgaria).

Dunderklumpen (by Per Åhlin for GK Films; Sweden).

Ruddigore (Copyright Halas & Batchelor; Great Britain).

The Little Island (Copyright Richard Williams; Great Britain 1957).

Fantasmatic (Copyright G. and E. Ansorge; Switzerland).

Adventure On ... (Copyright John Hubley; U.S.A. 1957).

How the Mole Lost its Trousers (Copyright State Film; Czechoslovakia 1957).

Cowboy Jimmy (Copyright Film Zagreb; Jugoslavia 1958).

History of the Cinema (Copyright Halas & Batchelor; Great Britain 1958).

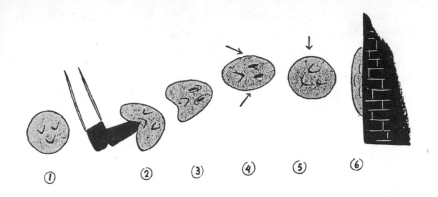

(1)   (2)   (3)   (4)   (5)   (6)

The essence of fluid animation is understanding the behaviour of any object to which the animator must give life and character. The physical laws of expansion and contraction and the effect of gravity on objects must be taken into account and exploited as a part of an animator's sense of action. While it is essential to understand such basic principles in just the same way as a figure artist must understand anatomy, the real craft of animation begins at this very point. He must know when to develop the normal position of an object (as in 1 above) into the abnormal (as in 2, 3 and 4 above) in order to emphasize the forces at work upon it—impetus, friction, gravity and impact.

the maximum in alarm and despondency before it soars up into the air and resumes its rounded shape and its look of contentment in the fulfilment of motion. Then comes the impact against the brick wall. The face is once again violently squashed into dismay before dropping disconsolately to the ground and bouncing feebly to a standstill. The ball may be sorry for itself, but it has fulfilled Newton's first principle of motion.

All the actions of ball-sport—bat-on-ball, racket-on-ball, club-on-ball, foot-on-ball—provide the grounds for such a cartoon exaggeration of the truth as this, for every ball which is hit loses its spherical shape at the moment of impact.

Consider next the time factor. In reality, it needs a high-speed camera shooting at, say, 120 frames minimum per second, to register the flattening of a golf ball at the moment of impact with the swinging club. The normal time unit of the animator is one twenty-fourth or one twenty-fifth part of a second. If he wants to show the reaction of the ball to the club in an animated film and he permits only one frame for the moment of distortion of the ball's shape, he will be greatly exaggerating the time-factor of the distortion in terms of actuality. But exaggeration is part of his craft; he will tend therefore to exaggerate the "squash" of the ball in both

57

time and amount. This will give him the comic pathos he seeks through a sharply dramatic emphasis of the truth.

"Squash" becomes, indeed, a technical term in animation, and indicates the high degree of resilience under duress of the figures he draws. In fact, he often designs them so that their shape should suggest this resilience. They look either fastastically immovable or fantastically mobile, and act accordingly.

In the accentuation of squash apparent weight as well as time is involved. For light objects squash may be reduced to a single frame, that is one twenty-fourth or one twenty-fifth part of a second; even so, as we have seen, this is in point of time a high degree of exaggeration. But given an object of great apparent or actual weight (a whale or an elephant, for example), the squash given to their movements may be exaggerated further, say up to five or more frames, that is approximately one fifth of a second or more. This makes the elephant "galumph" in his movements, and the whale "roll" like a wave.

The cartoon figures thus have their own elasticity which caricatures their motion without loss of character—in fact, with the cartoon there is always an emphasis of character. Very solid objects, like buildings, may be permitted a fully visible sway in the wind— no doubt to their obvious dismay, though real buildings like skyscrapers and towers do in fact sway considerably and are constructed to do so.

But if such solid objects as buildings are permitted the licence of visible motion when attacked by some force like the wind, then static objects such as trees or ships must be given a proportionate licence to wave and toss. Their design on paper must suggest this potential elasticity, and, like elastic, they must be prepared to distort themselves unevenly to give the right effect.

An even distortion implies a greater visible resilience at the point of impact than elsewhere. Let us go back to our dismayed ball. Where the toe impacts, the distortion obviously needs to be greatest. If a tree tickles because a woodpecker irritates it, it is at the point where the woodpecker is at work on the bark that it will react most sharply. If a whale turns in the water like a speedboat, then the distortion must flow through its frame in response to the fully realized action of its turning. If an elephant starts to slip while skating on an ice-rink, then the legs will distort first before the disaster is apprehended throughout the rest of its body.

It might be claimed that Salvador Dali's soft watches are cartoon watches tired out. They wrap themselves limply round the furniture

58

like rubber mats. So when solid objects come in contact with some more masterful surface than themselves they wrap themselves round it in obsequious obedience to Newton's Laws of Motion. A speeding train collides with some unexpected buffers and bulges over them with squash. A grand piano falls from the upper floor of a sky-scraper and spreads itself flat on the sidewalk before hastily re-assembling in proper form to play a funeral march. A car meets a lamp-post, goes soft with squash, and then winds itself round the obstruction like a drunken muffler.

Similarly, the motion of bodies may inter-react. A dog may charge a closed gate and by his efforts swing it open. But the gate has a spring on it. So it swings back on to the dog and hurls him into space. The gate will suffer exaggerated squash from the impact with the dog; and then the dog will suffer an equal degree of squash from the impact with the gate. This in animation terms is a "concertina movement"; it is the transmission of squash from one object to another, or from one part of an object to another part.

We have dealt so far primarily with objects which are static or moving in one direction only. Newton's second Law of Motion comes into force at this point. The static object is subjected to a force, overcomes its resistance to movement, moves in the direction of the force which impelled it, meets another force operating from another direction, and is thus deflected from its original path. In animation, all these changes must be reflected by appropriate emphases through distortion, attended by a "flow" originating from the point of impact with the force through to the remaining limbs or parts of the object.

The third of Newton's Laws of Motion—every action causes an equal reaction in the opposite direction—has like the first and second Laws its reflection in the process of animation.

Every movement can be reinforced where it is valuable to do so, by means of a secondary and opposite movement that derives from it. A car starts off at speed—the impetus of the fast movement can be emphasized by the outlines of a puff of dust starting from the ground in the opposite direction. The movement *back* of the dust emphasizes the movement *forward* of the car.

Thus it is wise in animation to give every movement its full visual value. Every action should have its preceding and succeeding phase. The cartoon car about to start pulls back like an elastic catapult preparatory to launching itself forward. When it comes to a stop it halts slithering on its distorted wheels. Animation demands this fuller realization of the physical laws of gravity and friction, this

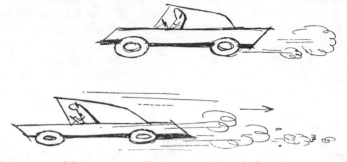

Even if the animated drawings are stylized in appearance the basic laws of motion must be observed. Three major factors have to be taken into account—the preparatory movement, the action and the reaction—in addition to these basic laws. In certain cases the reaction, because it is the pay-off of the animation, may well be the most important point. The art of animation depends on the inter-action of these various factors.

visual symbolizing of the natural forces and the results of weight and mass.

Yet natural motion should be avoided in animation. The laws governing such motion should be observed and understood as they affect the real-life counterparts of the drawn image, but then developed by the artist for his own ends, which are not the ends of nature. The art of animation starts when the artist interprets natural movement creatively without directly copying it.

The artist in animation starts, therefore, with the knowledge of how objects and living beings work, just as Leonardo da Vinci sought constantly to understand the bones and muscles within the structure of human or animal bodies. Leonardo, were he the instructor of the animator to-day, would be unlikely to permit him to develop the symbolization of movement in the form of mobile cartoon until he had understood how it worked in the practice of nature. Imagination follows on scientific analysis, taking its cues from what is real.

But the mere reproduction of nature is the denial of the artist's function. The artist is under an obligation to create something which goes beyond the careful manufacture of a carbon copy of natural forms and movements—the province of the live-action camera. The value of the artistic exercise starts when the artist puts pencil to paper and begins the fabrication of a graphic world which he alone creates.

5

ANIMATION: THE AESTHETIC PRINCIPLES

THE difference between cartoon animation and real life lies in the application of certain principles which are most appropriately called aesthetic.

An animator normally carries out his work by means of line drawings. With these drawings he outlines forms that indicate objects and figures which in real life possess volume. It is because of this that the physical laws already discussed must be understood in so far as they would affect these objects and figures were they to exist in actuality.

The artist may, however, choose to create forms other than line drawings with little or no counterpart in actuality. He may prefer to develop wholly or partially abstract shapes in motion. These shapes deal in essential movement—shapes for shape's sake, movements for movement's sake. As these abstract shapes take on certain forms which may hint at counterparts in reality (like the comic chicken figure in McLaren's *Blinkety-Blank*), the designs may begin to possess a symbolic value and cease to this extent to be wholly abstract. As soon as the hints of actuality creep in, the behaviour of the near-abstract shape which has now become a figure must conform to some aspects at least of the movements and character of its equivalent in real life. The figure has, in fact, achieved a sort of diagrammatic significance.

It suggests essential or rudimentary form and behaviour only, like the simplified diagram of a machine in a technical demonstration. In animated film there is a certain aesthetic link between the simplified figure (the pin-man, match-stick figure or the little embryonic beings that dance in and out of McLaren's abstract films) and the mobile diagrams of the simpler instructional films.

As the figures in cartoon films begin to approach actuality more closely, the physical laws affecting their real counterparts must be more strictly applied, even though they are still fantastically caricatured. The graphic beings in U.P.A.'s films are conceived in variously stylized outline, for example in *Gerald McBoing-Boing*, *Rooty-Toot-Toot*, *Madeleine* and *The Unicorn in the Garden*; they maintain an existence which is far from actuality in their quaint and angular outlines. Their movements are simplified, mechanized, grotesque. But they are funny because they nevertheless bear a direct relation to the human beings and animals that they caricature. Their legs may rotate like cog-wheels, their bodies may glide and wave like cloth—but through these *grotesqueries* of movement shines the light of human observation, the comic realization of the problems of human mass and weight, gravity and friction, the physical laws of nature. The aesthetic and the physical meet on a sublimated plane of comic imagination. This is seen repeatedly in the more intelligently designed comic fantasies for television commercials.

The style of most cartoons derives from the comic strip, and the comic strip deals in certain grotesque and simplified versions of human and animal bodies which go far back to folk art and its links with folklore. The artist has always been quick to seize on human weakness, eccentricity or ugliness. The reasons for this are as much psychological as they are aesthetic. They no doubt suit the artist's graphic convenience, and encourage a shorthand in drawing.

Ancient literature dealt in human and animal types before the more subtly observant writers of modern times developed the varied, balanced and flexible portrayal of character in depth in the so-called psychological schools of literature. Magic-men, mummers and actors wore masks in earlier times to typify in grotesque exaggeration the farcical, the comic, the eccentric, the pathetic, the tragic and the insane in human portraiture. Imagination went further still in the horrific faces created for demons, devils and malignant gods. The bodies of Greek actors were enlarged by padding and the high-boot, and their heads were crowned with masks of a disproportionate size. Devil masks in Africa are enlarged to stress their horror, and the natural proportions of the body are abandoned in the interests of dramatic or magical emphasis. There survive representations of masks used in the classical Greek theatre that might well be models for characters in Walt Disney's films, such as the terrifying witch in *Snow White and the Seven Dwarfs*.

The grotesque is developed in both primitive and advanced art forms. The horrific faces in the drawings and paintings of Leonardo da Vinci, Bosch and Breughel and in the mediaeval gargoyles show the urge the artist possesses to conjure the devil in human character by graphic exaggeration and grotesque representation. Such themes

62

are only a step away from the popular *commedia dell' arte* or the Punch and Judy Show. The more familiar animals also lent themselves obviously to caricature in picture and fable—the antecedents to the comic creatures dreamed up by Walt Disney or the M.G.M. cartoon studios.

The "type" is very important in this literary and artistic tradition. It gave rise to certain distinct figures in Greek and Roman comedy, in the "Characters" of literature and folklore, in the "Bestiaries", and in the *commedia dell' arte*. Creatures (human or animal) whose faces, motifs, modes and even "properties" were universally recognizable (Renard the Fox with his coat, Braggadocio with his sword, Bacchus with belly and goblet, Punch with hump and stick, and Harlequin with his chequered costume and black mask) became universally accepted, and in the twentieth century the products of a newer folklore, such as Felix the Cat and Mickey Mouse, shared a similar universality in popular recognition.

The economics of much cartoon film-making depend on the series, and this requires familiarity with recurring characters like Betty Boop, Popeye or Mister Magoo. Durable type figures are the root of cartoon, and can also develop interesting national characteristics in their graphic presentation.

For example, in cartoon film history the size of the head in proportion to the rest of the body has been developed quite differently in America and Russia. (Compare similar national differences in the tempo of movement described earlier on page 30.) As the American cartoon gathered momentum, the convention of making the head larger and larger has tended to grow with it, and audiences who thirty years ago would have been shocked to see a head drawn as big or bigger than the rest of the body are prepared to accept it as a graphic convention quite correct within a wholly artificial medium. Russian cartoon, on the other hand, has kept to the lines of observing a more naturalistic graphic style in the presentation of the characters in folk stories, even though Ptushko's puppets in *The New Gulliver* (1934) had heads approximately a quarter the size of their bodies.

The history of this kind of proportion in American cartoon shows a progressive tendency to exaggerate form.

Exaggeration in cartoon is largely born of function. The gesturing parts of the body—legs, arms, hands, feet—demand enlargement, and above all so does the head, as the principal feature in either human or animal kind. Within the head itself, the mouth demands enlargement through the gesture of speech, and so does the eye,

63

1/5   1/3   1/2

The tendency to exaggerate the proportions between the head and the body in favour of the head and eyes is a feature of American cartooning. This tendency derives from the fact that the majority of contemporary work is designed for the small television screen. These exaggerations are of importance for accentuating character and expression. In the figures above the proportion of head to body is approximately indicated.

because it is the most important means whereby mood, emotion and character may visually be demonstrated.

Finally, there is a technical reason in cartoon film-making for exaggerations and simplifications. When drawings have to be produced in large numbers and by various hands, some form of graphic economy through the emphasis of certain characteristics is essential to enable the nature of a figure to be maintained without any unwanted deviations which would be likely to confuse the clear markings of character.

It is a basic aesthetic principle of cartoon film-making that in the case of animal and human figures, characterization is achieved by the distortion of shapes and forms—big eyes, big mouth, big nose, large head, small body, etc. In the case of inanimate objects (furniture, for example, or commercial trade marks) a similar exaggeration is appropriate when they appear in cartoon, so long as their link with their original models remains sufficiently clear.

Characters in cartoon must look as they are and behave as they look. Exaggeration and associated simplification are therefore both aesthetically and functionally proper; they are vitally necessary to the medium.

When inanimate objects assume life in the pursuit of humour, the

64

need for exaggeration becomes even more pronounced. For example, the cartoonist may want to give an automobile the characteristics of a dog in its attitude to the fuel that its owner offers it. When it shakes its shaggy head in refusal to tank up with the wrong brand of spirit, then the whole body of the car must shake like a neurotic Saint-Bernard, and its head-lamps must become great eyes filled with a pathetic dismay.

In instructional films where comic exaggeration is needed for some emphasis of fact, even diagrammatic models may be permitted to acquire human or animal personalities, though exaggeration of this kind is only used to help make some important teaching point.

Visual symbols may have to be introduced to emphasize what cannot in real life be seen but only felt. The wind may enter the action in the form of the moving lines familiar in the strip cartoon; hot and cold may also require some kind of symbolic indication made by lines which surround a figure in order to indicate shivering or sweating. The exaggeration here lies not only in the experiences shown through the reaction of the characters, but in the way the graphic symbols are introduced and animated.

These graphic symbols are of the greatest value even in the most advanced films. What may have found its origin in the form of a few startled lines of halation round Felix's tail when it has got accidentally trodden on, may also serve to explain in a complex scientific film such as *Criticality* when the "critical" point has been reached in an atomic reactor.

The basic aesthetic principle in cartoons of graphic distortion is supplemented in entertainment cartoons by the fun that can be had at the expense of the physical laws of motion. The exploitation of actions which go beyond all normal physical possibilities in the real world have a powerful effect on any audience.

In Disney's pre-war cartoon *The Clock-Cleaners*, Goofy dances in an ecstatic daze brought on by the bells, and he gyrates and leans at impossible angles on the parapets of the bell-tower over the space which looms below with a savagely exaggerated perspective. Mr Magoo walks on air and defies all the physical laws proper to man on earth. To the audience sharing this graphic experience, horror at what may happen to these foolhardy creatures gives way to delight in their ability to frustrate the laws of nature.

Time is also a plaything in the cartoon—an action can be speeded to such a degree that round the world in eighty days becomes round the world in as many seconds. The chase motif of movie drama develops into a paroxysm of speed with a fine graphic flourish in perspective—the minute dots on the horizon hurtle with rhythmical abandon into vast blown-up proportions in the foreground all within three or four seconds. The cartoon uses slow motion far less than quick because its peculiar dynamics usually makes it move faster than life in everything it does.

For instructional animation, however, a slow speed is often desirable; the stripping down of a complex diagram to its inner sections may well require a slower-than-life rhythm—that is, were the sections of real machines being lifted apart for inspection. The diagram unpeels in synchronization with the commentary to meet the demands of clear and well-timed exposition.

In the entertainment cartoon, the animator has exploited dynamism for its own sake. The speed-dominated cartoon—for many people the only typical style in this branch of film-making—belongs by a kind of national right to American concepts of entertainment. Yet it is not obviously the only style, nor the only American style of cartoon production. The tempo of Disney's own films—especially those of feature-length—is very varied, as it must be in the course of an action lasting 60 to 90 minutes. However, speed is the highlight of American cartooning, and is totally at variance with the pace of, for example, both Russian and Far-Eastern cartoons. These have little or no feeling for speed as such, and permit an action to adhere fairly closely to its natural timing in real life.

It is of some interest that there is an almost entire absence of this kind of forced speed in those graphic films in which the painter or live-action film-maker rather than the animator is in control of production. Examples in Britain and America are Ronald Searle's drawings for *John Gilpin* in the film directed by John Halas, and Hazard Durfee's drawings for *Hook The Hawk* in the film by Abraham Liss. The painter coming freshly to the film medium thinks in terms of the play of the moving camera over his drawings after the manner of the films on art such as *From Renoir to Picasso* and *Paradiso Perduto*, made respectively by Paul Haessaerts of Belgium and Luciano Emmer of Italy. Here dynamics is achieved by means belonging properly to the live-action film—the speed of cutting tempo, the intrusion of the sudden close-shot showing some detail of action or expression in the still drawing or painting, and the movement of the camera away from or towards some detail selected as a starting or ending point of visual emphasis.[1] In cartoon films these dramatic effects are normally obtained through the various

---

[1] *The particular problems of making films entirely from still pictures are discussed, pp. 287-9 below.*

stages of graphic design and composition which the animator achieves on the drawing-board, and in the cutting room. The editing of a cartoon film is part of the process of animation itself, pre-determined by the order and timing of the drawn action before it is shot by the camera or handled by the editor.

The animator is, of course, aware of the visual dynamism proper to his medium. He naturally interprets whatever story or action he is producing in such a way as to use these powers to their maximum effect. He can rely now on a wide international audience which is visually trained through extensive experience of the cinema and television to accept the artificial graphic conventions of the most extravagant forms of cartoon film-making.

Even the abstract or almost-abstract films of Norman McLaren are completely acceptable as entertainment to large audiences of people who would never dream of visiting an exhibition of abstract painting. Yet their governing factor is purely visual. There is no literary, no dramatic, no story concept to help the audience relate what they are seeing to normal human experience. Shapes and forms are composed in a continuity which has no resolution except in the evolution of the shapes and forms themselves. McLaren permits, as we have seen in the case of the chicken in *Blinkety-Blank*, an occasional reference to actuality in his world of patterns and colours, but these references are subsidiary and incidental.

The imagist and symbolist film draws away from the purely abstract world of pattern into one where themes and concepts are presented by means of recognizable objects and figures. These rare films are counterparts of imagist and symbolist poetry, presenting abstract ideas and attempt to invoke intellectual or emotional reactions to images. *The Magic Canvas* is an example of this, in which the struggle of good and evil in the soul of a painter is develop-ed through symbolic images on his canvas.

More immediately understandable, though still essentially graphic in their style and treatment, are such films as *A Short Vision*, *Romance of Transportation* and *Balance 50*. Films of this kind are more numerous because the appeal of their subject-matter is at least equal to the appeal of their graphic style; nevertheless the graphic style, the visual element, forms a very important and at times a predominant part of their effectiveness with a responsive audience. In the best entertainment films from U.P.A. it is difficult to say which pleases more—the imaginative flourish of the graphic style or the story-action that it represents. Both live very much together on the surface. There is no inner mystery for the audience to solve.

The drama or the argument is vivid and apparent, however fantastic the visual style and treatment.

Drawing somewhat nearer to the measure of actuality are the more traditional American cartoons—the Donald Duck and the Tom & Jerry series, to quote outstanding examples. The short stories of these films bubble brightly on the surface; their rapid tempo, their violent action and their savage humour maintain an interest which often enough far exceeds any aesthetic value in the visuals themselves. Nevertheless, the graphic element in them is still very strong—the drawing and colouring have an economy and a visual impact that matches the overwhelming vitality and sometimes the crudity of the action and characterization.

Next in degree in the graphic path that leads from the abstract towards naturalism come the cartoons that are typical of the Russian studios—such as *Unusual Match*, *The Golden Antelope*, *The Vain Bear* and *The Snow Queen*. Here, as we have seen, the timing of the action and the treatment of the story are both realistic in concept. The fact that these films are made as cartoons at all seems sometimes to be incidental. With little change of style they could be transferred into live-action films.

This, too, might be said of the British feature-length cartoon, *Animal Farm*, each main sequence of which observes a naturalistic timing and employs a simplified, slightly stylized naturalism in its graphic presentation of both humans and animals. The argument of the film, like its origin, is literary in conception, and the use of the cartoon medium is justified in this case only because real animals could never have been brought to perform as serious a drama as this for the screen. *Animal Farm*, however, represents the outer limit of the animated film, the borderland before cartoon enters a region proper only to live-action.

This point of distinction is of primary importance. It is fruitless, uneconomic, inartistic and very exasperating to undertake the laborious process of animation in order to tell a story in a manner which could be achieved just as well or even better through a live-action film. A cartoon's virtues lie in simplification, distortion and caricature. It distorts for its own purpose and affects both character and behaviour. It observes the physical laws of nature only to defy them. It conforms wholly to naturalism at its peril, because it then invites comparison with something fit to be reproduced only by the live-action camera. As the animator draws away from naturalism the powers of his medium increase; there is nothing but the limits of his imagination and his technical resources to hold him back.

68

6

THE SOUND TRACK

SINCE the animated film is essentially a hand-made art, the relation of the visuals to the sound track can be made to fit glove-tight. This pictorial relation to the sound track, and especially to music, can never be made as close in the case of live action; hence the term "Mickey-mousing" used to describe the attempts in the live-action film to bring music and sound effects into the closest possible relation to the movement on the screen.

It is part of the joy of the animated film that it can be exact in this respect. Audiences love the precision with which picture and sound can be made to move together. Thus a high degree of analysis and calculation enter into the plotting of a cartoon in terms of action and sound.

There are three kinds of sound track to be considered as in the case of the live-action films: (1) the track carrying the voices, (2) the track or tracks carrying the effects, (3) the track carrying the music. These three main elements of sound in a well-made cartoon are blended and inter-played with the greatest exactitude. Wit and precision are allies here. The potentialities of each of these three elements on the track must be kept in mind, though not in isolation when an actual film is being thought out.

Whoever comes from outside to work for this medium must understand it fully before he can be of any help. This is true especially of the writer and composer. The animator himself—bound up in the visual creation of his characters—may in short films improvise any dialogue he needs for his drawings or puppets. In a long film he will want the help of a writer. The writer, in turn, must understand the peculiar limitations of utterance which bind the drawn characters, and if he has any responsibility for the storyboard he must appreciate the action in animated pictorial terms.

Music is virtually always of the greatest importance to the cartoon film—the composer is, in fact, frequently more essential to the animator than is the writer. (Possibly because he will find it more easy to claim to have writing abilities than creative musical gifts.) Again, however eminent and versatile a composer may be, he cannot help the animator unless he, too, understands the peculiarities of the drawn or puppet film. Mood music is not required of him; he will not be given (like the composer of a live-action film) timed instructions indicating the musical accents needed and to be related to specific sequences and action-points. For the cartoon the composer must be able to respond exactly to a continuous movement which carries its own accents and responses in every second of the score. And yet he must develop an unfettered melody which will captivate an audience and rouse it through its atmosphere as well as through its wit.

The Voice Track

The first characteristic cartoon voices were those of Mickey Mouse and Donald Duck.

Sometimes a fully-established cartoon voice may become more important, more established with the public in its immediately recognizable character, than the visuals themselves. The moment a voice like this is heard it will give the audience the essential, the immediate cue to the character. Donald's angry introductory squawk immediately established his cantankerous and interfering nature, and Mickey's quick squeak his impetuous efficiency.

Indeed in cartooning an idea for a character may start in the conception of its voice. Then it is a case of the animator matching the character of the voice through his drawing. So close is the relation of the animator to the voice of his character that Walt Disney (as is well known) decided to voice Mickey Mouse himself, and Mrs Lantz voiced her husband's cartoon character, Woody-Woodpecker.

In the case of figures such as Popeye and Magoo, their character is established equally by the voice and by the peculiarities of the drawing. Popeye, Magoo, Sylvester and Woody-Woodpecker are all examples of burlesque voicing, and the burlesque voice is normal in cartoon films because it fits best the exaggeration and distortion of the cartoon figure as it is drawn. Specialized players are often employed for this purpose, men and women with peculiar gifts for mimicry and for creating distorted or animal-like voices. The voice, in fact, completes the process of distortion which we have seen to be at the root of cartooning. Thus the design, the looks, the behaviour

70

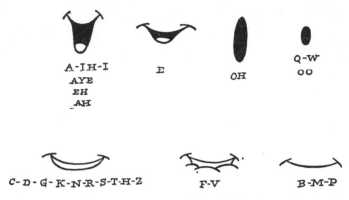

A-IH-I
AYE
EH
AH

E

OH

Q-W
OO

C-D-G-K-N-R-S-T-H-Z

F-V

B-M-P

Owing to the small television screen great liberties have been taken in simplifying animation of lips in speech. It is no longer essential to animate each syllable individually when the audience would be quite unable to appreciate such detail. The above Illustration gives the seven basic positions for the whole range of English speech sounds.

and the voicing all combine to create the artificial personality of the true cartoon character.

The special problem of animating the mouths of speaking characters has led to the establishment of certain conventions, which are again a simplification for the purposes of cartoon of what must initially be observed in nature. The cartoon mouths must mime with suitable distortions the basic positions of the natural mouth when uttering words made up of vowels and consonants. (Diphthongs are dispensed with altogether.)

There are seven basic or elementary positions of the mouth for this miming of speech.

The timing of this mime in the mouths of the cartoon characters is of obvious importance, but clearly developed gestures accompanying speech give both meaning and character to what is said.

More recently there has been a tendency to try out straight, or virtually straight voicing of cartoon characters as an interesting variant from the normal burlesque voice. The Piels Brothers' Commercials in America have been voiced by the comedians Bob and Ray, and in Britain Kenneth Horne and Maurice Denham have voiced the commercials for MacDougall's Self-Raising Flour. The voices of the MacDougall commercials are used rhetorically, and this relatively straight delivery of the "message" of the commercial establishes a greater realism of vocal (as distinct from drawn) character and so makes the delivery of the commercial itself clearer

71

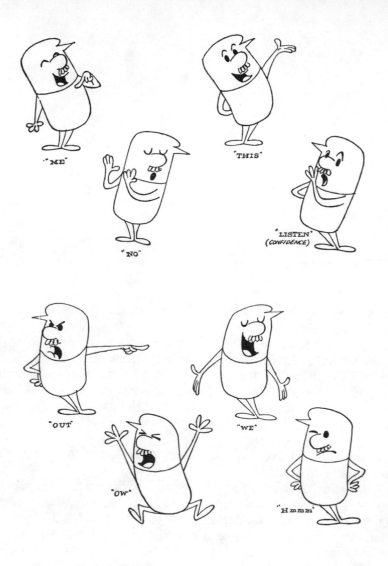

The animation of the lips is only a part of speech gesture. The remaining element is the animation of bodily reactions to what is said. The hands are obviously a predominant feature in this aspect of speech gesture. These eight illustrations indicate this.

Petroushka (Copyright Audio-Visual Associates; U.S.A.).

THE TELEVISION ENTERTAINMENT FILM

Mister Wister the Time Twister (Copyright Jean Image; France).

Gerald McBoing Boing's Show (Copyright U.P.A. for C.B.S.; U.S.A.).

Praise Be to Small Ills (Copyright EKO Co. Ltd.; Tadanariokamoto; Japan).

The World of Little Ig (Copyright N.B.C.; Halas & Batchelor; Great Britain).

Gerald McBoing Boing's Show (Copyright U.P.A. for B.C.S.; U.S.A.).

Gerald McBoing Boing's Show (Copyright U.P.A. for C.B.S.; U.S.A.).

The Butterfly Ball (Lee Mishkin/Halas & Batchelor; Great Britain).

and so more purposeful. In the same way George Pal used normal operatic singing for his puppet presentation of *The Barber of Seville*.[1] There are comic possibilities in developing as a side-line of true cartooning this kind of counterpoint between a "normal" voice and the simplified distortions of the drawn characters.

It is very important for the animator to concentrate on correct gesture, the sheer acting characteristics of his figures in their particular relation to speech. The audience is always more taken up with such gestures and actions than they are with any exact synchronization of lip and dialogue. Though this has its importance, it is a secondary one.

Another subsidiary characteristic of cartoon voicing which is worth further development is the way in which interesting continuity effects can be achieved by letting a straight-voiced commentator suddenly assume the voice of one of the characters on the screen. This has been done in the cartoon on alcoholism made for the United Nations Organization, *To Your Health*, which is basically a film with a commentary, though the commentator now and then voices the queries of the central cartoon characters with suitable lip synchronization. This has a much sharper, more emphatic effect than its parallel use on occasions in live-action documentary, when the commentator momentarily supplies the voice of an actual person.

The Effects Track

Effects can be made up of natural sounds, specially created artificial sound effects, and specifically musical effects.

The use of natural sound effects in cartoon films creates special problems. First of all, they make an unnatural contrast to the drawn image which appears to produce them; for example, the real noise made by a train when starting sounds odd when set against the simple image of a drawn train pulling away. Further, the tempo of real life reflected in the sound does not normally match the distorted tempo of the cartoon. Only in certain isolated cases of quick, violent noises like the scream of car brakes can real life sound effects enter more correctly into the cartoon environment. Natural sounds can, of course, be themselves used as the basis for artificial distortion, but in that case they come into the category of specially-created sound effects.

The specially-created effects were very fully developed by Disney

[1] *Called* Jasper's Close Shave.

in the earlier days of the sound film; his Sound Effects Department was made up of a group of keen specialists with musical training who, according to Professor Field,[1] amassed a collection of some 8,000 instruments and boasted they could produce any sound, natural or artificial, required for the most extravagant moments in a film. As Feild points out, every sound from the smallest animal scratching to the roar of mighty tempests must be contrived and then orchestrated on the cartoon sound track.

Whatever kind of sound is used, natural or contrived, it establishes the nature of the acoustic idiom which must be used for the rest of the picture. To start off a cartoon film with a natural sound implies that natural sounds should be used wherever relevant later in the film, whereas to begin by using special sound effects with an artificial quality to them frees the animator from this obligation. He must judge in advance what it is best to do for each individual subject. In general, he is likely to prefer to use wholly artificial sound effects because these are more congenial to his medium. He is then free to choose not only the nature but the exact timing of his effects in advance of fitting them to the animation itself.

The Music Track

The developed use of special effects is always trespassing over the border into the sphere of music itself. The effects are not only orchestrated carefully in association with the music; they can easily become part of the music itself. A superb example of this is the track for *Mickey's Moving Day*, in which the melody of the composer's music is punctuated by the quick urgent voices of Mickey, Minnie and Goofy and by the extraordinary noises which emanate from the piano in the process of being moved about and broken up.

The first approach of the animator to music may well be the temptation to use it solely for achieving effects. This is to confine it unwisely, and to lose one of the greatest assets of a good cartoon, which is a good score with inherent musical qualities.

Two composers in Britain are outstanding in this field—Matyas Seiber (with scores for over sixty films, including *The Magic Canvas*, *Animal Farm* and *A Short Vision*, the cartoon of the nuclear bomb made by Joan and Peter Foldes which so stirred audiences in the United States when it was shown on television) and Francis Chagrin (who wrote, among many scores, those for *Without Fear*, *All Lit Up*, *Fly About the House* and *Balance 50*).

[1] The Art of Walt Disney, *by Robert F. Field, Collins, London, 1944.*

78

In America brilliant work has been done by such composers as Gail Kubik and Paul Smith.[1]

The composer for the cartoon film has to accept the particular discipline of the close, second-by-second relation of his score to the action and mood of the picture while at the same time developing the continuous musical quality of his work. It requires a special musical imagination to achieve this. Some experienced composers of cartoon music prefer to create their broad musical line first, and then at a later stage to superimpose on it the particular accents required by the details of the action.

This brings us to one of the main controversies in the production of animated films; should the music be pre-recorded before animation is undertaken or, as in the case of most live-action pictures, should it be post-synchronized?

If we assume that music for the animated film is largely valuable on account of its potentialities for close synchronization, then we must also assume that to pre-record the music would be of far greater help to the animator than to post-synchronize it. Pre-recording will, of course, pin the animator down exactly—it is the price he must pay for the precise effects that he has chosen to achieve in a medium supremely adapted for the purpose. Therefore any kind of musical sequence in cartoon films where the animation is detailed and depends on close timing with the sound is bound to be pre-recorded before animation begins in any final form.

On the other hand, if any sequences in a film do not rely on this form of close synchronization—when, in fact, other elements in the film are more important, such as demonstration or instruction in a cartoon about a technical subject—then pre-recording may not be necessary. Consequently the animator will not be tied down to the same degree, for the usual procedure in theatrical cartoon work is to prepare a sound track giving a piano recording of the music to act as a guide to the animators for the progress of the rhythm. This recording is of great help to the composer himself when he comes to the orchestrating and conducting of the final score. But if the animator decides to do his work in advance of the recording he must be prepared to sacrifice one of the principal effects of his medium for the sake of gaining his freedom.

The various new experiments in creating sound and musical effects can be of great use to the animators. The principal systems at

---

[1] *Readers are referred to pp. 35-39 and 154-160 in* The Technique of Film Music, *by Roger Manvell and John Huntley in the same series as the present volume. Some account is given there of the work of music in cartoon films.*

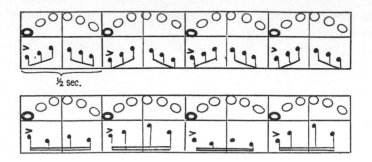

These diagrams illustrate the basic synchronization between music and movement in animation. Normally a far more complex relationship is established, especially in the use of such new sounds as electronic music and musique concrète. In the diagrams the upper sections represent the movement and the lower the music; each line is the

present are drawn sound (associated particularly with Norman McLaren's work in Canada[1]), electronic music and *musique concrète*.

Drawn sound has for long been a close ally of animation in a strictly limited field. Its application beyond the abstract cartoon film can only be occasional. Drawn sounds lack any warmth or humanity. They consist almost entirely of varied "plips" and "plops", "plinks" and "plonks"—sounds which are interesting and amusing rather than significant or in any way emotional in their appeal. At best, only a very limited aspect of human feeling can be expressed through them.

Electronic music is also limited.[2] It has no harmonics, which makes it seem cold and impersonal. *Musique concrète*, however, offers greater opportunities, with its wide range of frequencies and its attempt to raise sound effects into the sphere of expressive musical art. Its range of effects offers a chance to the animator to experiment with sound outside conventional musical forms; it can bring to the sound track new instruments with new qualities of expression which, however limited in themselves, serve the same purpose as the animator seeks to fulfil when he attempts with his composer to orchestrate both effects and music into a single composition of sound.

[1] *See pp. 169-177 in* The Technique of Film Music *for McLaren's own account how his system of drawn sound has been developed for his films.*
[2] *For a descriptive account of* musique concrète *and electronic music, see the articles by Reginald Smith Brindle in* The Musical Forum (*May and June 1956*). *Electronic music was first used for a cartoon film and most significantly by Honegger for Bartosch's* L'Idée.

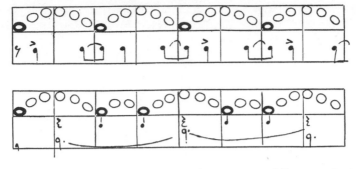

equivalent of two seconds' action on the screen. *Line 1:* Music follows exactly the rise, fall and impact of the animation. *Line 2:* Instead of following the shape of the animation, this depicts *MOOD* (busy activity). *Line 3:* Impact of animation and musical accent form a syncopated rhythm. *Line 4:* An irregular pattern is stressed by musical rhythm.

What the animator should avoid is imprisoning his imagination in a cul-de-sac, or entering a fascinating maze of experimental sound from which there is no exit. Sounds—musical or in the form of effects—are valueless to him when they cease to be expressive in their relation to his picture. It is useless destroying any reaction in the public to what is being put across from the screen, whether the animation is comic or serious.

The animator is responsible for the vision, the control of the total medium, including sound as well as sight. He must *think* sound as well as picture. He is only half an animator if his skill is limited to drawing. He must be able to maintain a close and inspiring collaboration with his composer, and this must often look beyond mere rhythmical synchronization.

The basic, most practical time unit in cartooning is half a second, that is, twelve frames. This is equal to one pace in normal walking. A number of these half-second units make up the basic rhythm of movement—a man walking. But if cartoon films observed this natural rhythm of movement and its equivalent in all standard motions of bodies and objects, the result would be monotonous— a visual monotony which is apparent enough in those cartoons which stay too slavishly tied to naturalistic timing. Therefore, the animator, having established his rhythmic unit, soon proceeds to break away from it in order to add interest and surprise to his pictures. He may therefore quicken the animation from twelve frames to nine or six, or slow it from twelve frames to sixteen or twenty-four, according to the effect he wants for his subject. An

81

exact relation of sound effect to image is not necessary; in fact an interesting counterpoint can be achieved by speeding up the vision at the expense of the sound.

The animator and his composer have to come to some understanding about this rhythmic relationship between sound and image. Once the time units have been established and charted, and the composer is able to observe these time units exactly, it is possible to post-synchronize the film. There is a danger of a very slight loosening of the bonds between picture and sound, but they are likely to be so small that no audience will be aware of them. For the more imaginative forms of score, the animator should leave the composer as free from the strait-jacket of timing as he possibly can. If, however, animation is undertaken before the music is composed or recorded, the composer must give the animator a very clear idea of the kind of music he intends to produce. The style as well as the rhythms of the animation must "belong" to the music once the two are brought together.

There is a further aspect to the relationship between music and image. The sounds produced by certain instruments suggest various visual forms and shapes.[1] This must be borne in mind by the animator when he learns that the music will feature, for example, bassoon or harp, violin or double bass, drums or cymbal. He should know whether his shapes must be crescendo or diminuendo; his movements andante or legato.

Instruments, too, suggest colours. This is more debatable because it is a much more subjective aspect of visual-aural relationships, but it has great dramatic and atmospheric importance in both the cartoon and live-action film. For example, the woodwind instruments may associate well with blue, the violins with yellow, the saxophones with red.

In all these considerations of fitting music to pictures, every film is necessarily a law to itself. What matters is that the animator should be alive to the possibilities of his art not only in design, but in the combined use of voices, effects and music as well.

Although the sound track is almost as important as the picture itself, it often fails to get equal consideration. This is particularly true in the case of the music tracks for television commercials; the

---

[1] *See an article on this subject by Chuck Jones in* Hollywood Quarterly (*July, 1946*). *The writer is mainly concerned with the relation of abstract mobile shapes to music. Another relevant article is that by Ralph K. Potter on "Audiovisual Music" in* Hollywood Quarterly (*Fall, 1947*). *The theme is the exploitation by means of film of patterns of movement and colour co-ordinated with established or original music.*

82

commentator's voice only too frequently overrides and dominates the sound track. The cartoon is weakened by such treatment.

The animator must be aware of the potentialities of a good sound track and conscious of what happens to it in the final mixing. In cases where there are music, dialogue and sound effects tracks, the final sound track may easily become overloaded with too much happening at the same time. For instance, confusion may arise if an intending client wants the name of his product emphasized all the time, or the composer wants his music to be heard above everything else. A proper balance must be achieved and the animator directing the film must be in control of the final shape of the sound track in its relation to the picture. Simplicity must apply to the sound track as well as to the animation.

Finally, there is now a widening range of synthetic sounds suitable for cartoons and many new tape-recording techniques for both effects and music. These should be developed so that the old routine jingles, with their dulling familiarity, recede from this branch of cartoon production.

7

VALUES IN COLOUR AND IN BLACK-AND-WHITE

THE audience watching a film has little time to study the aesthetic values of any one picture in the general continuity of the production.

A man lingering in front of a masterpiece in an art gallery has before him a still composition conceived for timeless contemplation. The composition of such a work must therefore be complete and valuable in terms of its stillness, however living the flow of its line, however vivid its balance of colours.

The film audience can only appreciate the composition of a picture in terms of its constant motion—not only motion within the individual shot, but the developing motion which comes as shot follows shot in the progression of the movie. The painter who is to become an artist in the cartoon film must instinctively respond to the needs and advantages of this mobile, progressive composition, this play of colours in time.

It is, in fact, an entirely new opportunity for the artist. He can now conceive his colours in terms of a time as well as a space dimension. He can evolve a drama of colour which aims at the unfolding of moods and the onset of emotional values, and he will in consequence find himself planning colour developments in time units and footages.

This essential difference between coloration in normal static painting and the cartoon film is the starting point of the cartoonist's work. If he thinks of the cartoon as a series of still compositions in which the colours are mobile merely because the characters bearing them move about, he is obviously unaware of the richest qualities in animation. Yet it was some time before this dynamic use of colour in cartoon work (as distinct from the dynamic movement of the characters and the action) began to be sensed and consciously developed as a fundamental part of animation.

It was, perhaps, first understood by Disney in certain climactic sequences of his feature films—in *Dumbo*, for example, when the

84

little elephant becomes intoxicated and sees a fantastic illusion of pink elephants, and in the case of the melodramatic battle of the stags in *Bambi*. It was also developed much earlier by Len Lye in *Rainbow Dance* and *Colour Box*, and by Hoppin and Gross in *The Fox Hunt*.

These films show some of the earliest examples of the dynamic use of mobile colours changing for dramatic purposes. Until such demonstrations as these had shown what could be achieved through the dramatization of colour-design, animators had been content to use colour only illustratively as it had been copied from nature in normal book illustration, especially in the more elaborately illustrated books of fairy tales with pictures by artists such as Arthur Rackham and Edmund Dulac.

Once the break had been made in one direction by Disney and in another by abstract artists such as Len Lye, the way was open for the more advanced colour developments shown in the more striking post-war work of British, French and American animators, and particularly in Hubley's early work for U.P.A. and McLaren's work in Canada. The colour plot of U.P.A.'s *Rooty-Toot-Toot* (directed by John Hubley) was an extreme example of what the dynamic use of colour can achieve to emphasize the dramatic quality of this kind of film.

The cartoonist working in the theatrical field must have, therefore, a strong colour sense. It is colour that hits the eye of the audience first. In *Rooty-Toot-Toot* the dramatic surprise is frequently established for the first time by the sudden colour changes that operate almost like music, flowing boldly through the picture anticipating the coming changes in emotional values. Here is a further break from realism, a further challenge to the imagination of the audience. The characters themselves, simplified to an absolute minimum in lines, angles and curves, are also presented in strong, flat and basic colours. Instead of a realistically-conceived coloration involving ten or twenty tints, two or three strongly contrasting colours help to develop Hubley's hard-hitting characterization.

This dynamic conception of colour reached the essentially popular art of the film from sources which had already for some time been affected by the more advanced design of posters, book-jackets, journal-covers, magazine and other forms of advertising. The attitude to colour of the Post-Impressionist painters had strongly influenced many of the best artists working in this field of commercial art in the nineteen-twenties and nineteen-thirties led by the artists of the Bauhaus, a centre for architectural experiment founded by Walter Gropius in Weimar, Germany, in 1923, and other advanced Continental schools of art whose teachers and pupils later found a fertile and receptive ground for their activities in the United States.

Notable designers of posters in Britain, France and America at this time were McKnight Kauffer, Cassandra, Jean Carlu and Paul Colin. The coloration of their work was as striking as its design, and its public display helped to prepare popular audiences to accept such work in the cartoon film. The avant-garde among the film-makers—notably Len Lye and, in the puppet advertising film, George Pal—helped to establish the dynamic use of colour and so furthered the freer graphic tradition already established in the black-and-white films of such artists as Gross, Hoppin, Moholy-Nagy, Fischinger, Man Ray and Hans Richter.

Here the European film-maker led the way, as the European painters had done long before in the Post-Impressionist movement. The dynamic use of colour by Van Gogh and Gauguin, who developed their own form of dramatic surprise by rejecting the merely representational use of colour and adopting colours wholly dictated by mood and feeling, became an example to the animators. They followed it crudely enough at first, but they have come to understand it with a new, increasing subtlety in more recent years.

8

ANIMATION AND THE COLOUR SYSTEMS

THE animator's work can only reach the screen through one or other of the colour systems available to him. The history of the cartoon film has been closely associated with the history of these colour systems which are still evolving.

Disney made his first colour cartoon, *Flowers and Trees*, in Technicolor during 1931. Technicolor used at that time a three-strip process in which three films were sensitized to record red, green and blue light. The cumulative colour effects were produced by the interplay of these three colour elements.

When Len Lye was making *Rainbow Dance* (1936) he worked in Technicolor's Laboratories in order to develop certain effects that he wanted during the process of printing, so side-tracking photography altogether. Later, Norman McLaren avoided the camera and painted his abstract films directly on to the celluloid. We are grateful to Bernard Happay of Technicolor Ltd. for giving us the following account of Technicolor's work with Len Lye:

The original material for this subject was a series of separate black-and-white images, some being derived from original black-and-white photography of live-action scenes and some being obtained from the photographic reproduction of certain drawn or stencilled patterns done by Len Lye directly on to strips of film.

All this material was assembled into a number of rolls of equal length, the material derived from live-action photography being sometimes in the form of negative and sometimes in the form of positive print derivatives. There were no colour separation negatives in the ordinary sense of the word and the resultant colour image was entirely produced "synthetically" by differential printing of the three matrices used to transfer the Y, C & M dyes.

Each individual matrix was multiple printed from selected reels of black-and-white material, the intensity of printing light being adjusted from scene to scene throughout the roll so as to give variations of colour, and sometimes two negatives would be run simultaneously while printing the matrix so that one, for instance a title, provided a matte reserving the title area against the appropriate background. When printing one of the other matrix records, a complementary title matte would be used so that coloured lettering of the titles was obtained, the colour depending on the relative printing of the three matrices.

The same sort of effect was obtained when printing from the live-action photographic derivatives as negative or positive, so that in some scenes the effect was obtained of a heavy colour positive image, for instance a dark brown-red, combining with a corresponding negative image in bright green. One or other of these images might also be combined with a moving pattern of lines or dots as well as titles.

The whole printing operation was very complex, and involved a large number of separate printings on the same three strips of matrix stock; but the result was certainly outstanding and the rhythmic effect of both image patterns and colour changes made a terrific impact on the viewer and was a tribute to Len Lye's amazing ability to visualize in such detail the effects which could be obtained by the utilization of such complex printing procedures.

While Technicolor permits a degree of control by the artist within each of the three colour bands, Eastman Colour is an integral three-layer process using a single strip of sensitized material. The artist's control, therefore, is limited to what he has created in advance graphically for reproduction in Eastman Colour. The same is, of course, true of other integral three-layer processes.

The cartoonist must be aware of both the advantages and the weaknesses of the colour systems at his disposal. There is no commercial colour system in which there is not some loss in colour values, but the nature of the loss varies with the systems themselves. Once the artist knows the system he is going to use for each individual film, he can favour in his designs the colours which are the strong suit of the system. If a subject demands a certain colour emphasis, then the designer should obviously try to use the colour system that favours this emphasis.

9

THE TELEVISION CARTOON

THE cartoon as seen on the television screen is the result of the projection of impulses in the forms of lines sprayed over the television tube. The laws of the persistence of vision operate to turn this series of constantly-retraced lines into a satisfactorily assembled image. But this image has its obvious weaknesses in range and definition. From the animator's point of view this is painting and drawing through electronics.

In live action there is a certain loss of focus in the televized image, and the greater the depth and detail in the original the greater the loss of quality in the transmitted image. The cartoon lends itself to projection through television because it can offer action by simply-outlined characters drawn without moulding, figures that are flat-surfaced and schematic in design.

The development of the colour cartoon designed specifically for television is limited at this early stage by the slow progress of colour television itself. Certain factors affect this medium, and the utmost simplification is needed if the image is to be at all appreciated by the viewer. There is also a loss of colour at both the white and the black extremes of the colour range. In fact, the fewer colours used the better, and those that are used should be as positive and strong as possible. Coloured figures must always be enclosed by very clear outlines; the subtle use of colour to indicate a figure without the further definition of outlines—a graphic form which can be so effective on the big theatre screen—is entirely lost on the small and less-defined television screen. The first stages of design for colour television seem to demand the use of the flat colours familiar in the comic-strip, enclosed by bold outlines, and the avoidance of those pale colours which fall out of visibility altogether in the process of transmission and reception.

The main development of the cartoon for television has taken the designer back to the early days of black-and-white animation. He can now study in the light of thirty and more years' experience the value for us to-day of the pioneer stages in cartooning—even that represented by Cohl himself. Also the shadow-films of Moholy-Nagy, the silhouette films of Lotte Reiniger (which she has herself developed afresh for television), the tonal-shapes of Fischinger's work and the firm, simple outlines of Bartosch's animated woodcuts all give their separate cues for useful developments in television cartoon design, alike for commercials and for straight entertainment. Colour is quite unnecessary for most kinds of simple burlesque which are dependent on the quick wit of animation rather than on any subtle attempts to establish mood.

We have gone back to the past for the cue, but what is being evolved now for television is essentially a modern, black-and-white cartoon idiom. The emphasis is on the outline set against a light-grey background. This light grey becomes the neutral, undazzling white needed for the television screen; pure white would burn out and be tiring to the eyes. Alternatively, clear white outlines can be used against a dark background, after the manner of some of Emile Cohl's films. In this case, the dark background must be some degrees lighter than black itself.

It is a useless and therefore an uneconomic labour to try to be too subtle on the small electronic screen. The graphic effects must all be broad and clear. But once the animator realizes these limitations and then finds that he can nevertheless create satisfactorily within them, the opportunities offered by television are very great indeed.

10

INFLUENCES AFFECTING THE FILM

SOMEONE must pay for it all! Either before or after the film is made, the costs of production and a reasonable profit for the film-maker must be found. This money may come from an advertising agent on behalf of his client, from an industrialist through his public relations department, or from a corporation, a department of some Government or an international organization. Or it may come from the box-offices of the theatres through a film distributor.

Whatever the source of the money, it talks hard to the film-maker and in one way or another affects the nature of his product. The so-called free cinema is the rarest form for either live-action or cartoon film-making—though it too exists, often on the borderline between amateur and professional production. An important example of this was Joan and Peter Foldes's celebrated cartoon *A Short Vision* or Bruno Bozetto's *History of Armour*.

The film-maker has to meet the needs of his patron—whether he is an advertising agent, a public relations officer or a distributor claiming to represent the tastes in entertainment of the general public—and the animator's approach to his work varies according to the nature of the impact of these other very differing interests upon his creative talent.

The Needs of the Advertising Agent

The advertising agent, like the journalist, is a much-abused character. At one moment he is the angel, the patron, the harbinger of employment. At another he is suitable only for a star part in *The Hucksters*. The animator working with an agency for the first time may find himself having an attack of nerves. The proper relationship between the advertising agent and the animator is still a matter of trial and error. It needs some understanding from both sides if the trials are not to become sore and the errors profound.

The animator has to realize that the film, or series of films, that the agent wants from him is, from the agent's point of view, most likely to be a part of a carefully planned advertising campaign, either new or already in operation. The animator may regard his film as an end in itself, but the agent will be interested in it only in so far as it crowns the work he has initiated in other fields—for example, his newspaper, magazine or poster campaigns on behalf of the same product. The cartoon, which for the agent may well be the most expensive single item in his client's budget, seems to him like the visible part of an iceberg. It only takes the form it does above the waterline because of the far greater proportion of ice that supports it below the surface.

The agent therefore tends to begin his discussions with the animator in terms of pre-conceived ideas. He will want his cartoon film to fit in with all the gimmicks he has thought up for his posters, his packaging and his press advertising. And the animator will indeed be lucky if he finds himself talking to a man who has made a real study of either the limitations or the potentialities of his medium.

He will probably be asked at one and the same time to give too much and too little as far as good cartoon film-making is concerned. He will probably be told precisely what the agent wants him to do, with the storyboard virtually if not actually taken out of his hands. He will walk out of the agency with a contract in his pocket and his heart thumping heavily in his boots. And the agent will look down after him from the office window thinking how difficult these artists are to convince about anything they have not thought up for themselves, however obvious its virtues may be.

In the case of the advertising agent and the animator the art of working together has to be evolved mutually. The animator must be responsive and appreciative of the problems of his latest and possibly most important patron, and learn how his versatile, flexible, responsive medium can fulfil the needs of an advertising campaign with delicacy, taste and skill. He must evolve his own aesthetic of the television commercial as well as that for the longer forms of advertising film for the theatre. These commercials are in any case going to be made in large numbers. It is better that they should be made well, that they should be satisfying, amusing and good entertainment in their own right.

The agent, on the other hand, must for the good of his own work, realize what a cartoon film is. This he can only learn from the animator, and if he does not consult him about how his work may best fit in with the campaign he is organizing, he will only be paying

92

Pages 93-95: *The Rope* (Copyright Playhouse Pictures for N.B.C.; U.S.A.).

SPECIAL USES FOR ANIMATION

ve and Below: *Cinerama Holiday* (Copyright Halas & Batchelor; Great Britain).

Butterfly (Copyright C.B.C.; Canada).

Round and Round (Copyright C.B.C.; Canada).

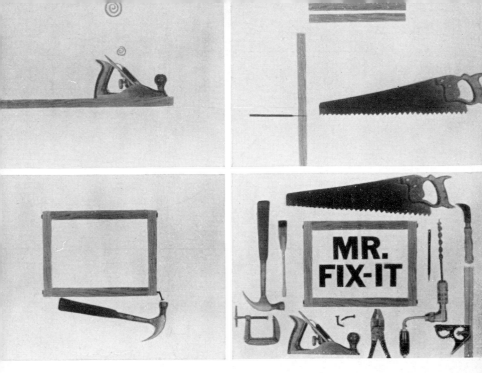

Mr. Fix-it (Copyright C.B.C.; Canada).

General Promotional Film (Copyright C.B.C.; Canada).

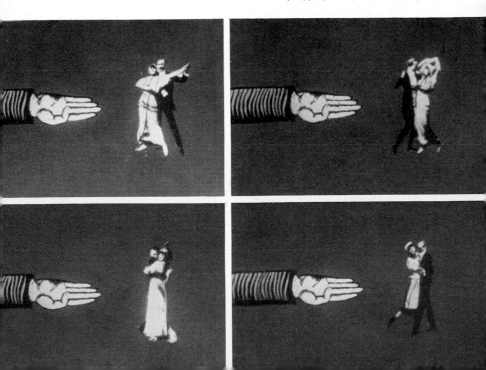

Around the World in Eighty Days (Copyright Michael Todd Productions).

Three backgrounds for credits designed by Saul Bass and animated by Shamus Culhane.

a great deal of money for an incomplete or ill-conceived job, giving satisfaction in the end to nobody. The public readily enjoy a good cartoon when they see one—they have been educated to do so for a full generation in the cinema. Their sense of entertainment is only frustrated and insulted by bad, crude work when it appears in the television or theatre commercial.

This bad work is only too common to-day. Sometimes it is the result of unskilled film-making. Often it is the result of a bad story-board, ill-adapted to the virtues of cartooning and imposed on the weaker film-makers by the agency. It is to be hoped that good cartoonists are not so needy nowadays that they must accept such travesties of their art as part of their anonymous output. (Every commercial should, in fact, carry the signature or trade-mark of its maker.)

The purpose of a cartoon commercial is to commend an advertiser's goods to the public. A bad commercial is simply not doing this job, and a cartoon may well be bad if it has been conceived, not by the animator himself, but by the team of script-writers, visualizers and art directors employed by the agency and actively trained only in the other branches of their profession.

The Needs of the Public Relations Officer

When the cartoon film-maker is approached directly by an industrial firm, government department or international agency to make a film, he is faced with an entirely different set of circumstances from those created by working for the advertising agencies.

First of all, he is dealing directly with his sponsor, and not working through an agency official, with artistic ideas of his own and a professional reputation to maintain before both the client and the film-maker. This simplifies the relationship considerably, for the sponsor regards the film-maker as a specialist in his own right, and is only concerned with the content or "message" of the film, together with its general purpose, length and cost. The sponsor normally employs a public relations officer who works directly with the animation production unit.

The kind of film needed is, broadly speaking, a single-reeler or two-reeler belonging to one of four main types of production:

1. The instructional film, teaching how something should be done;
2. The demonstration film, showing how a process works through the unique visual opportunities of the animated diagram or model;

101

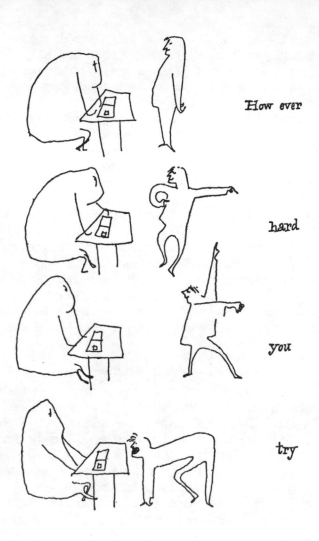

How ever

hard

you

try

Richard Macdonald, the British art director and storyboard artist, states his views visually on the relationship between sponsor and cartoonist.

it's impossible

to explain

storyboards

[almost all]
to some people
^

The storyboard has two possible functions—to explain the nature of the continuity of
a film project to a sponsor and to serve as a visual guide to the Unit itself.

3. The sales promotion film, usually designed for internal use by a large industrial organization for its sales staff;

4. The public relations film, which is either a prestige production to commend a company and its product to the public (rather than to sell a commodity directly, as in advertising), or a film designed to put over some information or propaganda from a government department or other public body (national or international).

In all these types of production, the film-maker normally finds himself working closely with an expert in the subject. Their relationship is a fluid one, with the film-maker constantly in need of information, either technical or general, which will help him to realize effectively the kind of film his sponsor needs.

In establishing his working relationship with his sponsor, he must find out as soon as possible why the sponsor wants the film and whom he intends to address through it. Only then can he make practical suggestions as to how he should design the production— with initial proposals for the presentation of the subject, the length of the film and so on. Matters arise which are not inherent in the advertising film as such, and which necessitate the film-maker drawing very close indeed to his subject, in fact himself becoming a temporary expert in it. This is obviously the case with the instructional and demonstration types of film, and the animator should have little difficulty in preserving the dignity of his medium in such circumstances. This branch of production is of increasing importance in widening the conception of the animated film and increasing its stature as an art.

The Entertainment Needs of the Public

Where the public alone is the animator's patron, nothing stands between him as a film-maker and his audience. There is no agency, no public relations officer, no technical expert, no wary civil servant. The sole purpose is to entertain and mostly to create naked laughter.

The tradition here is never to be without a gag coming up—a gag every ten seconds, so they say. But in cartoon entertainment there can be other factors besides the gag—dramatic feeling, lyrical and poetic values. Indeed, the gag has become a millstone round the neck of the modern animator—it has created an almost unavoidable tradition of winning quick, hard laughs or nothing. The result has been that the cartoon has become established in the minds of both the exhibitor and his public in the conventional form of a series of cliches which has gradually confined it as a branch of film entertainment and wearied its audiences through the sheer reiteration of a single style. While live-action films have been exploiting every kind of mood, the cartoon has become stuck with comic-strip humour and machine-gun tactics which are designed to shoot down its audiences with gags.

The pioneer now is the man who widens the moods as well as the styles of cartoon entertainment not only for the theatres but more especially for television, where the scope for experiment is considerable, not the least in the opportunities that lie in designing general programme material quite apart from the production of the commercials.

PART TWO

THE USES OF ANIMATION

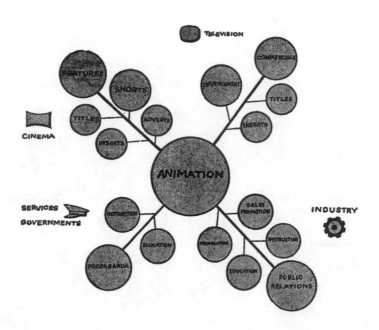

Animation has a wider outlet in terms of use than many people think. It serves the cinema and television as well as the official and industrial sponsor. The extent of the demand in any one field constantly changes in relation to the others. For example, in the United States the needs of television entertainment through cartoon have already exceeded those of the commercial and sponsorship by industry is increasing.

11

TELEVISION COMMERCIALS

Commercial television began in the United States in 1946, and since then it has developed on a scale which will eventually be world-wide. Already the countries with commercial television include, in addition to the United States, Great Britain, Canada, Australia, Japan, Western Germany, Italy, France, Holland, Brazil, Venezuela and many others. The motivation behind commercial television is to sell consumer goods, and this makes it, generally speaking, national, regional, or even local, in the narrow sense, and also very idiomatic in its style and approach. It contrasts strongly in this respect with the style of international cartoon film-making for the theatres.

Cartoons have particular advantages as commercials; among these advantages are their immediate entertainment value, their speed at making points against the severe limitations of time, and their ability to stand up to repetition when most live-action commercials tend to lose "face" by being repeated. Cartoons also have an important economic advantage in that the repeat fees to performers which have been negotiated by the unions are naturally far heavier in the case of live-action films using well-known personalities than in the case of the unseen players voicing the cartoon sound tracks.

Cartoons are said to have a certain recognized disadvantage because members of the audience can never identify themselves individually with the performers. This is the same as saying that it is a disadvantage to gin that its taste is not the same as that of whisky. They produce, in fact, a different kind of effect; they are entertainment on the level of fantasy and they put the audience into a good humour which is immediately associated with the advertiser who has sponsored such a pleasant way of putting over his product. Only the more exceptional, confidential and "genuine" live-action perform-ance by an actor or "personality" is in fact likely to generate a similar degree of "good-will", a feeling that he really means the recommendation he is making. Most people tend to react by saying "Turn the so-and-so off" because they know perfectly well that he is being paid, and paid handsomely to promote the goods he is pushing.

Nevertheless, it is best from the outset to recognize that the nicely-spoken young man, the smiling, pretty girl, the well-mannered middle-aged person with all the assurance of a mature authority can establish an immediate bridge of identification or respect with audiences that have not yet developed an automatic sales-resistance to the direct approach made by these smooth acting performances. These are the sort of people they like and trust in real life, and the virtues of the product are spoken by the performers in terms they immediately understand, and indeed believe to be on the whole true when spoken in this easy, confidential manner. This is one well-tried and often successful way of advertising, though the risks involved can be great because the more sophisticated audiences tend to react against what they hold to be the insincerity of the actors. The cartoon way is quite simply a different way, because it does not attempt to use the method of audience-identification or win confidence through that particular kind of human approach.

Cartoons are more expensive to make than live-action commercials, but they normally have a much longer life and cost far less (as we have said) to repeat in terms of fees to performers. They are much sharper in their impact; they can focus immediately on the product, and indeed bring the product itself into the action by animating the pack or the automobile or the can or the utensil or the apparatus or the food—whatever it may be! Familiar trade-marks come to life on the screen, and this, well done, obviously provides advertising of the most direct kind possible. Cartoons, too, can make a virtue out of their neutrality; no one is putting over an act. Cartoons are only drawings; puppets are only puppets. They can quite naturally and correctly perform to the advertiser's jingles without the frightening insincerity of many live performers. The animator is completely free to create a form of his own that fits the advertiser's message glove-tight.

But it must be faced that a bad cartoon commercial is normally excruciatingly bad! To combine true entertainment with advertising it is necessary to have the kind of imagination which really enjoys the work and takes full advantage of the minor artistic experiments which are most certainly possible in the number of seconds available. The pointed absurdity of the good cartoon commercial can be a delight, as was the case in John Hubley's famous series for Ford. The few seconds add up to a little drama in a world of caricature in which the invention of the artist fills the audience with delight and a desire to see it again for its own sake (which is also the product's sake!). The high degree of control in the timing of effects extends with equal ease to the sound track, and the punch-lines can be just as deftly controlled and emphasized as they are in the dynamic design of a theatrical animated cartoon. Even jingles can be made to seem more pointed and witty by virtue of the skill of the accompanying animation.

This, however, assures a sympathetic relation between the advertiser and the animation designer. Without that understanding the cartoon merely follows lamely in the wake of an advertiser's storyline or message. It does not light up. It has no fireworks. It could not sell a button. Any form of cartooning from stylized naturalism to the completely abstract can be readily adapted to positive salesmanship, provided there is a proper understanding of the medium by the advertiser as well as (of course) by the animator himself.

The idea behind the animation concept must relate directly to the purpose of the advertiser, whose own interests will be best served if he does not initially try to impose the wrong kind of concept on the animator. The cartoon is still magic, a box of conjuring tricks quick as sight itself, a sleight-of-hand within the given seconds. But it requires a particular kind of imagination to realize the advertiser's message in this way, and the best attitude to cartoon-invention is always to pursue an original and striking policy rather than to conform to certain recognized cartoon conventions. The 30 and 60 second commercial is in some respects an ideal length in which to carry out experiments. The selling capacity of cartoon commercials has, of course, been repeatedly proved.

The various national styles of cartoon commercials follow the patterns we have already described in an earlier section. There is no literary tradition in American cartooning; the background alike to the television commercial and the short theatrical cartoon is the comic strip technique with which the American public has grown up for nearly half a century. But the character of the American commercial has developed independently since it took over the skills of the theatrical cartoon after 1946, especially in relation to timing, the introduction of the jingle to establish the name of the product, and the general liking for sheer zany comedy—drawing and story alike putting the accent on oddity.

The idea behind the jingle is to leave in the memory of the audience an inescapable residue of sound associated with the name of a product. Its origins lie both in American jazz and in German close-harmony singing. On the threshold between conscious and sub-conscious thought the jingle tee-teeters on, pattering out its rhythms in little toe-beats or tongue taps. It joins the dangerous territory of "sub-think"—you many find yourself naming the product without conscious thought at all. But whereas "sub-think" implies a technique of implanting thoughts without the conscious acceptance of them in the first place, the jingle is an honest enough mnemonic planted with every degree of obviousness in the public ear.

By the time British commercial television began in 1955 it was natural that the technical experience gained in America would be studied and applied in the development of British commercials. Nevertheless, certain differences between the attitude to advertising of British and American audiences had to be kept in mind. The treatment of early commercials tended to be slower with a more marked storyline (as in the *Guardsman* commercial for Murray-mints). British audiences are more sceptical of advertising than American, and more susceptible to sales resistance; it was therefore more difficult for both the advertiser and the cartoonist to evolve effective methods of presentation which would not alienate audiences who from the start had been conditioned to suspect the more blatant American advertising method.

Apart from their long experience of theatrical cartoons, there was no rooted tradition of comic strip-cartoons in popular British culture apart from the mild little stories dotted about the picture papers. Even in the theatres cartoons had been gradually declining in numbers during the 'fifties and therefore becoming rather less familiar than before to the general public, and for the majority of people it was a great novelty to see short cartoons of any kind projected into their living rooms. Perhaps the biggest surprise of all was that the much-derided jingles actually became popular and seemed for these mass audiences in Britain to have some entertainment value. The style of the commercials, as in America, became very national in character, idiomatic in artistry, fairly realistic in graphic style, caricaturing comic British types with comic British voices. Their effectiveness as selling agents soon placed them in the forefront; by 1960 some 25 per cent of the commercials being used were cartoons.

The other distinct stylists in commercial cartoon film-making have proved so far to be the French; certain units there have

112

developed a unique style of their own, and have produced considerable numbers of these cartoons for use in British and American television. They have their own national pictorial flair and invention, a true Latin quality in their elegance of design, their wit and their glamour.

The American pattern, however, remains paramount in the television commercial. Its influence extends to Canada, to Latin America, even to Japan, where there is a strong indigenous graphic tradition, but little knowledge of, or background to, cartoon film techniques. The result has been that the technique of the American cartoon, in particular the Disney cartoon, has been copied in a setting where a distinct national style could well have been developed. And there is little of American wit, the American sense of vitality and fun, in these carbon copies—merely a plugging emphasis on the advantages of the product in improving the comfort and well-being of the purchaser. In Western Germany the television commercial has got off to a very slow start, using the old-fashioned, rather coy fairy-tale style which shows how life is changed (as if by medieval magic) once the product comes into use. German television commercials rely heavily on the artistic and technical skills of animation units in Britain.

The interchange of animators and designers between the United States, Canada and Britain encourages a constant germination of ideas and techniques, and a gradual movement towards a unification of styles between these countries. What is important now is to keep this lively if limited branch of cartoon film-making on the increase if only because it is the bread-and-butter of animation. Without this useful occupation, animation as a whole might well have faded to little or nothing during the period when the full impact of television on theatre attendance began to change the nature of the theatre programme as well as the ratio of theatre screens, and led to a severe curtailment in the production of theatrical cartoons.

12

ADVERTISING FILMS FOR THEATRES

ADVERTISING films for the theatres are confined mainly to the Western European countries; they are not greatly used in the United States. Their use began very early in European theatres, and some of the earliest cartoons made were in fact advertising films. There is a tradition in Europe that at some stage in the programme films of this kind will be shown, though their length tends to vary as between certain countries. The traditional length in Italy and Germany is 2 to 3 minutes, in France 2 minutes, in Britain 1 to 2 minutes, with short filmlets of as little as 15 seconds. The advertiser in addition to supplying the films pays for their exhibition in the theatres. It is unlikely, however, that this form of advertising film will expand in the future, as its place is being gradually and more effectively taken by the television commercial whose repetitive impact and wide coverage is bound to offer obvious advantages.

These films, as long as they last, must compete for public attention with the technical standards, showmanship and dramatic atmosphere of the feature and short films alongside which they are shown. It is essential, therefore, that they be well made, the equal in every respect of the normal theatrical cartoon film.

The purpose of these films is exactly the same as that of the television commercial—to sell a product by building up the goodwill of the audience through entertainment. Because of national differences in tradition and feeling, the style of these films differs very greatly as between, for example, Britain, France, Germany and Italy, but even here the American influence can be seen at work—that of Disney in Italy, Germany and France.

However, there has been some excellent and highly individual work done in this kind of cartoon by such units as that of the Pagot Brothers, Bruno Bozetto, and Maximillian Garnier in Italy, by Paul Grimault in France and Ivo Caprino in Norway, as well as Zagreb Films in Yugoslavia serving the Dutch market. Theoreti-

114

cally speaking this kind of effective advertising through animation could be expanded with advantage, even though it is very expensive, especially as it must keep abreast of current screen ratios and make effective use of colour. In practice, the chances are that the competitive impact of television will militate against such developments.

In these brief films it is essential that a more developed storyline is introduced than appears in the 15 to 90 second film for television. Two to three minutes may seem a long time without a story treatment, but although there is more room to expand than in the television commercial, these films are still very short compared with the normal eight-minute cartoon. If the film is to achieve its maximum usefulness as an advertising medium, then this story development must be closely connected to subject-matter directly derived from the product itself or constructed around it. As in the television commercial, the product must be featured at the close of the film—the pay off to the story climax. Up to this moment the product itself might be concealed from the audience, appearing as the *deus ex machina*! In television commercials there is normally insufficient time for this particular technique.

13

PUBLIC RELATIONS AND PROPAGANDA

THE public relations and propaganda aspects of film-making afford an additional outlet for animation.

The kind of film service developed by the documentary movement in Britain during the nineteen-thirties might not at first seem to offer any substantial place for the cartoon. But in *Night Mail* the documentary film-maker was already using the sound track with the same kind of calculation as the animator in his work, and the spirit of experiment that inspired the best sponsored documentaries in Britain at that time gradually extended until it drew in the cartoon itself—initially during the War years, when animated propaganda films were produced.

In America Walt Disney's films made during the same period were very successful. In Britain, anti-Nazi cartoon films were made for exhibition in the Middle East, and later Sir Stafford Cripps, when he became Chancellor of the Exchequer, personally initiated the *Charley* cartoon series which ran from 1945-48 and used a symbolic character representing the ordinary, sensible, intelligent and hard-working Englishman to show in a good-humoured way how the tasks of post-war Britain had to be faced.

Cartoons can make entertainment out of the presentation of facts, figures, systems and ideas. They can show quickly and imaginatively how an industry, a Department, even a Government Bill such as an Education Act operates. "Public relations" are an attempt at explaining how something works in the service of the community. It is obvious that the live-action film can do this well, but it frequently proves clumsy or cumbersome when animation could be quick, neat, amusing and, above all, absolutely clear. A film like *As Old as the Hills* can explain how oil developed in the crust of the earth in a very few minutes. A film like *Balance 50* can turn the dry figures of a balance sheet into a polished and witty demonstration of how the finances of a great corporation work.

116

Commercial for Ford, designed by John Hubley (Storyboard Inc.; U.S.A.).

THE TELEVISION CAMERA

Commercial for Philip Morris, designed by John Hubley (Storyboard Inc.; U.S.A.).

Commercial for Heinz, designed by John Hubley (Storyboard Inc.; U.S.A.).

Fuji Film Cassette Tape (Taku Furukawa; Japan).

Nervine (Jack Tinker & Partners Production, Samuel Magdoff; U.S.A.).

Screaming Yellow Zonkers (Hurvis, Binzer, Churchill Production, Samuel Magdoff; U.S.A.).

Commercial for Scotts Paper Napkins (Ray Pratin Prod.; U.S.A.).

National Colour Television (Shinichi Suzuki; Japan).

Men Who Did Something First (Renzo Kinoshita; Japan).

Brother Electron Organ (Renzo Kinoshita; Japan).

Commercial for Union Carbide (Academy Pictures; U.S.A.).

Commercial for Timken (Academy Pictures; U.S.A.).

Commercial for Kool Shake (Academy Pictures; U.S.A.).

Marching Vegetables, commercial for Heinz (Playhouse Pictures; U.S.A.).

Gondola, commercial for Ford (Playhouse Pictures; U.S.A.).

Stew, commercial for Falstaff Brewing Corporation (Playhouse Pictures; U.S.A.).

Commercial for Vitalis Hair Tonic (Shamus Culhane; U.S.A.).

Commercial for Esquire Boot Polish (Shamus Culhane; U.S.A.).

Commercial for the New York Telephone Co. (Electra Film Productions; U.S.A.).

Commercial for the New York Telephone Co. (Electra Film Productions; U.S.A.).

The *Guardsman*, commercial for Murraymints (Halas & Batchelor; Great Britain).

Made in Japan (Renzo Kinoshita; Japan).

The Snakecharmer, commercial for Shell Petrol (Halas & Batchelor; Great Britain).

Curriculumachine (Renzo Kinoshita; Japan).

Commercial for cheese (Nicholas Cartoon Films; Great Britain).

Commercial for Maxwell House (Biographic; Great Britain).

Commercial for cider (Griffin Animation; Great Britain).

Tango Time, commercial for Guinness (Eric Radage Group; Great Britain).

Commercial for Sunblest (T.V. Cartoons; Great Britain).

Commercial for Murray fruits (Guild Television; Great Britain).

Marathon (Commercial by Samuel Magdoff; U.S.A.).

Commercial for bacon (Halas & Batchelor; Great Britain).

Animation's ability to simplify essentials stands it in good stead when a complex process has to be dissected and yet at the same time kept alive. The economic situation of Britain in 1947—the absolute need to work for export—was shown in a little cartoon for the theatres called *Robinson Charley*; the new Education Act was explained in *Charley Junior's Schooldays*. The audiences in the theatres were shown how the wheels went round, or should go round, and then left to draw their own conclusion as far as they were concerned themselves.

In *Without Fear*, a film about totalitarianism, shock tactics were used to emphasize the psychological horror that results from a police state. In all cases these facts of life would normally be repellent or boring or unintelligible or at the least uncomfortable for the average citizen to absorb during his leisure—far too much like work or formal education for him to bother to look up from the sports page and take note. But these films were also entertainment and so made their point painlessly—either deriving a dramatic impact from the subject or winning the sympathy and good humour of the public because of what was in effect the aesthetic impact of the film, the graphic charm or force of its presentation.

This new branch of animation has developed particularly in Britain during the past fifteen years, and in the United States since the middle 'fifties. The British Petroleum Company (formerly the Anglo-Iranian Company) has sponsored a whole series of cartoons on the evolution of oil and the history of motoring and flying. These films inspired the National Film Board of Canada's *Romance of Transportation*, a charming and clever film about the growth of transport in Canada. In the United States, pioneers in the sponsorship of public relations cartoons have been the Dupont Company and the United Fruit Corporation, though the films made initially for them tended to be more for internal than external showing, like Dupont's cartoon on the working of their scheme for staff pensions. France is also beginning to use cartoon for public relations; an example is Jean Image's film for the French Coal Board, *Un Grain de Bon Sens*.

A beginning in this field has been made. As individuals we live in a physical world which is in reality very small and confined. What we can see and hear is limited. Animation, well used, can help to explain what is going on outside our personal sphere, and it can often do this more clearly than is possible through the live-action film, which suffers from the same limitation as the human eye and ear. Animation analyses and presents its subject through graphic symbols. Nor is it limited in its use, as the live-action film often is,

133

because it too obviously represents the people and the scene of one particular country and involves dialogue spoken in one particular language; what narration is necessary in a cartoon can easily be re-recorded in whatever language is needed, and a scene presented graphically is less specific than one recognizably photographed on a particular location. In other words, where live action particularizes, animation generalizes, and in the process makes what it seeks to explain universal.

14

THE INSTRUCTIONAL AND EDUCATIONAL FILM

THE instructional and educational film observes the same principles as the public relations film, though for animation the subject matter is narrowed down to achieve a more specific purpose—practical teaching. However, many public relations films are suitable for background in education and are used in schools and colleges, like the film on the search for oil *Down a Long Way*.

In the specific teaching film a complicated process or argument can be presented in its simplest, basic terms. Most branches of modern education, whether technical or academic, need the help of many different kinds of film, though good educational films are still not produced in anything approaching sufficient numbers or with sufficient thoroughness of educational purpose. This is especially true in Britain, where official sponsorship is sadly lacking. In America educational films are more numerous, but too often their intention seems haphazard and their technique elementary and unimaginative. The fact that animation is expensive means that few animated instructional films are produced for schools, and that the simpler technique of black-and-white animation will have to be adopted if sponsorship grows. Meanwhile, most of the animated instructional films which have been produced are intended for technical education in science and industry.

There is now no doubt at all that the carefully planned instructional film can add to the efficiency and clarity of teaching. The eye is the quickest sense through which the student can both learn and memorize technical details, especially when the significance of what is being seen is reinforced by words and sounds. Animation adds its own analytical clarity by simplifying down to their essentials processes which in actuality are either too complex, too fast, too slow or too concealed to be seen clearly when photographed in live action. Animation can focus attention on the basic movements, and bring the diagram into action when the more realistic representation

135

of a process is less clear or memorable. For example, the moving diagram is often the best and the quickest demonstration of how a machine works. The instructor using such a film as this can reinforce what is important in it by discussion with the student before the film is repeated on the screen.

It has been proved by experience that the shorter the film the more effective the instruction is likely to be, because of the intense concentration which the student must give to what he is both seeing and hearing at the same time. Animation can often help to shorten the footage of the instructional film without loss of content. The timing of the action in an animated film can be specially controlled in order to make whatever is being demonstrated more memorable.

The element of design in the graphic style of the film can itself be an aid to memory through the use of striking shapes and colours. There is a definite relationship between the visual presentation of facts and figures and their retention in the memory. The key moments in the animation of mechanisms and processes can easily be isolated to be made up into film strips to accompany the instructional film as part of a visual teaching unit.

The following are examples of animated instructional films, each with a note showing in what way the process of animation has contributed towards clarifying the subject:

Water for Firefighting. This film, made with three-dimensional simplified models, uses a form of animated shorthand to show how the forces of water delivered change in relation to the pressure applied by the pumps and the length and dimension of the hosing.

Longitude and Latitude. A mobile diagrammatic technique is used to explain the theory of the measurement of the surface of the earth by the system of longitude and latitude.

Digestion. This film uses a graphic demonstration of the process of digestion in the human body seen in section, in a way impossible if the film-maker were dealing with living organs.

Catalysis. A visual analysis of the composition of proteins in molecules, involving symbolic diagrams showing in magnification certain processes of change quite impossible to reveal through photomicrography.

Linear Accelerator. This film shows the radio-active properties of X-ray equipment in a manner impossible by means of normal demonstration.

A for Atom. The interior structure of the atom is demonstrated through visual symbols.

136

In addition to such full-scale animated instructional films as these, normal live-action films frequently incorporate sequences in animation to make some point of demonstration clear. Examples are to be found in *Criticality* (where diagrams show how criticality is reached in an atomic pile), *Approaching the Speed of Sound* (which shows how pressure on aircraft builds up as they approach the speed of sound) and *The World that Nature Forgot*, in which certain sequences using three-dimensional symbolic models explain the molecular construction of plastics.

The factor common to all these animated films, or inserted sequences of animation, is the invention of simple graphic symbols to represent matter in action or the forces behind some physical phenomenon, or even perhaps to symbolize the nature of some action as, for example, Disney's beating hammer used to represent military power in his film on the invasion of Germany. The common symbols of volume, weight or measurement are frequent enough in the diagrams of text-books, but they can be actively introduced into the instructional film; for example, the volume of a submarine in relation to its displacement of water can be symbolized by a weight and a counter-weight balancing against each other. So a complex phenomenon is simplified not only by the nature of the symbol itself but also by the nature of its movement.

There has never been a greater need than there is now to increase the use of films as visual aids in technical, scientific and academic education. A few good standard films of a general character are not enough. The education of the immediate future needs the careful grading of films on all essential subjects to meet the needs of each age-group and class of student from childhood to manhood, films designed for the most elementary up to the most advanced stages of study. The pressure to enlarge our technical knowledge and capacity is increasing rapidly with the growing need for more skilled working technicians and planners. Those responsible for the administration of education cannot afford to neglect the proper, organized use of films to help the teacher meet these urgent demands, and this in turn means the careful, planned production of instructional films of all kinds and grades. This has been recognized for some time in Soviet Russia, where technical films are produced on an extensive scale, with animation playing an important part in the technique of presentation. Only during the War (that is, in a time of national emergency) has either Britain or the U.S.A. used the film with an equal intensity to help quicken the reception of essential technical knowledge by large numbers of men and women. The urgency is still with us; we must still learn fast and use, among other things, the techniques of learning that the film places at our disposal. The speed with which Soviet Russia has pressed forward the education of her citizens in a single generation is largely the result of using every modern teaching device that she can mobilize.

The need therefore is for organized sponsorship in this field, and for a response by the film-maker and the technical expert. The sponsorship may come from the State or from industry, or from both together. There should be an annual production of a large number of responsible educational films, not the mere handful common to-day.

* * * * *

On the subject of technical films, Geoffrey Sumner, formerly Managing Director of the Larkins Studio, has contributed the following note for this book.

Technical films are the prose of animation. The ultimate aim is no more than the presentation of facts or the development of an argument. The difficulty is to make the natural process of visual demonstration suit with the development of argument or the natural style of verbal communication.

Broadly speaking, there are no subordinate clauses or conditional statements in visual communication. If verbal argument was limited in this way intolerable repetition would be the result. If anyone were to try to describe a complicated process without ever using "except" "unless" "if" "not", he would find it impossible not to repeat himself after the manner of "This is the House that Jack Built". All the information has to be reduced to a series of connected affirmatives, analysed into main headings, and additional related information. The overall argument builds up by accumulation, not by deduction and subordination. Therefore the material must be carefully framed and rearranged so that the argument develops in the right direction and the right order.

At the same time care must be taken not to distort, by this process of rearrangement, the shape and proportionate importance of the whole case being presented.

The effect of this process of rearrangement to produce an argument by accumulation is that factors which in writing may be closely linked (and films are usually devised from written material) have to be separated in order to appear in different parts of the film argument. In dealing with the behaviour of component parts of a machine it is logical to put all the relevant details of each —its operation and characteristics—under one heading. In film this will almost certainly not be the case. In fact it may be necessary simply to make only the briefest introduction of each component and then follow through the behaviour of the machine in a simple way. After that further characteristics of each component may be introduced by watching the whole machine, or some section of it do a second operation.

15

EXPERIMENTAL, AVANT-GARDE AND ART FILMS

THESE films do not represent a defined field of production. They are made by professional, semi-professional and non-professional film-makers for a variety of reasons, most of which originate in their enthusiasm for the medium itself and their desire to develop some technical or artistic aspect of it.

Norman McLaren, who has become over a period of years the best known originator of abstract or near-abstract animation, claims that his approach to each new film is experimental in the sense that he wants to explore some new technical invention alike of sound and image which will expand his own particular field of work still further. The nature of his films, therefore, grows out of their own individual techniques.

Other experimentalists may try to test particular powers of animation against some theme or subject about which they have strong feelings; Peter Foldes's *A Short Vision* grew out of a brief poem accompanied by sketches on the subject of the ultimate extinction of life by a nuclear weapon, the destructive power of which had no limit.

While most forms of animation serve the particular ends of advertising and propaganda, story-telling and entertainment, and so begin with an idea or a need that originated outside the medium, experimental films normally germinate in the heart of the medium itself. The discoveries made by the experimentalists are therefore of constant use to the professional animator because they reveal both in their success and their failure what the medium is capable or incapable of accomplishing.

In a medium as free and as flexible as the drawn film, the field for experiment is endless, and it is through keeping alive this sense of experiment that animation could avoid some of the stereotyped repetitions of established forms of design and technique to which it is so often subject. Although it is obvious that a considerable degree

139

of experiment is always possible in the course of normal commercial production, it is the "free" cinema (that is, film-making without commercial commitments) that allows those more extreme forms of work where failure or partial failure may be just as revealing as some successful new technical discovery. The professional animator should do everything he can to encourage the wilder shores of experiment in "off-beat", non-commercial animation, and should sponsor this work himself whenever he can.

It is one of the limitations of the medium that the total outcome of the work, its final artistic achievement, cannot be judged in advance of its actual realization—certainly in no sense as finally as the theatrical vitality of a play can be judged from its script or a still picture from its advance sketches. Too many essential elements— such as visual flow and continuity, the dynamic relationship of sound and vision—only emerge when the full work has been done.

This is why an experimenter such as Len Lye who concentrates for a period on some detached aspect of animation (such as shock-tactics in the use of colour and sound, or the relation of opticals to the drawn film) gives an invaluable service to his colleagues. He demonstrated initial forms of animation which can be developed more fully by others, as was the case when Norman McLaren used the work of Len Lye as the starting point for his own more advanced and prolonged experiments. It should not be forgotten that the boldest work of both Len Lye and Norman McLaren has been used frequently for very utilitarian ends, such as putting across official propaganda slogans for war-bonds or for the postal service.

The experimenter usually becomes a specialist in some chosen aspect of animation into which he researches further than anyone else until his success encourages the experiments of others. This deliberately narrow application of technical or artistic research (or both together) may, of course, lead into some cul-de-sac of the medium and then atrophy.

Night on a Bare Mountain (a short film exploring the varying pictorial images made possible by the shadows cast from the pinscreen's mass of closely set, movable pin-heads lit from various angles) is probably a good example of a cul-de-sac in animation; the result was both unique and effective, but disproportionate to the immense labour involved in resetting the pins for each frameexposure.

On the other hand, the devoted work of the mathematical filmmakers, Robert Fairthorne and Brian Salt, in animating diagrams to demonstrate geometrical propositions and other mathematical

140

problems and formulae helped to found a limited but very important branch of mathematical film-making capable of elucidating phenomena hitherto regarded as impossible to demonstrate because they remained mental concepts in the minds of trained mathematicians.

Further significant examples of experimentation in animation techniques have been:

Hans Richter's experiments with animated patterns inspired by musical rhythms (begun in 1920); and Len Lye's experiments in films hand-drawn directly on to the celluloid (commencing 1931).

Three-dimensional, stereoscopic animation designed by Norman McLaren, which is of particular significance for the scientific and instructional film of the future (1951). George Dunning introduced an impressionistic free-flow animation in *Flying Man* (1962) and *Yellow Submarine* (1967).

Luciano Emmer's and Enrico Gras's advanced work on the dynamic presentation of still paintings, demonstrating a new way of observing both the subject and composition of the painter's art (commencing 1948).

The early development of animation for serious propaganda, argument or the demonstration of ideas by Bartosch, Disney, Halas and Batchelor, U.P.A., Trnka, (*L'Idée, Dust-bin Parade, Victory through Airpower, The Brotherhood of Man, Spring-heeled Jack*) leading to a later school of film-making which presented abstract ideas through images and symbols (*The Magic Canvas*), or social-scientific exposition (Philip Stapp's *To Your Health*, John Sutherland's *A for Atom*, Disney's *Reason and Emotion*).

The application of a special "humorous diagram" technique with a mock-poetic commentary to make refreshingly clear the significance of a great industrial corporation's balance sheet (Larkin's *Balance 50*).

The first application of animation techniques to the new systems of film presentation, such as Cinerama (Halas and Batchelor); Cinemascope (Walt Disney); Todd A-O (Culhane and Bass); and Living Screen (Halas and Batchelor).

Lilian Schwartz experimented with abstract computer generated films in *Pixilation* and with Ken Knowlton (1969–1972), and John Whitney made abstract graphic motion films such as *Permutation* during 1970.

16

ANIMATION FOR THEATRICAL ENTERTAINMENT

In the theatrical cartoon the sole purpose of the film is to entertain, though a few cartoon films (such as *L'Idée*, *The Tell-tale Heart*, *The Magic Canvas* and *A Short Vision*) have introduced serious social themes into a medium which is virtually always comic fantasy.

The status of these cartoons in the cinema programme has always been a subsidiary one, and the cartoon feature is still an anomaly rather than a recognized branch of full-length film entertainment. Historically, when the live-action film developed in length from the one- and two-reeler, the cartoon was left behind because no one at that time could undertake the phenomenal labour of drawing a six-reel silent production. Although the cartoon became the most popular short in the programme, economically it has always remained the Cinderella of the industry, the odd film out.

As the technical proficiency of cartooning increased, so did the production costs. Unfortunately, cartoon rentals remained very low. The only way to match these increasing costs with increasing earnings was to establish world distribution. The Americans did precisely that during the nineteen-twenties and thirties, and so the American cartoon flourished during the great productive period 1930-50. Even so, the exhibitors paid little or even nothing for them, and some distributors even gave them away with the feature booking.

European cartoons then went underground and joined the avant-garde movement. Their makers were forced to use ingenuity and invention to overcome their lack of finance, and (as we have seen) they often developed new and interesting styles. But their work reached only a limited and specialized public. European animation came into its own again through the various forms of sponsorship developed during and after the War.

In countries such as Russia, Poland, Czechoslovakia, and more recently Yugoslavia, cartoon film production has been subsidized solely by the State itself. As a result of the provision of these State subsidies considerable technical and artistic developments have taken place. We have seen work from both Poland and Yugoslavia which not only is completely free from ideological propaganda but also in point of style and subject goes further in the degree of its stylization than any school of animation in the Western countries. Examples are *The Opening Night* directed by Nikola Kostelac and *Cowboy Jimmy* directed by Dusan Vukotic (both made at the Zagreb studios in Yugoslavia), and *Once Upon a Time* directed by Borowczyck and Lenica in Poland.

Around 1950, that is parallel with the fuller development of television, there came a recession for the American theatrical cartoon. Although on the face of it the audience always seems to want cartoons in the programme, the hardening of American cartoon technique into a continuous repetition of conventional styles had in fact dulled the appetite for these films, and as they were gradually withdrawn from the general programme structure, the audience, unfortunately, did not really miss them. Costs were rising; the studios in Hollywood were being reorganized; the production of cartoons (which for some companies had amounted to an unprofitable sponsorship) virtually stopped. Their exhibition became confined increasingly to revivals in the specialized cartoon and newsreel theatres. The animators, meanwhile, turned to the lucrative market of the television commercial, and are now hoping for an expansion into the pure entertainment field opening up in television. This regular production of theatrical cartoons for the theatres is for the time being at least, virtually confined to the State-sponsored industries of the Communist countries, where flourishing animation centres are being developed.

In America, by 1958, experienced animation units could command an advance of $10,000 or more for one minute of commercial television cartooning. The same units could only anticipate the eventual return of half that sum for the equivalent footage if they decided to make a long-term investment in purely theatrical work. By 1975 the price rose to $20,000.

In our view this is a deplorable position. Cartoon is the only important branch of film art which has been permitted to atrophy. In the various limited forms possible for television it is quite true that production has expanded. But the height of animation as an advanced art and technique within the general framework of the cinema has been reached solely in the theatrical colour cartoon. It is this advanced form of production which the present economic struc-

143

ture of the American, British and French industries no longer permits, apart from the occasional film made for love and never for profit by those companies which turn aside now and then from more profitable forms of animation to make films they have conceived and designed to please themselves.

There is, however, a new outlet growing rapidly for animation which aims only to entertain. This, once more, is television. So far the main hindrance to this development has been the limited budgets available for sponsoring the more complex forms of animation necessary for television programmes. In addition to this, animation seemed to be too elaborate a process to undertake for the limited number of repeats possible in the television medium, even allowing for expanding exports.

Many organizations have been developing various methods that aim to simplify the laborious traditional technique of animation without loss of standards. Certain artists have succeeded in both the U.S.A. and Britain; recently in Britain a method has been evolved which reduces labour costs to a fraction of those previously current for cartoons of theatrical standard. This method involves the use of plastic-based grease-pencils of differing colours which have been developed recently so that the animator can draw direct onto the cell; the intermediate stage of tracing is entirely eliminated, and all painting eliminated except for finishing. This process retains all the richness of animation, backgrounds and general treatment necessary for effective story-telling. It is obvious that the future of the entertainment cartoon lies in the development of techniques such as these which will permit extensive production within the television budget.

THE FEATURE-LENGTH FILM

ANIMATION has never secured a regular, recognized place as a branch of feature entertainment. Only Walt Disney has made a succession of feature-length animated films produced at gradually increasing intervals. Not all were great box-office successes, though some undoubtedly were and have also become a part of film history. In spite of this gigantic and mainly successful feat of organized feature production achieved by Walt Disney, both the public and the film industry have persisted in regarding the live-action film as the only form of feature entertainment.

The work of Walt Disney and of those few other producers in America and elsewhere who have succeeded in making the occasional feature-length cartoon has been accepted by audiences as a kind of *tour de force* in film entertainment quite outside the normal stream of full-scale production. Therefore no tradition of feature-length cartoon production and exhibition has been established, and in spite of the adult appeal of most of Disney's work, his feature productions based on fairy-stories, fantasies and folk-tales have been regarded as entertainment mainly for children. Only *Animal Farm* and (to some extent) *La Bergère et le Ramoneur* could be said to have been designed specifically for adult audiences. *Fritz the Cat*, made in 1971, and many of the Japanese features exploiting trends in eroticism have also claimed to be the first-ever animated features for adult audiences.

If there could have been a tradition established of the regular production of feature-length animated films, there seems to be no reason at all why they should not have become a normally accepted part of film entertainment. But with less than 200 productions of this kind realized during some fifty years, and these made in several countries and in several languages, each production has had to break new ground with audiences when it was finally exhibited.

In any case the number of units capable of undertaking the

sustained and devoted labour necessary to complete a sixty to ninety minute cartoon has necessarily been very few indeed. To undertake the work at all represents normally a major sacrifice of profitable production in the many fields of short cartoons, as well as the risk of a capital sum which is at least equal to that required to make a generously-budgeted live-action feature. Moreover, this capital must be risked without any degree of assurance comparable with live-action production that the public may respond well at the box-office. The question always arises whether the effort is worth while, considering the enormous time and labour involved compared with that needed to make a live-action film of equivalent length. Also one must question whether any but the most exceptional cartoon designers can build and sustain audience interest in their medium over a period of sixty to ninety minutes.

Animation produces, in effect, a shorthand of action; it tells its stories through simplified shapes and forms which convey a rapid flow of events to the eye and the mind. Since compression is the virtue of animation, the demand made on the audience in a given space of time requires a higher degree of concentration than is normally needed for following a live-action film. The presence on the screen of the human actor inspires varying kinds of identification between himself and each member of the audience, a sense of identification which it is, as we have already shown, unusual to find inspired by the drawn actor. Cartoons must depend, therefore, mainly on the appeal of movement and action, and the dramatic emphasis of atmosphere; they cannot rely upon the extended scenes of dialogue and acting, the revelations of mood and character that belong very properly to the live-action drama. This compression, simplification and lack of immediate human identification withdraws the cartoon film to some extent from the immediate human sympathies of an audience seeking an easy way into a soft and undemanding dramatic experience.

Cartoons are more akin to poetry than prose, using graphic images for their symbolism, and poetry is more readily acceptable to most people in its shorter forms unless a special taste for epic poetry is developed. The cartoon legend of feature length is pitched into an heroic, artificial mould that might lie in its appeal anywhere between the levels represented by Scott's once-popular epics and those of Homer himself. And such appeals are not particularly attuned to our times.

The degree of skill required in the animator to hold and develop audience interest through the extended time occupied by a feature-length drama is of a completely different order from that needed for the various forms of short cartoon. The feature animator must become a special kind of dramatist sensitive to a new kind of dramatic form. An eight- or nine-reel cartoon is not the sum of a series of eight or nine shorts. In fact, almost all the feature-length cartoons have depended so far on the appeal of established legend and fantasy, the fairy-tale or folk-tale with which the audience is already familiar and which they delight to see retold in an entirely new way.

But the animator has also at this stage in animation technique to learn how to sustain his own creative interest through the months and even years of concentration on the same familiar tale. *La Bergère et le Ramoneur* was in all some six years in production; the Disney features and *Animal Farm* each took some two years to produce. Often the weariness of labour shows in threadbare sequences that flag or that fail to flow, sections of the story that lack the lift of any real graphic imagination. Every new art form has to find its own natural shape, its own best method of approach when work on such a scale is attempted.

The feature cartoon lies like a great continent unexplored except for its coast line and the mouths of its rivers. To explore the hinterland requires courage and exceptional resources. Meanwhile certain shorter forms of expedition can be very useful and instructive, the kind of expedition represented by Disney's *Man in Space*—a featurette which was an excellent piece of documentary science fiction. It seems obvious now that animation should set itself free from the cosy old world of the fairy-tale and the folk-tale and grasp at bolder themes that are impossible for the live-action film to realize. Science fiction is one field. The mystery story and the fantasy are others. The exploration of strange, imaginary worlds created especially for cartoon could supply a new experience in entertainment challenging the curiosity of a public that has become overfed with the more repetitive forms of live-action story. The test for the cartoon subject is always the simple one: is it something that a live-action film simply could not do? The cartoon feature will achieve its maturity when it creates its own original subjects—the stories "out of this world" that offer some new feat of the artist's imagination.

Feature cartoon production, in contrast to normal live-action film-making, demands far greater skill, talent and experience on the part of its producer if an acceptable result is to be achieved on the screen.

The contribution of a star performer is invaluable to the director

147

of a live-action picture. In cartoon, the building up of a star character depends on the skill of the animator, and at present there are too few animators capable of carrying out the required task on the scale of a feature film.

Even so, the greatest problem of the feature cartoon is story construction. We have already seen that cartoons tell their story at a far greater speed than live-action, owing to the visual simplifications of the process. Also, few writers have an understanding of the medium. The routine formulae for live-action stories are, fortunately, wholly unsuitable for cartoons. In addition to realizing this, the story writer must understand the entertainment needs of an audience which is relatively unfamiliar with the medium and can easily tire of the film after the first ten minutes. For this reason the story should as far as possible reach a climax by the 15th and again by the 45th minutes of the action, since these are usually the critical periods in the audience's attention to a cartoon feature.

The possibilities of animation, both dramatically and artistically, are very great indeed, and this branch of production should not be left unexploited. Furthermore, the wide screen processes are bound to give added impetus to the spectacular cartoon. We can only hope that the medium will live up to its great artistic potentialities.

John the Hero (Marcell Jankowitcs, Pannonia Films; Hungary).

ANIMATION IN THE THEATRES

Tyrannie (Philippe Fausten; France).

Happiness for Two (Zlatko Grgic, Boris Kolar, Ante Zaninovic, Zagreb Films; Yugoslavi

Pirrot (Takchiko Kamei with Amina; Japan).

Out of an Old Man's Hat (Per Åhlin and Gurmar Karlson; Sweden).

Triumph (Borislav Sajtinac, Neoplanta Film; Yugoslavia).

A Film for Philips (Estudios Moro; Spain).

The Line (Yannis Koutsouris, Nassos Mirmiridis; Greece).

Diagram (Daniel Szczechura; Poland).

Sisyphus (Marcell Jankovics, Hungarofilm; Hungary).

Diary (Nedeljko Dragić, Zagreb Film; Yugoslavia).

The Battle at Kerzsence (By I. Ivanov Vano & J. Norštein; U.S.S.R.).

The Nine Lives of Fritz the Cat (Robert Taylor and Steve Krantz; U.S.A.).

PART THREE

CARTOON ANIMATION

We come now to the actual process of animation, and some account of the work of the artists and technicians who are involved in making animated films. We should emphasize at once the distinction between the experimental animator who undertakes all or most of the work of production himself as a single artist-technician, and the producer who, even though he is a creative worker, achieves the production of his films with the help of either a small or a large staff of assistants.

18

PREPARATION

THE initial conception of an animated film grows out of the animator's knowledge of the particular audience for which it is intended and its specific purpose as it has been interpreted to him by the advertising agent or the sponsor. Once this has been understood, it is the animator's task to bring to bear his own instinctive feeling for his audience, and begin to create his storyboard. The storyboard is the visual presentation of the idea in a series of sketches.

The Storyboard

The purpose of the storyboard is threefold. For the film-maker it is the first visual test of the idea to see how it works out, what promise it has for film development. For the film-maker's own staff it acts as an initial demonstration of the work to be done. For the sponsor it shows the kind of film he may hope later to have.

First comes the idea, and out of the central idea the supporting ideas. Ideas are the root of the entertainment cartoon, which needs a ceaseless flow of invention, comic or lyrical, poetic or dramatic. There is a constant inventive process going on in the mind of the animator; there is no let-up for him, unless he delegates this essential task to others and ceases to be his own initiator. Ideas for the sponsored film are born of its purpose, of the technical explanations offered to the animator by the specialists, or the general response of his imagination to the various tasks and directions he is given.

The sooner the animator gets down to drawing the better. Different artists work differently—some prefer to begin with a few words put on paper expressing the core of the idea and intended for a first discussion with the sponsor; others prefer to begin with sets of thumbnail sketches. Here, for example, is the verbal "core" for a public relations film on economics and productivity.

159

THINK OF THE FUTURE

A film eventually completed by Halas and Batchelor, from a script by Joy Batchelor.

Theme: How to get prices down (or to keep them from rising).

Audience: *Western European technicians and factory workers.*
Essential to avoid any approach which will offend, such as talking down or another device on the part of "management".

Approach: Suggest that instead of showing productivity simply in terms of "if you work harder you get more", admit right away that many of the processes involved in mass production *are* boring, but on the other hand, the *pre*-mass production era was not only boring but poverty-stricken. It follows that one cannot go back, but should go forward with a positive attitude (not the present negative one).

Storyline: George (or any other multilingual name) is sick of his job in the factory (he makes chairs or cookers). As a good craftsman at heart he feels wasted. He longs for the good old days, and while nodding off at his machine finds himself back in them.
With pride and joy he chisels a chair (or hammers a cast iron stove) and at 6 sharp downs tools only to find factory hours in 1850 go on until 9. Nor does he have a bicycle to ride home on. Nor gas nor electricity when he gets there. Nor as much protein on the table. Nor running water in the kitchen. George wakes to reality prepared to co-operate and work his way up from being a bicycle-rider to a motor-cycle owner.

Notes on character:
1. (a) He must be likeable.
   (b) Or is there anything to be said for making him thoroughly disagreeable? People might like him better, but it might embarrass the sponsorship.
2. (a) He can be international, living in an undefined but Western European environment. His name, George, Georges, or any other translation according to country of distribution.
   (b) He can be national but divisible, singular or plural. George lives in England; his counterpart, Georges of France, is the hero of "How to get prices down (or stop them from rising)" and so on.
3. Do we have him married or not?
   Singular or plural.

Opposite are the few rough drawings that followed up this verbal outline.

In the smaller animation unit, the responsibility for producing this germ of the film rests with the producer himself, possibly in association with his key animator. Only the few bigger companies have set up a Storyboard Department to initiate these starting points. It is preferable that this essential work should not be delegated, and the fact that it has been in certain cases is one of the results of the increasing specialization of function in the production of animated films which we have discussed earlier.

160

The ideal start for the creation of a cartoon film is to have not more than a page of words fully developed visually by means of many drawings. But consideration must be always given to the particular needs of individual creators.

Certain advertising agencies have set up their own storyboard departments. When these are controlled by imaginative men who are experienced in cartoon work, no damage is done provided there is true agreement between the agency department and the outside unit undertaking the animation. It is obviously convenient for the agency to exercise this high degree of control over the production, but if their storyboard designers are not experienced cartoon men, the potential damage they can do to the medium by imposing their inexperience upon it is incalculable. The exception is the case when a true animator heads the agency's storyboard department and, having created the storyboard himself, passes the animation on to a unit in creative sympathy with his ideas and style.

The storyboard should normally be fluid rather than precise at this early stage in the conception of a film. It gives the logic of the idea in terms of a pictorial action or story, with its key visual "gags" or "gimmicks". It should also begin to show the style and shape of the film, its choreography or motion-continuity.

The animator must acquire his own skill in constructing these initial storyboards. They will soon come to show very cogently his particular graphic style, his own handwriting. He must develop an instinct to pull out the salient drawing from the action operating in

161

his imagination—the drawing which shows the highlight, the peak moment coming out of what has gone before but is not yet drawn at all.

The storyboard at this stage is concerned with the simple projection of the idea or ideas for the film. It must be capable of being quickly understood and absorbed. The animator should be prepared to draw and re-draw his sketches until he gets them right.

It is not without interest that the makers of live-action films have from time to time used the storyboard method of preparing their films. An example of this not uncommon practice which has been published is the series of drawings prepared by John Bryan for the striking opening sequence of David Lean's film of Dickens's *Oliver Twist*.[1] When Walt Disney first turned to the production of live-action films, he used a storyboard to illustrate on paper every camera set-up.

The storyboard, then, is the exploratory stage in any animated film. It shows the main visual outline of the action and the main characters involved. But even at this early stage of rough sketches strung together in sequence it is useful for the animator to test, or feel out, certain sections of the film by elaborating them. This means increasing the number of his sketches perhaps to the extent of producing as many as 30 to 40 drawings for each selected minute of action.

The essential quality in all this early work is its fluidity—its adaptability to the various purposes the animator has in mind. He may want to show the storyboard of a commercial to a client; the sketches will then have to be more finished in their appearance than they need to be if the storyboard is required only for the animator himself and his immediate associates. The quality and quantity of the drawings are matters for the individual to decide according to the way in which he develops his own particular graphic shorthand.

In the case of a film involving quick-moving or violent action, more sketches are needed to pin-point the key moments of movement than is the case with a film of technical exposition, where the sketches may only indicate phases in the evolution of animated diagrams. It is the texture of the action that determines the number and the nature of the sketches involved. The animator is searching for the continuity of motion which will achieve the greatest effect on the screen, the modelling of a graphic action which will eventually exist in time as well as space.

[1] *A section of these drawings are reproduced in* The Film and the Public, *by Roger Manvell (Pelican Books).*

Like the human body, a film of this kind must soon reveal its due proportions; its head, its torso and its limbs must all bear a correct relation to each other. The storyboard is the stage to discover the correct phasing of the action, these points of balance. The artist can literally stand back from the wall on which his sketches are pinned in order, and see the action set out in the whole of its continuity. He can tear down sketches and replace them to fill out this section or concentrate that.

The storyboard is an event requiring great creative energy, ready invention, continuous excitement and lively discussion. For example, in the case of *Animal Farm*, the novel by George Orwell from which the action was being derived contained three fights which were all included in the initial storyboard. But seen in sequence in the storyboard sketches, three fights proved unwieldy in dramatic terms. A single climactic fight was then considered. This was seen to concentrate the action too much. At length it was decided to include two fights. (The final storyboard for *Animal Farm* contained some 2,000 sketches for 75 minutes of action, an average of 26 drawings for each minute. These 2,000 drawings themselves derived from a total production of 10,000 sketches all of which had taken their place on the storyboard at one stage or another.)

Although the storyboard is an essential part of the origination of an animated film, it must not be considered as possessing the same qualities as the film itself. It has no movement, no voices, no sound effects, no music! It is not of the same nature as the end product; it is merely a means towards reaching it. But the more vitally it can anticipate the future animation the better.

Every animator will evolve his own shorthand methods of indicating how his still sketches and drawings are intended to move when the stage of animation is reached. His imagination endows the sketch with a life it can never in itself possess, and he may cover it with symbols to indicate how that life will operate on the screen. But the storyboard is only a chrysalis to be left discarded once the discussion has ceased and the real work of animation has begun.

The Cartoon Characters

It is the characters that have been invariably the main attraction to audiences—ever since the beginning of the movie cartoon. The long procession of famous stars of the animated film demonstrated this, from Felix the Cat to Mister Magoo. The storyboards for their cartoons have obviously been designed to create effective vehicles for these star characters which were either in the process of becoming or had already become established with their audience.

Nowadays, many cartoons, especially those designed as television commercials, do not have the advantage of featuring characters which are well-known favourites with the audience. The character in a television commercial, indeed, may well be only a face superimposed on a cigarette or cosmetic pack. But even a trade-mark must be made to acquire a character of its own the moment it is featured in a cartoon film. The sponsors of television commercials normally expect to see the characters clearly developed at the same time as the storyboard of the action. In any case, characterization must inevitably run parallel with the action itself.

How can a cartoon character emerge? The strength of a character lies in its ability to contain within itself the peculiarities of its type. The *average* man or animal cannot be a character; he cannot in fact exist.

For example, let us say there are a million sailors in the world. Collectively they create a sailor-type in the public mind, a type which can be seen sometimes approximated in live-action films: a salty strength and vitality form an essential part of this type-image. The cartoon sailor is Max Fleischer's Popeye. With the aid of spinach he conforms to type: he becomes super-strong. But exaggeration and distortion give him his own peculiar character over and above this type-quality that he shares with the general conception of sailors as a whole. The essential value of Popeye for cartoon purposes is this exaggeration of the sailor-type with the addition of a screwball eccentricity. He is an oddity, but his anchor is firmly fixed in what everyone is supposed to recognize as the sailor-type.

Popeye also had his characteristic voice, as salty as a piece of old seaweed. Cartoon characters are not only distilled through the drawing but can also acquire great individuality through their voices, which must be made to reflect the vital facet of their characters with appropriate exaggeration. Once established, the style of drawing and voice must never vary, and the character must never be required to do anything outside his accepted range.

An endless amount of research goes into the forming of these characters—human and animal—which eventually become international stars whose natures are known and understood throughout the world. It has sometimes been the case, however, that a cartoon character has not come to full fruition until the series in which it features is well established, after the first half-dozen or more films.

Certain cartoon characters deliberately reflect the emotional needs of their audience—especially their sadistic needs. But actions which could never be tolerated in the case of living persons turn merely comic when associated with the figures of cartoon. It is argued that audiences experience an emotional release when a cartoon character is squashed flat, tied up in knots, sliced into sections, thrown into space, frozen in ice or lit like a bonfire. The audience meanwhile conjures up all the fantasies it would like to enact in relation to unloved wives, husbands, children, and parents-in-law. Perhaps this is so. Or perhaps Henri Bergson is right when he suggests the more charitable view that comic characters express through their inde-structible resilience in adversity the veneration we have for the life force.

The character designed for a single appearance in a specific cartoon must be equally simplified. Here the focusing of individuality within a known human type is essential—the doctor in *Gerald McBoing-Boing* or the lawyer in *Rooty-Toot-Toot*. Such characters are simplified and distilled—they are immediately recognizable both as types and as individuals. They are established the moment they are seen; they are known for what they are within a span of seconds. Sometimes such characters have to be imposed upon trade marks—a difficult process.

An additional, very important factor is that all cartoon characters must be designed in such a way that they are readily reproducable. Many hands will ultimately have to share in their animation. If the characters are well-constructed—that is, harmonious in their general proportions and justly balanced in respect to their implications of weight and bodily form, they will usually prove to be all the simpler to reproduce when the time for animation comes.

In the design of cartoon characters, the animator should keep in mind the broad conception of human and animal types which the public will instantly recognize. The hero type is characterized by his muscular development, his fine, blown-up chest; the villain by his spiky, angular physique, his long hands and feet, his sharply pointed fingers. The type of the heroine has a rounded face; she is wide-eyed and has a softly moulded body. These are only generalized conventions, and it is often desirable to ignore them. After all, a character may turn out to be all the more effective because it does not conform to type.

These types carry through into animal cartooning. The fox and wolf and eagle are cadaverous villains, while Felix and Mickey Mouse were built up into athletic heroes, little supermen. Pigs,

165

lambs and deer are normally soft and innocent. Lions and horses are normally developed as heroic figures.

Type figures also extend into a variety of moods. The happy figure is round and fat, a symbol of good living; he has small eyes and a wide, smiling mouth. The miserable figure is lean, bent, wild-eyed, crooked-mouthed.

A further starting-point in character design emerges from the habits the characters have acquired, and their background. This affects, for example, what they wear. The jolly man wears a bow-tie and a little cocked hat, the business executive a long, affluent tie and a large or tall hat.

Their colouring also differs—light, bright colours for the jolly man, dark colours for the solemn executive.

These generalizations—which are in no sense rules—may well be insufficient for the particular situation which the character may be required to sustain by the plot of a cartoon. The animator must, therefore, think up accessories or extensions to whatever general points he gives his character. For example, the thin, cadaverous villain in his dark robes might carry a vulture on his shoulder where-ever he goes. The nicely rounded society lady might hug an elegant little poodle. The hero might ride or lead a horse, which is itself an heroic animal.

In the joint development of characterization and storyboard, the size of the characters (whether human or animal) in relation to each other is of great dramatic significance. The element of distortion or exaggeration applies here, as it applies in every other aspect of cartooning. The villainous animals or humans grow larger and more looming as their villainy becomes more apparent. The heroic animals or humans achieve a more mighty stature as their need for strength is emphasized by the action.

We have already seen that the bodily proportions of all cartoon characters are an important factor in their design. Two main principles govern the practice of animation, which is the projection of sketches and designs for a figure into an active, dramatic, mobile creature. The first principle is that the character must be capable of retaining his visual identity when he is seen from any viewpoint. The second principle is that the nature of his design must make him easy to handle by the staff of animators who will take him over from his original creator.

The initial design of a highly simplified character may well break down into a definite pattern made up of circle, cylinder, cone or disc.

166

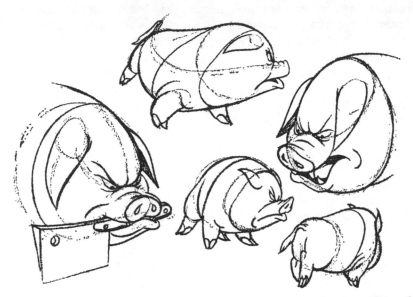

Initial action sketches for poses from the feature film *Animal Farm* for the guidance of animators. Such sketches should indicate extreme facial expressions and main characteristic gestures.

The figure has fixed proportions which are indicated to all involved in his animation. The task is at once regularized and animation by many different hands will be greatly simplified. The length of the head is the normal unit of measurement. In this way, the proportions of the body—head to trunk, trunk to legs, feet, arms and hands are established and retained throughout the film, unless there is some dramatic reason to vary them at specific moments.

The model-sheet should analyse the proportions of the head, indicating the sizes and distances involved in the relationship of the eyes, nose, mouth and ears.

A fuller model sheet is needed to show each character from at least three positions—front, side and back.

It is of additional help if characteristic gestures and facial expressions can be roughed out on these model-sheets.

If, for example, the hands or paws of a human or animal member of the cast have any important part to play in his active characterization, then this should be indicated by showing how they might be seen to move from one position to another.

It is necessary during the process of characterization to decide on the general size relationship of the characters, though this can be to some extent varied at crucial moments in the drama. If a relatively realistic style of animation is needed (as, for example, in *Animal Farm*), then the actual movements of the real-life counterparts of the humans or animals must be implied, in however simplified or distorted a form.

In many modern cartoons, however, with their less spherical, less moulded anatomical design, the virtue of the movement is purely graphic. The characters of *Gerald McBoing-Boing* look like drawings and behave like drawings; that is their privilege. But, although it may not at first seem so, the animation of these angular figures is often more subtle than that needed in semi-realistic cartooning.

The storyboard and the model sheets, the music sound charts, the dialogue and the script together form the essential research for an animated film. They are the elements out of which the future film is born. There are certain forms of animation which do not require this elaborate approach. This is the case with artists who tend to work by themselves, do not delegate animation to others. Often the particular nature of the animation these artists undertake requires a more highly individual and specialized approach to the task of preparation.

In normal procedure, it is the director of animation who must now provide the vision that turns this mass of static pictures and charts into a film that has both mobility and art. The test of quality, the test of true animation still can only begin at this point. All that has gone before is research, and it is valueless labour if the director cannot use it as the springboard from which he takes off into the medium itself, to sink or to swim, to fall or to fly. In animation, the only substitute for genius is a very high level of talent.

Sound

The silent sketches of the storyboard must anticipate sound as well as vision.

As the animator works at his drawings, he may well find himself beginning to make the noises that are to go with them—the exclamations, the snatches of dialogue, the explosion of key sound effects, the lilt of a tune or the rhythm of a phrase of music. The cartoon director with his storyboard pinned up in front of him will probably act out the dialogue or narration with the storyboard-artist, so that both the visual and the aural continuities can be explored together. The spacing of the music as a rhythm or as an extension of sound in time, can begin to form its future relationship with the action, and an action chart can be drawn to help the composer.

168

Everything done or said or played or performed has length. Length is basic to all film-making—and more especially to the cartoon film, in which the editing process is undertaken in advance, as a part of the design of the production completed before the shooting stage. Cutting in the sense of shaping a sequence from a collection of alternative shots is obviously wasteful in the animation studios. The vital effects of editing are achieved in the process of planning the continuity of the picture.

The director of a cartoon may employ a storyboard-artist to help him elaborate his sketches, but it is the director alone who must undertake the responsibility for anticipating the detailed relation of picture to sound, which the composite medium of the film involves. Music constantly underpins, glues together, punctuates the cartoon film—except in the case of television commercials, which quite frequently have no special music linked directly to the animation. Dialogue and sound effects are non-continuous elements; music is seldom absent, though it may withdraw momentarily in favour of these other elements. The animator must consult his composer as soon as the storyboard has reached a stage when it can provide a stimulus to the composer's imagination.

Nevertheless, it is a necessary part of the animator's own art to develop a good musical sense himself, to know what music can do for his films and what combination of instruments will be most suitable for each individual picture. He must be able to talk to the composer intelligently about the kind of score he wants. The composer's first contribution to the storyboard may well take shape as he sits at a piano and works out melodies, phrases and musical effects, while the director keeps his eye on the sequence of drawings. The composer may use a metronome to help him work out an initial rhythmic pattern to conform to the anticipated pattern of the visual action suggested by the sketches.

In very few cartoon production units is the composer a member of staff. He is normally brought in on a commission basis, and the director is therefore free to invite the collaboration of the composer whom he believes to have the most appropriate talent for the kind of film he is planning.

The application of sound to the storyboard has certain difficulties. The length of time required for sound to make its particular contribution may well over-stretch the visual action the animator has in mind—especially if this be very quick, as it frequently is in a cartoon. Experience shows it is always better to cut the number of words in dialogue or narration rather than to stretch out the timing

169

of the animation. If a film in general becomes overlength through the addition of essential sound, it is usually better to consider cutting out a complete sequence rather than try to compress the whole film by quickening the speaking of words. But everything should be done to avoid adding unwanted length to the animation in order to accommodate every word that seems necessary in the script.

As we have seen, the convention of speed has grown up with the development of the animated entertainment film. The audience brought up in the tradition of the American cartoon, expects every second to be jammed tight with action; over the years the cinema audience has developed a quickness of eye to catch every nuance of motion the animator packs on to the screen. But there is obviously a limit to what the eyes and the brain of the more average member of an audience can in fact absorb against time, and to carry over on to the small television screen the convention of a break-neck speed of action can lead to an entirely unintelligible rush of images.

The finally approved storyboard, charted with its accompanying sound, should have the dialogue printed beneath the sketches and the rough timing of the action indicated. Sufficient copies should then be made for everyone in the unit to see this outline of the film on which he is due to work. It is always better for the staff to know exactly what the film is about before they immerse themselves in the details of the production.

Some studios go so far as to reproduce the storyboard sketches in the form of a film-strip and record on tape an impression of the sound track. This may well be worth doing, and is a highly effective way of demonstrating the storyboard to a client. Done well, this method of presentation anticipates as fully as is possible without animation itself the way the finished film may shape.

19

THE PRODUCTION PROCESS

In all film-making there is the first stage of preparation and the second stage of realization. The producer of both live-action and animated films who wants to protect himself from becoming involved in any form of expenditure beyond what is necessary, naturally hesitates to enter on the second stage before he has tested out everything he possibly can during the period of preparation and planning.

In other words, the actual production process is like a military campaign every phase of which must be forecast. But since campaigns are not won on paper, the time must arrive when production must begin, and the storyboard preparation be put to the test of actual animation.

We shall describe first of all the main stages through which an animated cartoon film has to pass in the course of production, and then the contributions that are made by each artist and technician to this process. However large or small the studio, however wide or specialized the contribution of individual artists, the process of production has to remain the same for all normal forms of cartooning.

For convenience we will divide this process into twenty successive stages:

1. *The Work Book.* The Work Book is derived directly from the final storyboard, and is an analysis of each shot and sequence on a frame-by-frame basis. In this way the exact timing of every individual movement is determined, and its inter-relation with all other movements fixed at any given moment.

The Work Book must also show what in a live-action film would be called the camera movement—any movement, that is, which is the equivalent of a tracking-in, panning or tilting shot.

It must also show how each shot or sequence is to be punctuated, whether by a straight cut, a fade or a dissolve.

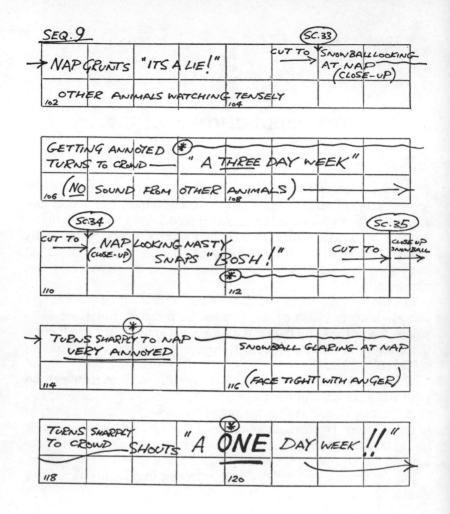

SEQ. 9

A Work Book is prepared by the Director who indicates in the upper line of squares the action of the film in terms of time units and the dialogue. In the lower line of squares he shows the types of sound needed to accompany the action. The Work Book also defines the length of each shot; in this case each square represents a half-second time unit.

172

Filling the Gap (Copyright Halas & Batchelor; Great Britain).

Dustbin Parade (Halas & Batchelor; Great Britain).

Abu's Poisoned Well (Halas & Batchelor; Great Britain).

The Winged Scourge (Copyright Walt Disney Productions; U.S.A.).

Brotherhood of Man (U.P.A.; U.S.A.).

Springheeled Jack (Copyright State Film; Czechoslovakia).

Charley's March of Time (Halas & Batchelor; Great Britain).

Romance of Transportation (Copyright National Film Board of Canada; Canada).

L'Aventure du Père Noel (Jean Image; France).

It's a Crime (Copyright National Film Board of Canada; Canada).

En Pourtant (Berthold Munschler; France).

Earth is a Battlefield (A Larkins Production; Great Britain).

Speed the Plough (Halas & Batchelor; Great Britain).

To Your Health (Philip Stapp and Halas & Batchelor; Great Britain).

Of Men and Demons (John and Faith Hubley. Copyright IBM; U.S.A.).

Disgusted Binchester (Nicholas Spargo; England).

The basic proportions of a character must be clearly analysed before production. Both body and hand proportions should be clearly defined.

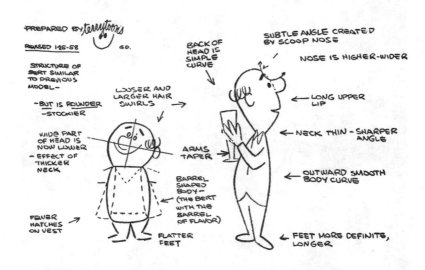

The animator requires as full detail as possible for the visual treatment and characteristics of a figure (Bert and Harry, from the Piels commercials).

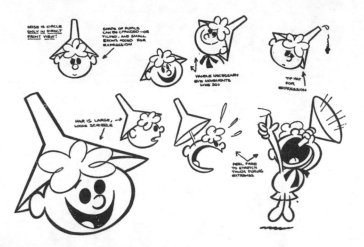

Details of characterization for *Tom Terrific*, a television entertainment series produced by C.B.S. Cartoon Film Unit.

Pre-production poses designed to guide the animators. *The Old Pro*, designed by Playhouse Pictures of Hollywood.

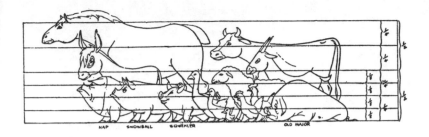

NAP   SNOWBALL   SQUEALER   OLD MAJOR

In the case of a feature production such as *Animal Farm* it is essential to establish the size relationship between one character and another. Charts showing the proportions of the individual characters are prepared; these analyse in detail the differences between all the major characters. These differences need not reflect those of nature, but should emphasize other distinctions of character, such as the innocent goodness and strength of the horse, Boxer, and the slinking slyness of the pig, Squealer.

The creation of the Work Book is the responsibility of the director, though he will naturally seek the advice of the principal artists and technicians with whom he is collaborating—in particular, the key animator, the designer, the composer and the cameraman.

The cameraman can be of great assistance during this first stage of production. The process of drawing is by its nature totally different from the process of photography, yet the camera will be the ultimate instrument through which the animation is recorded. The cameraman can often suggest ways in which a particular effect may be achieved with much greater economy by purely photographic means than would be possible through animation itself. For example, a complex superimposition of moving smoke or cloud might be both more effectively and more economically obtained by means of camera rather than animation techniques.

2. *Models of the Characters.* The preparatory drawings showing the characters from their various aspects and in their due proportions (head to body, body to limbs) must be made final, with separate drawings for heads, eyes and hands. Characteristic gestures must also be determined to guide the animators. It is also useful to pass

183

Comparative sizes of Snow White and animals from Walt Disney's production *Snow White and the Seven Dwarfs* (Copyright Walt Disney Productions). It is interesting to notice that Snow White and the deer are conceived as one unit, which helped to establish the characteristics of sympathy and innocence that they shared.

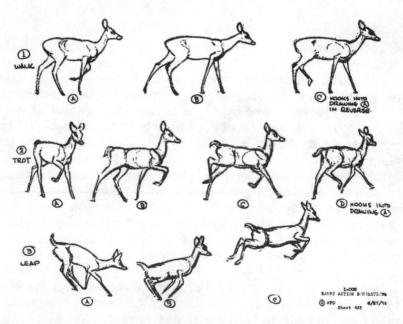

When movement is a special part of an animal's character, as in the case of *Bambi*, a detailed analysis of his basic movements should be provided for the animators. (Copyright Walt Disney Productions.)

184

on suggestions for action, especially if the model is required to perform complex motions. The exact size-relationship between the different characters is fixed.

This work is normally carried out by the director himself, probably in collaboration with his designer. Only the bigger studios employ full-time character artists.

3. *The Design and Lay-out.* The designer must set the style and decide the pictorial presentation of the film. So far the storyboard would exist only in the form of rough pencil sketches. Now the shot-by-shot colour and tone continuity has to be worked out and the relationship between shapes and forms in the background and foreground has to be arrived at. The exact pictorial appearance must be made final.

This work is the responsibility of the designer under the supervision of the director. Together they reach a decision whether the broad style of the film will be, say, in a surrealistic or some other modern graphic form or in a realistic tradition.

In the smaller units the designer also acts as the lay-out artist and in this capacity purely aesthetic considerations give way to technical ones.

In order to make sure that the Work Book is practicable in terms of animation, the director's proposals for tracking shots, pans and angle-shots are probed by the lay-out department.

The lay-out artist makes drawings which give a graphic impression of each shot from the point of view of angle and composition. He must also establish that the continuity will be smooth from shot to shot, making a satisfactory *developing* composition or visual choreography.

He tests the sizes, shapes and forms of whatever must be included in each shot, for these too must be satisfactory in their general continuity. They must be easy to accept by the audience, unless some visual shock is deliberately needed to achieve a special dramatic effect, like the sudden enlargement of a figure, or the rapid movement of a character from the far distance to a foreground close-up. The director and his lay-out artist have to keep in mind that their scenes should always be visually intelligible to the audience, or clarity will be lost and the continuity of interest destroyed.

The lay-out artist is also concerned with the essential problem of *match-line*, which is the exact relation in size and position of the moving characters in the foreground to their background. This background may be mostly static, but not necessarily so. In any case,

185

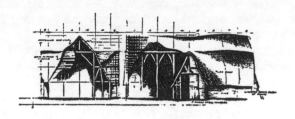

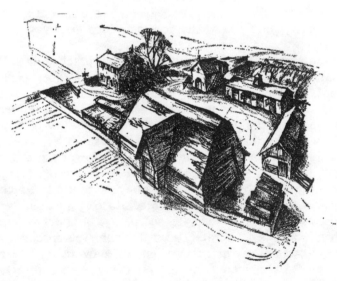

The nature of the design for the backgrounds in an animated film should establish both atmosphere and mood. In a feature film it is almost as essential to develop design in this way as to develop character. Considerable research was undertaken to achieve this before the production of *Animal Farm*; atmosphere sketches for the backgrounds for this film are shown here. The construction of buildings, the proportions of the exteriors and interiors of barns, farmhouses and stables had to be determined by visits to locations, as would be the case with a live-action film. Sometimes the backgrounds must serve a dual purpose; in the case of *Animal Farm* the barn not only had to look like a barn but also to give the right atmosphere to the animals' meetings of self-dedication to their movement, which in a sense turns the barn into a place of worship.

186

The working drawing of the raised platform in *Animal Farm* from which Old Major addressed the meeting.

the characters as they move must blend well with the background in terms of visual composition and dramatic continuity. The lay-out department completes relatively finished drawings of the settings, but only sketches the characters.

At least two copies of the lay-out drawings are completed, one of which is passed by the director to the animator with other relevant material, and the other to the tracing department to serve as advance technical information for such matters as match-lines.

4. *Recording the Music.* If we assume that the music is to be pre-recorded so that the animation can when necessary be tied directly to the track, the composer must provide the score in advance so that it can be recorded before the animation itself is begun.

The composer needs, of course, a copy of the storyboard and work book before he can produce the final score. He is normally responsible for producing all copies of the music required by the instrumentalists and for assembling the orchestra for the recording.

Because of the need for the exact timing of all the purely musical effects which have been agreed in advance with the director, it is

187

always best for the composer himself to conduct the orchestra at the recording session. The recording session for a one-reel cartoon lasts normally three to four hours; that for a one-minute commercial one to two hours.

5. *Recording of Voices.* The director must carry out voice tests of the actors he has decided to cast for his various characters.

These tests are the first actual realizations of the characters, and they may well affect the nature of the animation itself. The vocalizing of the future drawn figures must be based on a study of their model sheets, as well as on the storyboard and the work book. The director's understanding of the characters must be sufficiently well grounded by now for him to guide the actors into giving him the right voices, though it is true that there can still remain reasonable flexibility to permit for changes in the light of new developments and ideas.

Unless the director is using actors who are already established in the parts of characters whom they have played before, it will probably be necessary for him to give auditions to a number of players before he gets the most effective voices and renderings.

Experiments may be carried out to test the advantages of using special kinds of distortion, such as slowing down or speeding up the voice artificially, or recording with an echo.

6. *Charting the Music and Dialogue Track.* An analysis of every film-frame in terms of its sound can now be prepared as a guide to the animator. This guide shows the length of each phase of sound and its characteristics. In the case of the music chart, it should show the length of each bar, and the beats within the bar. It should also indicate the intensity and atmosphere of the music.

In the case of the speech chart, a distinction can be made between words spoken "off-stage" and dialogue directly uttered by the characters while in vision.

For "off-stage" speech and commentary, the length of each sentence only might be required on the chart. For dialogue spoken with the characters in vision each word must be charted syllable by syllable, and the nature of the speech shown in addition so that the animator can match this in his drawing.

Although the animator can hear as often as he likes the music and dialogue played back, only by means of this frame-by-frame charting of its progress will he in fact know exactly where he is both visually and aurally frame by frame.

188

7. *Preparing the Camera Exposure Chart* (*the Dope Sheet*). The director is now almost ready to give out the first scene to the key animator and the actual physical production of the animation can commence. He has completed his work book, which must next be elaborated on a different set of printed sheets, generally known as camera-exposure charts or dope sheets. This work can be carried out either by the director or the key animator, according to the routine of the individual studio.

Information on musical and dialogue accentuation, the choreography of the action, and the specification as to the type of animation required are all indicated in detail on these charts. The dope sheet becomes the detailed blue-print for the animator, a numbered frame-by-frame guide to the job for which he has already received his general briefing through the storyboard, work book, lay-outs and model sheets.

The animator also has disc recordings of those sections of the track which he must animate very closely for words or music.

8. *Key Animation.* As we have seen, the storyboard, the work book, the lay-outs, the model sheets, the sound-track charts and the dope sheets collectively prepare the ground for the artistic and technical work of animation. They are successive stages and facets of preparation for the final art of animation which will turn what have been so far still drawings or verbal descriptions of action and characterization into pictures with a closely disciplined movement and a style, life and personality of their own. It is a tense and exciting moment when all these weeks of preparation are brought to the final test of motion.

According to the way each studio is organized, the key animator will start work on the salient poses only (leaving the interlinking or in-between drawings to his assistants) or he may carry out the whole work more or less by himself. He might, for example, draw every fifth, seventh, ninth, thirteenth or twenty-fourth pose, leaving the rest to the in-between animators. The organization of the studio and the quality of the subject will together determine how much detail he undertakes.

In the case of very complex or subtle animation, the instinct of a good animator will be to carry out every drawing himself. According to the nature of the film, the key animator does his initial work either in rough pencil lines or with the cleaner, harder lines which from the start are intended to be suitable for the final tracings after the line- or pencil-testing has been completed.

189

Unlike live action film-making, it is customary for animated films to be made in the direct order of the action from beginning to end, especially in the case of television commercials of from fifteen to sixty seconds. In the longer film it may be necessary to select certain sequences which are directly linked in style or subject and animate them during the same period of work.

9. *In-between Animation.*   Following both the spirit and the mechanics of the principal poses, the in-between artists work on the frame-by-frame movements of the characters and objects, filling in the gaps left by the key animator, who supervises their work and keeps it in line with his own. All these animation drawings are carried out on sheets of thin paper.

When the key animator and his director are satisfied that a sequence (or a section of it) is ready for testing, a line-test (or pencil-test) is prepared.

10. *The Line- or Pencil-Test.*   In the larger studios a special camera and rostrum is reserved for this testing of the critical sequences of animation.

The drawings at this stage are all on paper, of which there may be two or more layers according to the sectionalizing of the animation as between the different principal characters. At this stage the contours only of the backgrounds are drawn on similar paper so that when viewing the line-test one should be able to see the relationship of the foreground movement to the background. The combined sheets of drawings are strongly lit from underneath to show up the lines.

The most economical form of line-test remains in negative only, showing therefore white lines on a black background when projected. The cheapest form of stock can be used, such as sound-recording stock, which is non colour-sensitive. The director, key animator and, sometimes, the in-between animators view and discuss the test, examining its suitability to character and subject, and its fluidity of movement. It is at this stage that the animation can be checked against the music and dialogue by means of double-head projection.

The line-test is, in effect, the last stage at which it is economical to introduce any but the smallest changes in the animation.

11. *Cleaning-up the Rough Animation.*   Some of the smaller studios omit this stage in the process by anticipating it at an earlier phase in

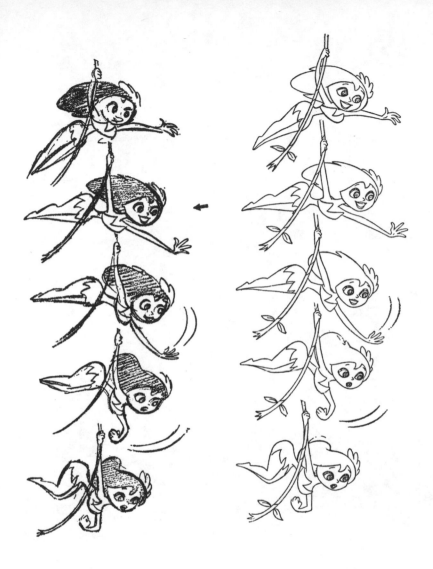

According to the organization in each individual studio and the system of work adopted by the animator, animation is prepared either in clean or in rough form. On the left the initial drawings are shown as a sequence of roughs; on the right the same work is shown drawn over to achieve a cleaner finish for tracing. The arrow indicates a key pose. There is no preconceived formula in fluid movement for what determines a key pose in relation to the in-between phases of animation. Practically every single phase could be as important to achieve fluidity as the key itself.

191

An excellent example of tracing from the Czechoslovakian film *The Creation of the World*. This style of tracing employs an even line throughout which is somewhat different from the normal approach, which gives emphasis to curvature by means of thick and thin tracing lines.

192

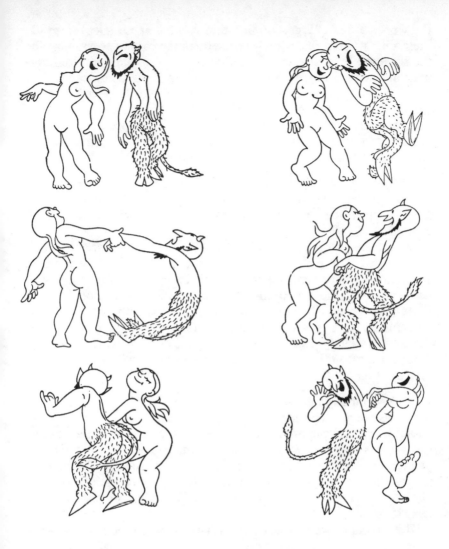

Another point worth noting is the use of texture in the tracing of quick action, as seen in the gyrating movement of the dance. During recent years the animation industry has gained new mechanical means to carry out the task of tracing animated drawings, which also allows the free use of texturised animation.

193

the work. But the larger studios find it more economical to grade their animation in this way—especially in the case of story-films for the theatres. It means, in effect, that they can make the initial animation drawings more rough than they intend the final drawings to be. These rough drawings (which are suitable for line-test) must be subsequently re-drawn with cleaner and more precise outlines—the key animator perhaps introducing certain improvements and subtleties in the process. The final work is therefore a refinement of what has been done initially for test purposes.

12. *Preparing the Backgrounds.* When the director feels confident that the animation is working well (both mechanically and aesthetically), he instructs the background artist to complete the backgrounds in detail.

By now he knows precisely through the line-test the scale of each background required—for example, the simple cases of the static shots, and the more complex cases which must allow for tracking in and out, tilting, and panning shots, where long strips of drawing must be prepared. He will paint his backgrounds to match the tones and colours of the objects and characters which will be animated on the cells, watching precisely the match-lines shown on the lay-outs.

He must also take great care to keep his work within the colour-system of the film.

13. *Inking the Animation Drawings on to the Cells.* The animator's drawings are next traced in ink on the thin celluloid sheets (the cells) with a maximum picture area of 15 × 10.9 inches or, in the case of the various forms of wide-screen in some other, a proportionate picture ratio. (The basic dimension of 15 × 10.9 inches has replaced the earlier customary ratio of 10 × 7 3/11 inches, since it allows for greater detail and camera flexibility in the case of tracking-in.)

This inking process is carried out with pens or specially-prepared brushes, and ink is used which has the property of permanent adherence to the cells. Tracing is a relatively mechanical stage in animation, and it is undertaken by a special department or group of artists in the studio. Because the work calls for a mechanical accuracy, certain larger studios favour using a newly developed electro-photographic system to transfer the drawings to the cells, such as the Ozalid or the Xerox systems.

14. *Painting or Opaquing the Cells.* The cells then go to the next group of artists, who paint them with opaque paint which is applied

194

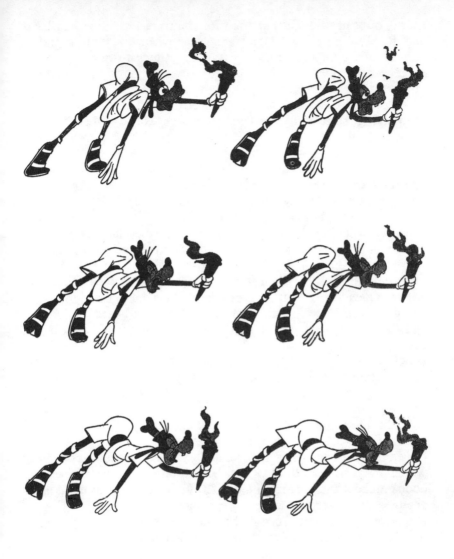

This series of fully traced and painted figures comes from the original cells for Walt Disney's *Clock Cleaners*. They show the finished work which has passed through all the technical and artistic stages prior to photography. (Copyright Walt Disney Productions.)

195

on the opposite side to that used for the traced outline in order to avoid obscuring them. (There are cases when opaquing could be carried out on the same side as the outlines to achieve special effects.) The colours have, of course, been previously planned and approved by the director or his designer.

According to the nature and style of the film various techniques of applying the paint can be used from airbrush to drybrush.

15. *Checking.* Before the photographic stage is reached it is normal to have a matching rehearsal, during which the various layers of cells are superimposed set by set on their appropriate backgrounds to test accuracy in assembly and any inadvertent mistakes in matching animation to background.

The cells are kept in an exact alignment with each other by means of standard perforations at their base which thread on to registration pegs on the animation desk and so enable the cells to be kept uniformly in position when they are set on top of each other. The backgrounds are kept in correct alignment either by pegging or by being fixed to a mechanically propelled panning board.

The checking department rehearses each line-up of the cells and their backgrounds, and enables the director to avoid any delays which could be very costly if mistakes were discovered after the photography had already begun.

16. *Photography.* Once the cells and backgrounds have been checked, the animator is ready for the camera.

Each exposure involves the cameramen in setting up the action cells and backgrounds in accordance with the original dope sheets which are passed on to them by the animators. The cells are given code numbers and the movement (if any) of the non-animated backgrounds (which remain on art paper) are indicated in fractions of inches or centimetres. During photography effects such as dissolves, double exposures, pans and tracks are also added.

17. *Viewing the Rushes.* The rushes are viewed as they come back from the laboratories to discover if any inaccuracies have escaped previous detection, and to see whether the animation is ready for editing.

18. *Editing Picture and Sound.* Editing in animation does not mean cutting the film in the sense of trial and error through montage; it is the final assembly of the picture track and sound tracks.

196

1.(TEA TIME IN ENGLAND)
(80 DAYS AROUND THE WORLD
THEME)

2.(WIFE POURS TEA)

3.(FORD MOTOR SOUND)
HUSBAND:(DECIDED ENGLISH ACCENT)
"IT'S THE '58 FORD. . ."

4.WIFE: ". . .WITH THE MOST
EXQUISITE STYLING."

5.(WIFE RUSHES OUT TO SEE FORD
AS TEA POT CONTINUES TO POUR)

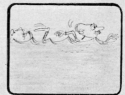

6.(FILLING ROOM WITH TEA. HUSBAND
SWIMS AFTER HER)

7.(WIFE STANDING BY "AROUND THE
WORLD" SYMBOL)
WIFE: "PROVED AND APPROVED. . ."

8.HUSBAND: ". . .AROUND THE
WORLD."

9.BOTH: "SEE IT AT YOUR FORD
DEALER'S!"
(TRUCK AND PAN OVER TO SYMBOL)

10.(SYMBOL ANIMATES TO "FORD")

197

storyboard INC.

CHICKEN: (clucking sound...)
TUP -- TUP -- TUP --

TUP -- TUP -- TUP --

TUP -- TUP --

(EFX: Sound of roaring traff

(EFX: Car guns past . . .)

(CHICKEN REGISTERS QUANDARY..

198

(CHICKEN observes source from
whence these new cars come...

CHICKEN: To get to the other side!

TUP - TUP -- TUP --

T - U - P - M - A - N!

TUP - TUP - TUPMAN

TUP - TUP - TUPMAN

TUP - TUP - TUPMAN!

200

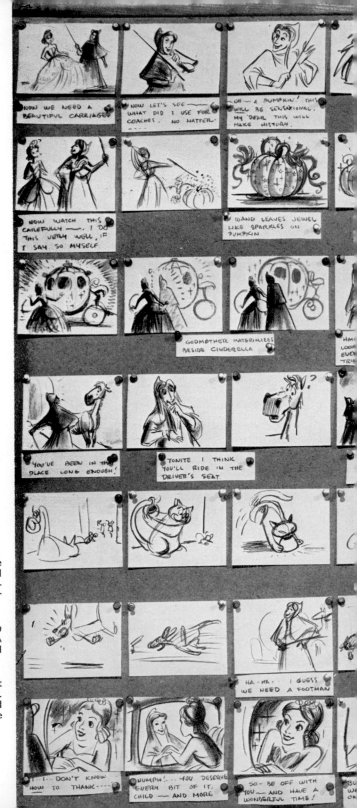

CHICKEN: WHY DO I WANT TO
          CROSS THE ROAD?

(EFX: Long blast of horn...)

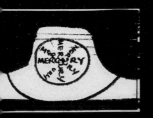  

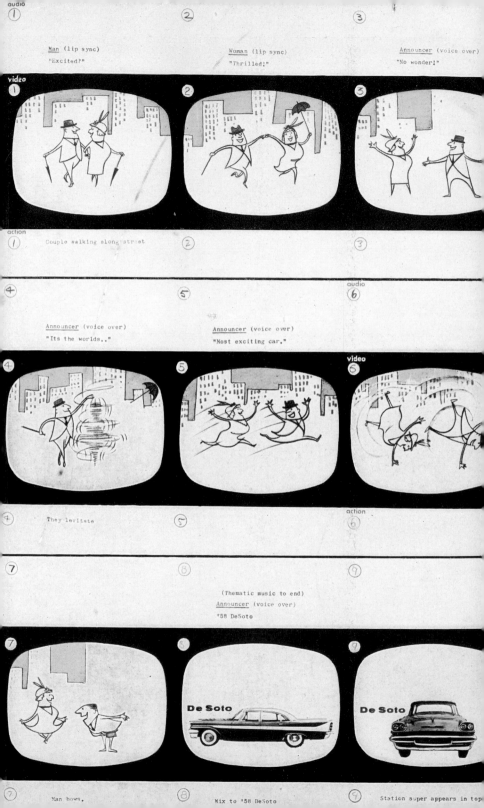

Man (lip sync)
"Excited?"

Woman (lip sync)
"Thrilled!"

Announcer (voice over)
"No wonder!"

video ①   ②   ③

action ① Couple walking along street   ②   ③

④   ⑤   audio ⑥

Announcer (voice over)
"Its the worlds.."

Announcer (voice over)
"Most exciting car."

video ④   ⑤   ⑥

action ④ They levitate   ⑤   ⑥

⑦   ⑧   ⑨

(Thematic music to end)
Announcer (voice over)
'58 DeSoto

⑦   ⑧   ⑨

⑦ Man bows.   ⑧ Mix to '58 DeSoto   ⑨ Station super appears in top

The editor has already joined the individual line or pencil-tests in sequence continuity and tested them against the sound. This process of assembly can begin sequence by sequence as soon as the work has been passed by the director after viewing. The film is gradually built up sectionally as it is completed, and the line-tests replaced by the final colour rushes. Music, dialogue and effects tracks are still kept separate but tested in synchronization with the picture.

The cutting copy (run multi-headed) may then be shown to the sponsor, whom we can only hope will be overjoyed with the result. The sponsor (if he can be trusted to look far enough ahead) may also have been shown the line- or pencil-test from which, like the director and key animator, he can judge to some extent what the finished film will be like.

In any case, he will see how different the storyboard is from a film; artists and technicians have interposed their talents and techniques since the time the original discussions between sponsor and producer were held over the continuity sketches. An idea has become a film; a series of sketches has become a drawing that walks and talks.

19. *Track-laying and Final Dubbing Session.*   The final set of tracks required for dubbing are laid, and at the subsequent dubbing session these are run simultaneously and balanced together and amalgamated on to one single sound track. This sound track is then married to the visual track.

The process of recording is carried out almost entirely magnetically, only going to the optical stage after the first dubbing.

20. *Final Show Print.*   With all his material now in the hands of the laboratories, the director should see that the colours in the final show print are reproduced as he intends. If any opticals are required, the director should also watch that these are carried out satisfactorily. The final show copy should reflect as exactly as possible all the art and labour that has been put into every foot of film that runs through the projector.

Artists and Technicians

We come now to the individual artists and technicians who make the animated cartoon film. Methods of procedure will to some extent vary with the kind of organization that is favoured by the producer and his senior creative artists, and it will also vary according to whether the film is being made in a large or small studio.

Most animated films are in fact now being made by comparatively small units. The larger studios employing a staff of, say, over fifty are very rare. The average fully established animation studio may well give regular employment to about a dozen people.[1]

Whatever the size of the unit, the work to be undertaken is fundamentally the same. The difference is that the larger companies produce more of it and possibly have a more elaborate system of organizing and grading the work of so many hands.

The following are the main executives, artists and technical assistants who contribute to the process of making an animated cartoon film under the supervision of the producer. In the smaller units an artist or technician may fulfil more than one of these functions.

> The Producer
> The Director
> The Designer, Lay-Out Artist and Background Artist
> The Key Animator
> The Assistant Animator
> The Inker and Colourist
> The Checker
> The Cameraman
> The Editor
> The Studio Manager

The composer is normally employed in a free-lance capacity by most animation studios.

Only a few of the larger units will have their own sound departments; the smaller units will hire sound recording facilities as they need them.

The Producer

We have spoken throughout this book of the animator; we have seldom, if ever, mentioned the producer. The word animator has been used as the general term applicable to the film-maker whose specialization is the creative work of animation. The producer of animated film is frequently, in fact normally, himself a practising animator or a former animator who has become an administrative producer of animated films.

In a number of respects, the producer in this field of film-making is not doing the same work as the producer of live-action films. He

[1] *The animation studio organized by one of the authors of this book, John Halas, associated with his wife, Joy Batchelor, called the Halas and Batchelor Cartoon Film Unit, was founded in 1941 and employed, during the war, an average of twenty artists and technicians. After the war, the staff gradually increased to its present level of seventy-five.*

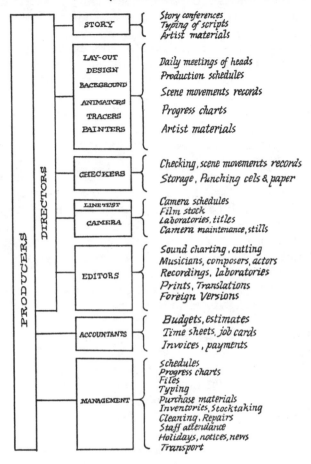

PRODUCTION STRUCTURE *(Management)*
(UNIT OVER 50 ARTISTS AND TECHNICIANS)

While the majority of the studios in the world include not more than twenty artists and technicians, the above diagram of the Production Structure of a commercial studio shows the disposition of some fifty or more technicians, and the division of responsibility between them. Although the essence of any cartoon studio lies in its creative work, it cannot avoid giving prominence to the administrative detail that results from the employment of labour and complications of contractual obligations.

211

is in no sense an impresario. He is the administrative and very often at the same time the creative head of his studio—half the time an artist and half the time a business man. Only in a certain sense is it true to say that he is simply responsible, in the way the producer of live-action films is responsible, for bringing together the two factors that make production possible—money and talent.

The producer in animation controls the main moves in maintaining a smooth flow of production for his unit in far greater detail than is usual in the case of the producer of a live-action subject. He may have created the storyboard himself and will play an essential part in guiding the animation through its technical stages.

As a business man, his "deals" are in any case on a relatively small scale. Production nowadays is virtually confined to shorts, playing from a few seconds to a few minutes only. These shorts are now almost entirely sponsored, so that the producer's business transactions may well be confined to satisfying his clients that the budgets he proposes are reasonable for the work his studio is capable of producing. Also, as we have seen already, he must be skilful in explaining the special qualities his medium has to offer to the various clients who may want to use his work.

We have already seen the producer at work creating the storyboard and discussing it with his sponsor. He is always his own representative outside the studio; inside it he may have a studio manager responsible to him for the supervision of his staff and the routine organization of their output.

Once the project has been approved at the storyboard stage, it must be costed. This is the producer's responsibility, in consultation with his accountant and his studio organizer. (The particular problems of costing a production are discussed in a later section of this book.)

The budget involves the producer in a series of commitments. He must go back to his client with a price for the production as it is envisaged in the storyboard and an estimate of the time the film will take to make.

The producer nominates the director, the chief animator and the team who will work on the film. If it is a small unit, he may direct the production himself. However this may be, the producer must know how long it will take him and his staff to make the film, otherwise he cannot assess the cost of the work. He has to measure up the raw material of the film as the production team gradually produces it.

Once the work has begun, the producer must be in a position to

212

check progress easily week by week. He must be able to see the production in some perspective or he will be unable to supervise it.

Each studio will necessarily have a scheme of controls, or check points, which enable the producer to see what is happening. There are three points in the various stages of production when the producer can exercise his opinion:

(i) *The Test Stage.* The director is responsible for controlling the animation, but the producer must judge the final quality of what is being made. The director, as in a live-action film, is immersed in the detail of the subject. The producer should try to see how the film is shaping as a whole, as the sum of its parts. The director brings his line- or pencil-tests to the producer at the stage when he is satisfied with them himself or feels the need for advice. This is the stage when it is still possible to effect radical changes.

(ii) *The Recording Stage.* The producer selects the composer who is to work with the director. He is also responsible for the quality and the suitability of all other contributions to the sound track—the writing, the acting, the effects. The producer can exercise his judgment on quality at the recording stage.

(iii) *The Rushes.* The producer sees the rushes of his films in the form of individual shots without sound, as they come back from the laboratories. The work of animation is now at an advanced stage, though complete only in small fragments. Improvements can still be effected by remaking individual shots, if the producer sees fit.

After this point the film can only be altered as a major undertaking, which will play havoc with both schedules and budgets. Therefore the producer must have satisfied himself by this time that the work is of a satisfactory standard. He must be able to forecast how the picture will shape at the earliest possible stages. In any case, most animation producers are self-employed and would not be foolish enough to waste work and money by making drastic changes late in production.

At the final stages of the work, the producer must see and approve the cutting copy and later screen the show print to the sponsor. It should be a proud moment for him. It sometimes is.

All through production, the producer acts like the conductor of an orchestra. He must know the score by heart, how much he can expect of his players, and the potential responses of his audience. The way the work is played will prove whether or not he is a good conductor, getting the best out of his orchestra and his audience alike.

The producer is, therefore, required to do much more than sign cheques. Like the conductor of the orchestra, it is best if he can himself do many of the jobs he now delegates to his team. If he has once done detailed work in animation himself he will be better able to understand in advance where things may go wrong in this delicate series of operations. His quality as a producing animator is that he can function on a broader plane, planning work for his unit which will widen their activities to the limit of their talent.

The Director

Once again it is necessary, in trying to visualize the range of work to be undertaken by the animation director, to distinguish between the large and the small studio.

In the small studio the producer is normally also the director and possibly the key animator as well.

Studios employing a staff of more than twenty soon find that they are obliged to plan the organization of their work in such a way as to maintain a smooth flow of production, and this results in varying degrees of specialization. Such studios as these will have one or more animation directors who are qualified to be the creative force behind the whole process of producing an animated film. While the producer will have approached the film from its broadest aspect, the animation director must not only appreciate this but also be able to follow the film through to its final detail.

Thus he has to be a very expert technician with a thorough knowledge of the mechanics of all the stages through which an animated film must pass. As in a live-action production, he is responsible to his producer for making the film; he must therefore show his understanding of its purpose and content in the way he organizes the storyboard, plans the process of production, and instructs the team of artists who will look to him for creative guidance and leadership.

Ideally, the director should participate from the start in the invention of the ideas for a film. If this is not possible, then he should at least spend as much time with the storyboard artists as is necessary to ensure his mastery of the technical implications of the storyboard. If by any chance he has to work from a completed storyboard, then his skill consists in his ability to assess the production problems of the film by studying the project as it has been sketched out for him.

214

The next stage comes when he begins to feel his way into the film through the creation of his work book, timing it and analysing each shot both from the visual and the aural points of view. This work book will become the guide used not only by himself but by his lay-out artist, his key animator and his composer. The work book becomes, as we have seen, the central source of information about the production, giving a reasonably accurate indication of the length of each shot and the spacing of the commentary, music and effects in their relation to the action. On the technical side the director is responsible for indicating in the work book the positioning of tracking shots, pans, dissolves, cuts, field-sizes and the general relationship of the camera to the subject-matter.

When this is done, the director is ready to allocate the work on the individual shots to the various artists in his unit. Before they begin their tasks, the animators, designers and lay-out men will discuss the storyboard and work book with the director, who, in addition to explaining the action to them, will show them the degree of stylization which he feels the film needs.

From now on the director becomes the controller of his unit's activity. He works closely with the lay-out artist, who in most studios is also the designer.

The lay-out sketches are passed to the director for his approval by the lay-out artist. These sketches are then handed over to the key animator, together with the chart of the sound track which gives frame-to-frame information about the characteristics of the music and the dialogue, when these have been pre-recorded. It is advisable to provide, in addition, a recording on disc of the track if the dialogue is very detailed or the music complex in order that the key animator may be able to play it as many times as he needs during the long process of drawing a character to match the voice of the unseen actor.

The director's first briefing of the key animator is an important occasion. He not only hands over the technical material to the animator, but uses this opportunity to inspire the animator—a chance not to be missed! The attitude of an uninterested animator soon spreads down through his department, and the work suffers. No two animators are alike, and since even a one-minute film breaks down into many shots, the director should divide these shots among the animators according to their capabilities. This is type-casting and must be done tactfully. Usually the director's sound chart, work book and model sheets are sufficient material for the animator to prepare the more concise camera exposure sheets, which are

215

based on the sound charts and information contained in the director's work book.

The director's next contact with the animators would normally be at the stage of the rough pencil-test of the animation of a scene. Each pencil-test is shot on negative and projected in loops so that it can be viewed over and over again. If the director decides to make any alteration other tests are made until he is satisfied. Both the camera exposure sheets and the work book must be adjusted to any alterations that are made.

The film having passed this crucial stage, the director influences and controls the subsequent work although he is not personally involved in the production process. These stages lead from the rough animation through to the cleaned-up animation, from the cleaned-up animation to the tracing and colouring, as well as the work involved in the final designing and background painting and photography. The director then views the rushes of each individual shot of the film.

He is, of course, available to the editor during the process of assembling the shots with their various sound tracks and, when he is fully satisfied, he can present the work for the producer's approval.

The Designer, Lay-out Artist and Background Artist

The designer of a cartoon film is responsible for the graphic impression of the film. The live-action art director, having designed and built his settings, is then in the hands of the director and lighting cameraman. The cartoon set designer is more fortunate. He has more control over his medium; he can assess the result of his work immediately by seeing the designs in actual use soon after they leave his drawing-board.

After designing the storyboard and other relevant material with the director, the designer makes a considerable number of atmosphere sketches and rough plans. In these he attempts to embody the many ideas possible regarding the visual conception of the story. A good designer always finds certain elements in a storyboard that he can emphasize—for example, the starkness of a locality or the opportunities that lie in contrasting colours. His job is to discover the best possible pictorial interest to be found within the scope of a given storyboard.

The storyboard is broken down into convenient sequences to facilitate handling. An eight-minute film might consist of three sequences, each containing twenty to thirty separate scenes. These are marked up in numerical order.

216

When the designer and his director are satisfied that the pictorial continuity of the atmosphere sketches conveys the right mood and emotions, the lay-out artist produces the lay-out of each scene together with the finished line drawings of the settings—including sketches of the characters and their size in relation to their settings, and the camera movements within the scene.[1] These drawings ensure that one angle cuts smoothly to another, while constantly preserving the audience's sense of time and place.

In planning the finished lay-out of each scene and staging each individual piece of action, one sometimes finds that the storyline demands a change in the location of a basic set. On such occasions the set has to be changed from its original lay-out; in fact, there is a period in every cartoon film when the settings are in a continual state of change and compromise. Both the designer and the lay-out artist should bear in mind all the miscellaneous action taking place in any location throughout the film and work with this in mind.

Therefore, one can modify one's ideas as one goes along with the production, but even a slight change of angle within a lay-out means new sets of drawings. Furthermore, such changes involve the problem of continuity in each drawing; for instance, every shape of stone, every subtlety of texture must be identical seen from each angle. It becomes necessary to simplify in order to reduce the amount of work required to reproduce every detail in these preliminary sketches; pet ideas may have to be discarded and, like any artist, the designer or the lay-out artist is sometimes reluctant to change what he feels to be an eminently satisfactory piece of design. But the main aim is to make the sets workable in relation to the total content of the film. Therefore, both the designer and the lay-out artists are dependent on the basic idea of the film, and they turn yet again to others to make final their own individual contributions, this time to the background artists.

The background artist works from the lay-out drawings and the designer's atmosphere sketches. In smaller studios this work is done by the designer himself, especially in studios producing only television commercials. In any conditions, however, the settings of each scene are the basis for their backgrounds, which are rendered either in black-and-white tones or in colour.

A feeling for mood and overall texture is essential in each painting. The background painter can make or mar the designer's work; the effect required can either be overstated or completely lost. When

[1] See the Appendix: "Mathematics in Aid of Animation," by Brian Salt.

the initial conception of the design becomes lost through the poor quality of the backgrounds, the first rough sketches often have a life and excitement that never reaches the screen.

The designer can work comparatively free from technical obligations, but the lay-out and background artist must conform to the registration system of the studio. This registration system centres round a peg-bar with three registration pegs each 4 inches apart. The animation drawings and subsequently the celluloids will be registered to these pegs, and obviously so must the painted backgrounds. But variation is possible in positioning the peg-bars as between the backgrounds and the celluloids to achieve greater camera mobility and save studio work. It is possible, for instance, to fit the backgrounds to either diagonal or top registration pegs and allow the celluloids to be registered to the bottom pegs.

Therefore, it is essential that both the lay-out and background artists should know what registration manipulation is possible under the camera, and in addition they should have some knowledge of mathematics in order to calculate tracks, pans and other possible camera movements.

A further point to consider in designing backgrounds is the compensation of colours in relation to the number of layers of celluloids which will be photographed with them. It is not uncommon in a scene to use as many as five different layers of celluloids, and considering that each layer darkens the background by approximately five per cent, it is easy to realize the potential loss of effect if there is no compensation for this during the original painting. Each individual shot must be analysed by the background artist in terms of colour continuity, the number of celluloids to be used in combination with the final art work, and the system in which it will be photographed.

The background artist should also bear in mind the characteristics of the colour system which is to be used when the film is photographed.

The Key Animator

The animator's work is governed by the dope sheet, which he has received from the director.

The dope sheet is divided into frame-units of one twenty-fourth part of a second, and indicates precisely the exact frame where the points of accent in the music, effects and the dialogue occur.

The animator should always refresh his memory of the total continuity of the film by looking back over the storyboard in order to

218

see how and where the individual scene on which he is working fits into the general action of the film.

He will instinctively search for the key patterns for each movement of his subject, and so prepare himself to start roughing out the action of the chief character. For example, a character batting a ball would have the beginning and end of the swing as obvious key positions; but the position of the batsman when striking the ball would also be a key position, because it is an extreme one for the movement of the ball.

The general timing has been devised by the director, but in order to maintain exact timing some animators use a metronome. The metronome set, for example, to a speed of a half-second interval, can influence an animator's drawing; his interest is stimulated by the rhythm.

On each key drawing the animator sketches a scale-diagram which shows the time relationship of this drawing to the next. This scale-diagram is to guide the assistant animators; it shows the number of drawings that have to be inserted between the two key drawings, and their relative positions. As each picture is shown on the screen for an identical period of time, the number of drawings between the two key drawings will determine the time it will take to move from one position to the other, while the positioning of the drawings will determine the speed—for example, if the succeeding drawings are crammed against the first key position, then the action will begin slowly and end quickly, and vice versa.

In representing unhurried movement (e.g. walking, turning, lifting, sitting, climbing and other actions undertaken at this speed) each drawing can be photographed twice instead of once; instead of using ten different drawings photographed in succession thus: 1, 2, 3, 4, 5, 6, 7, 8, 9, 10, the animator could use five thus: 1, 3, 5, 7, 9, and have each of them photographed twice. In this way he can achieve the same action in the same film time, but in only half the working time. The resultant movement looks sufficiently smooth due to the persistence of human vision and its inability to pick out the details of fast movement on the screen.

In actions of average speed, such as walking or turning, the consecutive drawings overlap considerably. The area covered in common by any two consecutive drawings is over two-thirds.

In more violent actions, such as running, falling, hitting or the flights of a ball, the area covered in common, if any, is usually less than two-thirds. To use the same drawing twice would now cause jitter. So a separate drawing has to be made for every frame.

If the area common to the drawings is, even then, still less than two-thirds, then dry brush effects can be used to join the two objects. For example, on drawing two dry brush would be used from it to drawing one, on drawing three dry brush would be used from it to drawing two, and so on.

In very fast actions, such as revolving propellers or the wing actions of humming birds, the object is not drawn at all but is replaced by blurred or dry brush or air brush effects which, when repeated or alternated, give the appearance of this kind of motion, which it is beyond our capacity to see in detail.

Again, to make a cartoon person or object convincing, it is, of course, necessary to know how they would act in a given situation in real life. But the skill and imagination of the key animator must enable him to realize how to put actuality aside for the sake of achieving some effect of movement which is right for the medium of cartoon. For example, when a character changes direction at speed, his hair, tie, jacket-flaps, as well as the top half of his body will be carried on some way before they follow his legs along their new path.

But when anthropomorphic principles come into conflict with any other laws or principles, the former usually take precedence. For example, if a character has been projected upwards by an explosion and then sees that he is heading for the predatory jaws of some bird of prey, he has to be made to express fright. The laws governing inertia, air resistance and gravity all insist that the loose appendages of the character should drag or flap back along the way he has come, but anthropomorphism suggests that they should defy gravity and aid the expression of emotion. His hair could stand on end, his eyes bulge, his tongue, collar, tie, fingers and feet stick out, and so on. Depending on the degree of emotion to be emphasized, the physical principles are abandoned for the anthropomorphic ones, or, to take a less complicated example, a lighthearted character could be made to float upwards to demonstrate his heart's condition in simple defiance of gravity.

Physical phenomena such as these may be observed only in high speed photographs, but unless they are allowed for in animation (although they only last for one or two frames) the action will look wrong, even though the lay viewer would be unable to say why.

A movement or effect can only be seen clearly when it lasts for six frames or more (that is, a quarter-second). Because of this, when the animator wants to emphasize a pose or mark a static position which comes between movements, he should hold it up for this length of time. For example, a cartoon character might be required to run away and then occasionally glance back fearfully at his pursuers; not counting the frames used in turning his head, the glance back itself should last for at least six frames.

These are the kinds of convention that the key animator should keep in mind. But he is also very much concerned with style. He must be able to reflect his director's or designer's style of drawing or sense of colour, which may be either traditional or advanced. There is all the difference between putting motion to characters conceived in the style of U.P.A. cartoons or in the style of Walt Disney.

The British animator John Smith has expressed this contrast in animation style as follows:

Generally speaking, the overall aesthetic attitude favoured in Disney's cartoon films is balanced in the following way. Complexity of detail is matched by complexity of movement.

For example, when a figure walks, his tongue may flap, his hair flop, his ears wiggle, his eyelids shutter, his adam's-apple oscillate, his whole body down to his feet fluctuate with added movements. The rich, even sugary colouring and bulbous forms are matched by movements that resemble a bladder of water moving (if it could), floppily and sensuously. The sentimentality of mood is matched with coy, cute, sprightly, easy movement, and sadism by excessive distortion and squashing. In general, life is portrayed as it might move in a land where people had brains and bodies of soft sorbo rubber.

The matching of pictorial form and mood to design in U.P.A. films is, of course, very different. U.P.A.'s artists favour simplicity of form and simplicity of movement, the essence without the frills. Acid colours and sharp forms are matched by a movement resembling the way in which cane, glass and wire would move (if they could), springy, whippy, staccato. The wit and cynicism of these cartoons is acted out in slapstick of a high but blasé kind. In general, this is life as it would be led in a land where people had brains and bodies of sheet metal.

The Assistant Animator

The assistant animator is responsible for the in-between drawings in the animation.

In-betweening, as the name implies, is the creation of intermediate drawings between two given key drawings in the sequence of an action. The two key drawings are placed in register on the light box; a clean sheet of paper is placed over this and an intermediate drawing is made. This may be flicked alternately with the other two in order to simulate a rough feeling of movement, and so check whether the break-down is a suitable one. This new drawing is then checked in the same way in order to break down the movement still further until the final number is reached.

The animator makes a chart on the key drawings which indicates how many in-between drawings are to be completed and in what

221

relationship to one another. The type and speed of an action will determine this; a number of drawings close to one another will slow down a movement, whilst the opposite technique will have the reverse effect.

In the completion of these drawings, the artist has to visualize the character chosen in a number of varying positions, and in order to assist him in this specialized work a model sheet is used. This sheet will show the given character in a certain number of positions with its proportions and other details given as a guide to drawing the in-between work. It eliminates such problems as loss of characteristics or proportion, and the accidental disappearance and reappearance of details such as buttons or fingernails. It is essential at this stage of animation that careful attention should be given to a figure's character and proportions, because the success of the work will depend on true and accurate representation of the character in its many scenes and actions.

The flicking of several drawings in sequence will again help to check that the figure is moving smoothly. This will show whether or not the movements occur out of sequence, and it will reveal whether the proportions swell and diminish without cause. The details may be studied and altered through flicking until the animator is entirely satisfied with the fluidity of the movement.

When an in-between drawing is being made, lines are not merely drawn between other lines in what appears technically to be a half-way position; the character must be reconsidered in each phase of his movement as subject to certain laws of gravity which will determine the positioning of each individual drawing. For example, a piece of flowing drapery may perhaps overlap its position on a previous drawing in order to simulate the smooth and delayed curving of its edges whilst in motion, or a sleeve may drag away from the leading edge of an arm as soon as the arm is raised, and not gradually move over. These are gravitational laws which must be remembered, even though animation is an artificial process.

Various exaggerations in drawing may be deliberately employed to emphasize a mood or movement. Whilst these may look ugly or incorrect when isolated as single drawings, their true value lies in their contribution to a total phase of animation.

All of these points should be understood by the assistant animator. It is through his work that the figures really achieve their life, and a smooth piece of animation, without any change of proportions or loss of detail, is the mark of good in-between work.

222

The Inker and Colourist

In spite of the effort that has gone into making the actual animated drawings, the audience in fact never directly sees this work. What they see are the tracings made from the drawings on the celluloid transparencies.

The technique of tracing requires great accuracy and skill in handling both a pen and a brush, and furthermore a considerable understanding of the technical demands of the medium. The animator sometimes leaves a large proportion of the figure undrawn, which the tracer is required to complete. Where the moving parts of the figure meet the static sections of the body, the utmost accuracy in tracing is required, otherwise the figure will appear jerky in its movements. A very smooth and accurate line is essential. The contour of a figure depends on its lineal enclosure, which is provided by the tracer. Good tracing can add both style and a better flow to the movement. Inaccuracy in tracing can easily destroy animation; great care is especially needed when a character is speaking or expressing himself through his eyes.

A tracer should be able to work with black and white inks, with coloured inks and with other paints. He should be able to adapt himself to using the thick outlines that are predominant in television cartoon techniques as well as the thin lines that are predominant in theatrical work.

The tracing supervisor is responsible for giving out and collecting the work. He is also responsible for seeing that the dye of the celluloids is correct and the positioning of the perforations accurate. It is important that the supervisor should allocate individual scenes to individual tracers and not subdivide the work.

The supervisor also checks the accuracy of the final tracings against the original drawings, and sees that the tracings are reassembled in the order set out in the camera exposure chart or dope sheet. They are then sent on to the colouring department. (Colouring is termed "opaquing" in the U.S.A.)

By the time the work reaches this department, the director will have approved the colour keys for the production. The colours chosen for individual figures are related to code numbers for each individual shade of colour or tone. The colour mixer has advance information on this and also on the amount of colour which should be prepared. The colour mixer is normally a full-time member of the departmental staff, and works under the direct supervision of the head of the colouring department, who is responsible for handing out the traced cells to the individual colourists with the necessary paint.

While in America there are several organizations specializing in the manufacture of celluloid paints, in the rest of the world studios still have to find their own solution to the problem of the best paint to use. The essential requirements of this paint are first, that it should have the right degree of opacity, second, that it should possess sufficient durability to prevent flaking, and third, that it should be quick-drying. In Britain both waterproof oil colour and emulsion based colours are used. Owing to the fact that several layers of these celluloid transparencies must be laid one on top of the other, colourists must apply their colour so that its consistency is absolutely smooth.

Attached to most tracing and painting departments is a special-effects painter with a certain skill in reproducing such texturized surfaces as speed-lines, smoke, water and sky effects. In the U.S.A. the work of tracing and painting is frequently sub-contracted to free-lance artists; this system has not been developed elsewhere.

Inkers and colourists are mostly women. The work requires great patience, accuracy and cleanliness of handling, and women have proved the best technicians.

Animators consider the present technique of tracing and painting a limiting factor in their work because only flat tones and shapes can be achieved. The more recently developed system of photo-electric transfer of animated drawings to the celluloids (such as the Xerox machine developed by the Haloid Company and the Ozalid process) can, of course, reproduce any form of texture or painting which appears in the original drawings. This new method, when it has to some extent been simplified, will eventually give a great impetus to the technical process of animation.

The Checker

Checking is the last phase before a cartoon film reaches the cameras.

After all work has been completed by the animators, tracers, painters and background artists, the checker, following the camera instruction chart, examines each frame of each scene in the film to see that all the cells are there. Even in a very short commercial, which may only take seven seconds to show, the number of cells involved can amount to well over a hundred. Each cell, of course, must be correctly numbered with the production and scene clearly marked, otherwise this could cause confusion at the shooting stage.

This is only the beginning, for the checker must also see whether the finished work has been done correctly and, in particular,

224

whether the tracers have adhered strictly to the drawings given to them by the animators. Failure here could cause the movements of a character to jitter when the image is projected on the cinema or television screen.

Painting, too, needs to be scrutinized. It is essential that each cell should conform to the colour keys which are supplied by the design department for each section involved in the production. Sometimes paint has to be mixed to conform to the various layers of the cells. It is obviously important that there should be no unwanted variation of colour in the middle of a scene.

Backgrounds are also scrutinized by the checkers. They must conform in size to the field the lens will include and also the area it will cover should either the background or the camera have to move.

It is also necessary to see that the characters match properly. For example, if a character should appear to be sitting down on a chair which has been painted on a background, the tracer must watch the matching of the animation lines very carefully in their relation to the static outline of the chair.

Small errors are usually adjusted by the checker himself, but major faults have to be sent back to the department concerned for correction.

Most of all it is important to examine the camera instruction chart, since this shows all camera and rostrum movements to be undertaken by the cameraman. The checker must have a comprehensive knowledge of the camera and be able to follow the script and see that the mechanics of the scene will work. Sometimes there are as many as six different camera moves in a single frame, and any fault that is not discovered in time could ruin an expensive sequence.

Cleanliness of the cell used is also taken into account. The cells must be polished thoroughly, since any dust or dirt marks are noticeable in the photography.

The same applies to the cell lengths. If, when the cameraman has nearly finished shooting a scene, he finds he has insufficient length of cell to work with, it may mean that the scene has to be entirely reshot.

The Cameraman

The cartoon cameraman's work is very different from that of his colleague who is responsible for live-action motion picture photography. The basis of his work is frame-by-frame exposure of the background and cells as a series of static combinations. He is

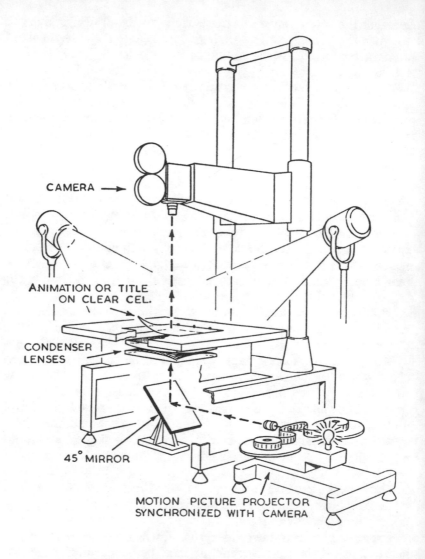

CAMERA →

ANIMATION OR TITLE
ON CLEAR CEL.

CONDENSER
LENSES

45° MIRROR

MOTION PICTURE PROJECTOR
SYNCHRONIZED WITH CAMERA

The Oxberry Animation Camera with the new aerial image rear projection. This camera set-up is capable of projecting a live-action scene on to the plattern glass and can, in conjunction with top lighting, superimpose flat cartoon animation over the live-action image. This is a considerable improvement on the matte system normally employed. The rostrum set-up is capable of controlling electronically both the movement of flat art-work and the vertical movement of the camera. The rostrum is also capable of selecting movement and transferring this movement electrically at a pre-determined speed. It has an automatic follow-focus throughout the entire range from 2 inch to 34 inch field size without the operator having to adjust the lens. The camera itself is capable of changing over from 35mm to 16mm and a wide-screen lens attachment can also be added.

226

responsible for the general standard of photography and table work such as smooth tracks, pans and dissolves, which can make so much difference when the final film reaches the screen.

His responsibilities begin with recording the finished drawings and cells on to film in the correct sequence. Either the director or the key animator responsible for the sequences provides him with the necessary camera exposure chart. This shows the combination of cells for each frame and also where effects such as dissolves, double exposures, pans and tracks occur.

Modern rostrum camera technique has developed substantially in recent years. The contribution of the cartoon cameraman can be a very important factor in production. With the skilful use of lens technique, much work can be saved, and in addition, striking visual effects achieved which help the animator.

Additional technical equipment for the rostrum camera is constantly being developed, especially by the outstanding engineer, John Oxberry of New Rochelle, New York. This equipment introduces new ideas for cartoon photographic technique. In addition, new lighting techniques achieve more interesting effects of colour.

In order to save time and labour and to provide additional facilities to improve the standard of camera work, modern animation tables are fitted with back projection which enables previously filmed backgrounds or live-action scenes to be superimposed on to the picture which is being photographed by the animation camera, thus enabling the live-action and animated pictures to be mixed together by the cameraman.

Other refinements include automatic follow-focus which enables tracks to be made without the need for the cameraman to do any focusing himself during tracking in and out. Such follow-focus should operate from the smallest to the largest fields possible.

Electronic control of movements at various speeds in all directions may be provided for and change-over facilities from 35 mm. to 16 mm. shooting and from normal to widescreen are also very useful additions.

The normal operational sequence is as follows:

1. Study of the camera exposure chart for all the camera moves, tricks, the number of cell levels and arrangements, and the length of each scene.

2. Once he is absolutely certain he has mastered these details, the cameraman prepares a schedule of each scene before starting to shoot. This will include notes on whether he is to shoot forwards or backwards, whether he is to use back projection and at what point

he will come to camera mixes or superimposition. In addition, he takes note from the camera instruction chart of all scene movements which he has to calibrate in terms of camera and rostrum movements.

3. The actual photographic operation can now begin. This requires the utmost concentration and freedom from interference. Briefly, the cameraman, following the camera instruction chart, fixes the background in the predetermined position on the rostrum table beneath the camera. He then places the appropriate set of cells over the background; both cells and background are held in position by peg-bars. Subject to the chart, he can then expose this particular frame. The lighting for each scene is static, predetermined by various factors which are described later.

4. After completing the frame exposure with attention to every technical detail, the cameraman records it on the exposure chart, and prepares for the next frame. This may involve him in re-adjusting the peg-bars in a predetermined direction in order to achieve movement in the background, and also in readjusting the rostrum table, if the scene so requires. He may also have to re-adjust the camera-lens and possibly the camera itself for other effects of movement in the scene according to the calibrations he has previously worked out.

5. When the whole scene has been completed and the negative material unloaded, the cameraman prepares detailed instructions for the laboratory. He must state the kind of film used, the length of each scene, and other relevant information affecting processing.

6. The cameraman checks the rush print.

In the production of animated films, it is often desirable to produce special effects, and many of these can be done during the process of photography. This saves the expense and time of having them done optically in the laboratory.

Most animation cameras are fitted with some means of reducing the exposure gradually from frame to frame, and by far the best way of doing this is by means of a variable shutter; that is, a shutter which is composed of two overlapping leaves which can be moved in relation to each other to give a maximum aperture (about 170°), or no aperture at all.

Other methods are either: (1) gradually to close the lens iris (this has the disadvantage of increasing the depth of field and general sharpness of the picture as it is closed down), or (2) gradually to reduce the lighting with a dimmer. This method cannot be used in colour photography, since a reduction of light also results in a reduction of colour temperature.

Fades are achieved simply by reducing the light gradually from frame to frame, either by closing down the shutter aperture or using other means provided until the point of zero exposure is reached.

Cross dissolves can be used to fade out one scene while the next one simultaneously fades in, or to fade out titles or part of a scene whilst leaving the remainder of the scene unchanged. This is done by closing down the shutter aperture over the desired number of frames from full to zero, and then reversing the camera without exposing, to the frame where the shutter started to close. The scene is then changed or the unwanted parts are removed and the camera is run forward again. This time, however, the shutter aperture is gradually increased over the same number of frames till full exposure is reached again. The overall level of exposure must remain constant for each frame of the cross dissolve, so the shutter angles need to be carefully adjusted to give 100 per cent exposure throughout.

In animation camera work, it is usually possible to expose the negative in two or more stages and this proves to be very useful if sections of the picture only require partial exposure, or if still titles are required to be superimposed on a picture which is moving through the screen area, or similarly, if moving titles are required to be shown on a still picture. By making separate exposures, titles and picture can be photographed at different distances from the camera, or title backgrounds can be diffused or put slightly out of focus if desired.

Titles for superimposing are usually painted in white on a cell and photographed against a dense black background; the cell is either painted black on the underneath surface, or else black flock-coated paper is used. Black carbon-surfaced paper is not suitable when fast panchromatic films are being used, since the carbon rubs off and the film receives a considerable extra overall exposure.

When parts of a scene require to be photographed with reduced density, the whole scene is usually photographed twice (in exact register) with percentage exposures, the reduced parts being removed during one exposure. In this way, for example, shadows, fire and smoke can be given a certain amount of transparency. The background or other parts of the picture will show through, since they will have had full exposure. Mist or fog effects can also be obtained by giving a very low extra exposure on a light grey card, either moving or still as desired. The mist can be faded in or out entirely independently of the remainder of the picture. When

229

planning scenes to be photographed in more than one exposure, however, care should be taken that parts of the scene do not show through other parts where they are not wanted.

The cameraman must have specialized knowledge of the techniques required to handle effectively the different colour systems. Among the many available, the two principal systems are Technicolor and Eastman Colour.

Photography in Technicolor is carried out on colour sensitive panchromatic film as used in black-and-white photography. It is a negative separation process. The process necessitates the use of a standard set of Tri-colour filters with suitable neutral density filters to balance the exposure for the type of light being used. The filters are geared to the camera mechanism and are automatically brought into position in sequence (Blue, Red and Green) either in front or behind the camera lens as each frame of film is exposed. The camera driving mechanism is adjusted to expose three frames (one with each filter) between stops, so that the exposed single strip of negative has a Blue, Red and Green filter record of each frame in Black-and-White. After exposure, the film is despatched to the Technicolor laboratory, where it is developed and the final colour print is made.

Photography in Eastman Colour is carried out on Eastman Colour Negative film. This is a multi-layer film, having three colour sensitive layers of emulsion together with suitable colour couplers, on one base. The top layer is sensitive to blue light, the second to blue and green, and the lower layer to blue and red. A yellow filter layer is placed between the top and second layer to isolate the blue light from the green and red sensitive layers. The film is made for use with a light colour temperature of 3.200° Kelvin. For light other than this, it will be necessary to use a suitable filter on the lens to balance the light to 3.200° Kelvin; photography is then as for black-and-white, but the exposure needs to be accurate.

The following are the main photographic systems in normal animation:

Technicolor	Colour sensitive panchromatic film such as *Plus X*.
Eastman Colour	Eastman colour negative.
Black-&-White Photography	*Plus X* or similar types of negative.
Line-Tests of Animator's Paper Drawings	Non-colour sensitive film of high contrast and clear base such as Sound Recording Stock. (The developed negative is projected.)

230

Exposures used are as follows:

Plus X—Technicolor	160 foot candles Direct Light, using standard *Wratten* Tri-Colour filters, ½ second at *f*2.8, with polarized screens.
Plus X—Black-&-White	120 foot candles. ½-second at *f*9.5, with polarized screens.
Eastman Colour	160 foot candles, colour correction filter (Blue) 2/3 stop increase—½ second at *f*2.8, with polarized screens.
Sound Recording Stock (*reflected light photography*)	120 foot candles, Direct reading, Black-and-White background = *f*4.5. White on Black background = *f*3.5 at ½ second.
Line-Test Exposures	32 foot candles of light transmitted through papers = *f*4 at ½ second exposure—not polarized on lens.

The main danger of rostrum tracks and pans is jitter. The following notes on how to avoid jitter when designing panning scenes have been compiled for this book by Bill Traylor.

Jitter is caused when objects of constant shape and size are moved through the screen area in steps, and then held in a still position while the exposures are made on the film.

It is much more common in animation than in live action, because in the latter the objects are moving during exposure. This invariably results in the image on the film being blurred, but in spite of this, objects appear quite clear and sharp when the film is projected on to a screen.

In animation it is not often practicable to move the drawings or cells during exposure, and when the movement is considerable between each frame persistence of vision enables the eye to see a clear picture of the position in which the object is being photographed, and a somewhat blurred image of the position on the previous frame; the object therefore appears to move across the screen in a series of jumps—which is, of course, what it really does.

The jitter effect will be proportional to: (*a*) The amount of movement of drawings for each frame, in relation to the field size at which the scene is photographed; and (*b*) The amount of contrast in the drawings.

Jitter is always most apparent on the edges of light tones which are at an angle of 90 degrees to the direction of movement: that is, verticals when the movement is horizontal, and horizontals when the movement is vertical.

On our standard 5 inch field, pure white will begin to show signs of jitter when the movement is only about .050 inch per frame, but if the tone is lowered to something considerably off-white, the distance can be increased to .100 inch or .200 inch per frame, according to the amount the tone is lowered. It should be remembered also that large areas of white show more jitter than small areas, but there is a danger that thick white vertical lines on horizontal pans may do so as well.

When objects are panned through the screen areas, jitter always appears to be worst (on standard 5 inch field) when the distance of movement is between .125 inch and .500 inch per frame; at speeds greater than this, however, the object moves through the screen so quickly that the jitter, although still there, will be so short that it does not appear to be objectionable. When an object with a complete outline in very light tones, and occupying about two-thirds of the screen area, is panned right across the screen in about one and a half seconds, it will appear as two complete objects—although there is only one image on each frame of film.

Fairly light colours do not jitter so much as white, and it therefore seems advisable to use colours whenever possible on fast panning scenes, reducing the tone of the colour and lowering the key of the drawings generally to suit the speed of movement. This of course will mean that if the same objects appear in adjacent scenes which are not panning, the tones will have to be lowered to the same level for these scenes.

It is doubtful if large areas of pure white need ever be used at all in drawings for films (except lines, titles or other material for superimposing by an extra exposure), as the camera exposure has to be adjusted to record the darkest tones and pure white is always over-exposed in any case.

It has been noted in a previous paragraph (*a*) that jitter is affected by distance of movement in relation to field size; if therefore the camera tracks in to a smaller field size during the panning movement, the contrast should be adjusted to prevent jitter at the smaller field size.

On fast panning pictorial backgrounds, such objects as trees, posts, etc. can often be sloped back slightly from bottom to top, and the edges can be softened; this will help to eliminate jitter.

The Editor

The work of the editor in animation goes well beyond assembling the film. His work begins at a stage which might be termed pre-editing. The director is obviously responsible for determining the exact timing of each shot, but he consults his editor throughout the planning stage.

The editor can advise the director on matters affecting the length and timing of music, dialogue and effects, and so help him in the preparation of the work book. Also, before production starts, the editor is often asked to carry out experiments with sound effects as well as to pre-record voice tests which will help the director in choosing the right cast for the sound track.

After the work book is completed and before animation starts, most animated films require some pre-recorded tracks. This even applies to films in which the music will be post-recorded. It is the editor's responsibility to see that these initial recordings are carried out satisfactorily from the point of view both of their content and their quality.

Since the introduction of magnetic tape, the editor should have some technical knowledge of the characteristics that belong to this form of recording in addition to his previous experience of optical recording. At some stage later in the production process he will be the technician chiefly responsible to the director for the sound recordist's handling of the tracks when they are transferred from the magnetic to the optical sound system.

232

The various elements of sound that will eventually make up the sound track (the dialogue track, the effects tracks, the music track) are examined by the editor in order to supply the animation team with an analysis of their contents, especially when these tracks have already been recorded and the animation must be synchronized exactly. This analysis is called the charting of the sound track and is a very detailed frame-by-frame examination. It is helpful if the editor draws attention to any particular points in the pre-recorded tracks which could be a source of inspiration to the animators. Similarly, he should also be prepared to discover and point out any defects the tracks may contain.

In animated films the first pictorial material which will reach the cutting-room will be the pencil- or line-test. The editor assembles the line-test following out the shape of the future finished film.

The sound tracks that have been pre-recorded can now be tried out in synchronization with the line-tests. Both the work book and the camera shooting charts are his guides as regards the length of each shot and their visual accentuation.

The editor's function as a cutter differs from work in the live-action studio because the order and length of each shot are pre-determined on the drawing-board. In spite of this, however, in practice an editor may find that the shifting of a few frames forward or backward may well tighten the action. This, of course, only applies to music and effects; dialogue must always remain exactly synchronized.

The whole film will eventually be assembled by the editor in line-test form as this first test stage in the animation is completed. Some of the sound tracks (for example, music and effects) can be laid now with the line-test—that is, a certain proportion of the final sound track is mixed before the first rushes of the finished animation come through.

It is customary for the editor to assemble the rush prints of the finished animated shots to the pattern of the edited line-test, and it is then possible to complete the mixing of the sound track. The editing of the sound tracks is in fact as lengthy and intricate a process as the production of the visuals.

The Studio Manager

We have seen from the many functions described in the production of an animated film that there must be some central organization to co-ordinate and administer the work. Without this not only time of creative workers would be lost, but the quality of the work

233

itself could easily suffer, and lose its sense of direction. This applies even more to animation than it does to live-action film-making because the majority of the artists and technicians are concerned with only a small section of the total production. It is therefore very necessary to have a studio manager who is responsible to the producer for the smooth running of the work.

The principal work of the studio manager is to assist the producer by presenting a day-to-day record of the progress of all current productions for comparison with his schedules, and to save time which might be wasted by staff directly employed on production by relieving them of non-technical duties.

He is responsible to the producer for the smooth flow of work in each department. By keeping in close touch with the heads of all departments, he can assist in preparing work schedules, draw attention to impending hold-ups and bottle-necks, and suggest remedies. He should, therefore, be kept informed of all matters affecting the progress of production in the studio, camera room and cutting room.

He should also handle all letters to the laboratories (concerning processing), place orders for film stock, supply information about completed films as required by the Trade Unions and the music copyright societies, and order all materials needed in the studio.

As soon as an animated film studio employs labour, it is obliged to organize its staff on an industrial basis. The studio manager takes over the task of scheduling staff matters such as welfare, attendance and holidays. In addition, he checks the invoices and delivery notes for stores, identifies the current productions for the accountants for invoicing, distributes and collects time sheets, issues artist's materials and arranges for servicing of equipment. Finally, he records deadline dates for line-tests, rough cuts and answer print screenings, and reports the sponsors' reactions.

Specialized Technical Animation

As an example of a radically different method of animation, in this case for highly specialized films of a scientific and technical nature, we are grateful to Francis Rodker, Director of Animation and Special Effects for the Shell Film Unit in London, for the following statement:

At the Shell Film Unit a system has been developed so that the animators, under the supervision of the director of animation, do their own drawing and shooting, thus acquiring a complete, first-hand grasp of the technicalities

234

involved at each stage. Working closely with the director, we prepare test shots before actual animation or model work commences.

I have always had a tendency to cut down on "cell" work and achieve motion where possible by manipulation and multi-exposures. This is particularly suitable to our method of individual working because the animator draws and works to his camera and calculates his shooting accordingly. It is also possible to add last minute refinements, or even cover up errors, should they occur, at a moment's notice. A great proportion of the work at Shell is of a precise nature, and in most cases the manipulation of one drawing can achieve this accuracy better than numbers of separate ones.

I have always been an advocate for using the animation rostrum for special effects, the kind of thing that should really be live action. During the War I had the opportunity of producing scenes which would normally be the function of the special effects department in a film studio. Such scenes as night bombing, wrecked aircraft, submarines under water and flying through cloud were done with one or two drawings, a little wood-carving, cotton wool and the full use of single and multiplane shooting on the animation rostrum.

During the War we were extensively engaged on War Office production. Films on submarine warfare required long footages of animation showing attack and defence methods nearly always involving ships moving at their natural speeds. Often a ship one inch long would have to take 240 frames to travel its own length; a submarine on the same set-up probably travelling more slowly and both craft manoeuvring all the time. The ships were drawn on cells, manipulated by hand and with magnifiers on the scaled tracks set off-screen; no pegs were used for multi-cell work (I have rarely used pegs) only surface registration, which is really accurate. Much time and drawing were saved by designing movements which utilize each cell perhaps twice or three times in different positions.

We have never adopted peg registration for several reasons, among them being the difficulty of exactness for mechanical movements, the wear on register holes in cyclic animation, swinging cells and the very varied nature of our work.

When one is designing, drawing and shooting, many short-cut methods are possible. Flexibility and freedom from transmitting detailed instructions to someone else to shoot, plus the "feel" of the job help to produce a high standard. One also tends to design for one's own capabilities, knowing well in advance what risks are involved.

I have designed a special rostrum to cover the variable nature of our work. The flexibility and simple construction of these machines make them readily adaptable in a very short time, and enable us to add extra units such as rotascope and back projection. We find we are using these accessories more and more and that they offer greater scope for new techniques. Even at the time of writing, our colour back projection unit is proving invaluable for colour flooding effects which would have been tedious and cumbersome to produce by more conventional means. We have also been able to cut out a great deal of optical work by obtaining all the effects on one negative in the animation camera.

Whatever technique is used it has always been our practice to keep the picture as simple as possible building up the story piece by piece, sometimes from a blank screen or by directly matched superimposition so that continuity is maintained. Whatever the technique employed one must never lose oneself in techniques for their own sake and produce a bag of tricks, for it is the clarity of the story on the screen that counts.

1. "Malaria"—1941. (See Still page 244.)

Here is an example of the way animation has been used to portray a process hitherto unrecorded by motion picture or even still photography (at the time the film was made). It is part of a continuous sequence showing the life cycle of the Malaria parasite and its transfer from insect to man.

235

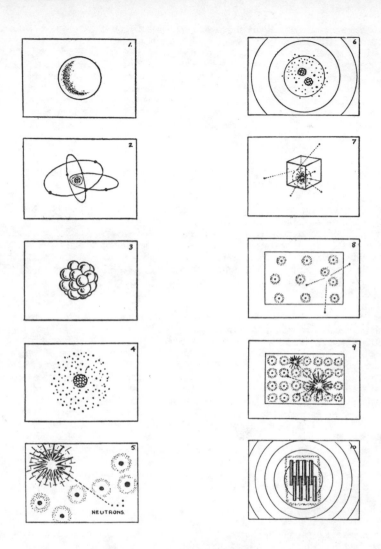

Sequence of drawings from *Criticality* (Larkins' Studio, G.B.) Commentary:

(1) The atom used to be thought of as a minute billiard ball, indivisible and indestructible. (2) Now visualize it as something like a tiny solar system with electrons revolving round ... (3) ... a nucleus consisting of several types of particles, in particular protons. (4) Uranium has 92 Electrons and 92 Protons. (5) Neutrons can split the atom releasing vast amounts of energy. (6) The collision divides the nucleus, releases more neutrons and generates radio activity. (7) Some of the released neutrons cause further collisions and so the process continues. (8) If the uranium atoms are widely spaced, the action peters out. (9) If the atoms are in a certain density the action is continuous and the mass is "critical". (10) Rods of uranium are regulated and controlled to establish criticality.

After I had collated my information from all sources (including, of course, the facts given me by my technical adviser), I decided to use the system of animating actually under the camera, using one or two cells only and cut-outs. This saved a great deal of time since there was little advance preparation necessary in the form of drawings, but it must be recognized that this system involves the risk that mistakes will only be discovered after the photography has been completed.

2. The Gas Turbine—1954. (See Still page 245.)

The technique employed here was to use an actuality film showing an engine in section, and then to superimpose animation on it to demonstrate its workings.

Since it was not possible to show gas and air flows on this engine by means of live-action, animation had to be used to show this. By combining actuality with animation an added force was given to the demonstration. Once the engine was stripped down to its shaft, with the compressor and turbine revolving slowly, the next step was to fit the animation to the sequence.

Direct photography by means of back projection plus three extra exposures for animation combined to produce everything required on a single negative. This technique avoided the use of opticals and reduced unsteadiness to a minimum. In addition, we were able to superimpose a section of the revolving shaft that was invisible on the original take and to block out unwanted parts of the machine that could not be dismantled on the engine. The process of back projection is not, of course, a new one. All that we have done is to apply it to animation in order to demonstrate a process more clearly.

3. The Search for Oil—1954. (See Still page 245.)

This was a chance to use a continuation of live-action and diagram to show one of the methods of strata survey. The scene opens with a full screen live-action back-projection shot which zooms to a miniature, revealing a diagram background of strata and river in cross-section. The weighted springs represent the gravity instrument used by the survey team in the boat. A separate exposure was necessary for the miniature by back projection spring and background, respectively.

4. High Speed Flight—1957. (See Still page 246.)

To demonstrate that an aeroplane flying at near the speed of sound may at sea-level be slightly slower than sound but in the stratosphere be slightly faster. A split screen effect using pure animation demonstrated this point, live-action being impossible.

The Composition and Recording of Music for Animated Films

The authors are grateful to Francis Chagrin and Matyas Seiber, both highly experienced composers in animated films, for the following descriptions of their different methods of approach to the intricate creative work of composing and recording music for this branch of film-making.

Francis Chagrin is concerned with the difference between composing music for animated and live-action films, and especially the problem of integrating the sound effects and voices with the total musical composition.

Matyas Seiber describes the relationship between music composition and the style of a film, and also the technical problems of timing and conducting the recording of the music.

Francis Chagrin writes:

It would be a gross over-simplification to imagine that cartoon film music is only one particular kind of music, but there is a possibility of finding one common denominator in its use and application: it is the only kind of film music that is—as a rule—always carefully planned ahead, usually before the actual art work, or at least the animation, is started; which is discussed in the greatest details by producer and composer; where the musician has to work to specification and where his contribution is not—as sometimes in feature films— a necessary evil used to cover up deficiencies of direction or production, but, on the contrary, eagerly awaited as a basis for the actual production of the film.

I am not referring to the fact that, more often than not, the music is actually recorded first, then measured carefully (or charted) and all the exact points of emphasis marked and handed over to the animators. What I mean is that sound and vision have equal importance; they are equal partners, aiming at an ideal married-print status and preparing for it scrupulously by synchronizing their moods and their movements; and, supreme marital bliss, by both telling the same story at the same time not only without ructions but in perfect harmony and with single-mindedness. I do not mean in unison; the harmony may be brought about by parallel movement or by counterpoint.

As in the ballet, there must first be a preliminary "engagement"—an engagement of two forces, two minds, two artistic forms of expression, trying to find the ideal *modus vivendi*, ready to make concessions and also to demand them; but once the basis has been agreed upon in detail and in general outline, it is the music that takes over temporarily to create the *modus operandi*; the musical score, in which all the ideas agreed upon will be incorporated has to be finally written before the choreographer or the animator can make their contribution. But here the comparison must nearly end.

Ballet—as well as cartoon film—uses music as a basis for movement. Whereas in ballet the movement is performed by one or several dancers whose movement is governed by their skill and the law of gravity (amongst other limitations) the movement in cartoon film is completely free from such considerations.

A change, in cartoon films, can be instantaneous; no need to take out the *corps de ballet* to have an empty stage: the cartoon character has only to stretch out a hand and it will hold—at will—a bunch of flowers, or a wheel, with or without car attached, and so on.

Only music has the ability to change so quickly and so completely in a split second. And this is one of the foremost functions of music in cartoon films: to be the perfect mould on which the action will be cast.

May I jump from these generalities to a technical detail which is the very basis of synchronization and which must be very clearly understood when settling down to writing the score for any film, but even more so for a cartoon film. The equivalent of one second is 24 frames, that is 24 different drawings, one of which may require the special emphasis that has been agreed upon. It is essential to remember that music starts from 0 seconds and that the frames start with 1. Thus, supposing the music to be played in 2/4 and 1 second = 1 bar, the four quavers will be played at: 0: 1/4: 1/2 and 3/4 seconds respectively and charted at 1: 7: 13 and 19 frames respectively. In a 3/4 bar of the same duration the three crotchets will be played at: 0: 1/3 and 2/3 and charted at 1: 9 and 17 frames, respectively.

The next thing to be aware of is that every section begins at 0. The composer should always insist on being given lengths for each detailed sequence, as well as the total length of the section from the beginning of it up to and including the latest sequence.

Section 1

	Duration of Sequence	Total						
		0						
Sequence a	2 sec.	2	starts at	0	ends at	2
„ b	3 „	5	„ „	2	„ „	5
„ c	7 „	12	„ „	5	„ „	12
„ d	2 „	14	„ „	12	„ „	14

Section 1

Total duration	0	2	5	12	14 sec.
Sequence	/ a /	b /	c /	d /	

Since film-music in general and cartoon film in particular can only have a *raison d'être* if it is perfectly synchronized with the action, a clear understanding of the very simple facts stated above is essential.

Unnecessary mistakes and time can be avoided if the composer knows: (*a*) how many seconds the sequence lasts (it may be a wild race which has to stop dead); (*b*) at which moment during the sequence there should be a special effect, or climax, or pause; (*c*) the total timing from the beginning of the full section (a section being a part of the music which is recorded by itself).

Only after being quite clear on these mechanical details do I ever start actually writing the music. This does not mean that I will not have jotted down in the meantime a number of possible musical ideas which I then consider carefully as to mood, movement, style, basic rhythm, total length of the musical phrase, etc., before I select the one which is the most apposite.

Words in relation to Music

If it is essential that perfect harmony should reign between sound and picture at any given point, this is only possible if there is no conflict of loyalties in the sound department itself. Any composer knows that, whenever words and music are supposed to be together on the sound track, the words are given unfair and unnecessary prominence and the music is "despised and rejected". The fault is not only that of the recording engineer, who will automatically (and sometimes rightly) consider that words must be clearly understood and so plays safer than is really necessary. Often the composer himself is to blame for considering words as the enemy.

This problem has always preoccupied me: how to find a way which will make everybody happy; how to write the music in such a way that it is not submerged when the spoken word invades the sound track. The solution was simply to do the polite thing and retire, submerging the music intentionally by altering the orchestration for as long as a word or a phrase is spoken and come back to normal as soon as it is finished. If the music is written around the words it comes down or up by itself much more naturally than if it is turned down or up by the sound engineer's knob, and without any loss of quality.

In one of my early cartoon films, for instance, *T for Teacher* (Direction: Peter Sachs; words by Roger MacDougall) I experimented further; I gave each syllable of the very witty text a time value, as if I had been going to set it to music, and then divided the whole text into bar-lines. The action was intimately bound up with the text, and for special emphasis I introduced bars or beats of rest, where the spoken word would give way to some special effect. There were, in addition, also passages of pure action, such as in the introduction, when a storm takes place, and various others, during which no words were used.

The final score looked as if it had been written for a solo singer with orchestral accompaniment; and, apart from the fact that it was spoken and not sung, this was the way in which I did actually record it.

Music without Words

The real joy for a composer is to have the whole sound track at his exclusive disposal. This is a challenge for the artist as well as the composer: words may be a nuisance on the sound track but they can be very useful in conveying a clear meaning. Drawings and music must take over all the implications. And the music, which has often to be subservient to the words, in intensity as well as significance, comes much more completely into its own.

Music and Effects

Cartoon film is larger than life because of its much greater freedom from reality. The emphasis, both in drawings and in music, must sometimes be exaggerated; or at least conveyed unmistakably. In many cartoon films the effects track can assume a significance parallel to that of the music track. But, unlike effects in feature-films, the effects in cartoon-films must be integrated in the musical score, even though they may be recorded separately. I have always insisted—usually successfully—that no effects, other than those written or decided by me in consultation with the director, should be added. To make this unnecessary, I have provided carefully for every single emphasis and—if necessary—written a separate effects track.

Two examples come to my mind: *Train Trouble* (Halas & Batchelor) had a passage where the main character, a squirrel who was a station-master, was always late—before he was converted to corn-flakes for breakfast. We wanted to convey the feeling of urgency, of fighting against time, of impending disaster, in the shortest possible space. Two trains were converging from two opposite sides and we first prepared, from records, a track which brought the two trains nearer and nearer; inside his room the squirrel was pacing up and down impatiently listening to the trains coming nearer. We decided to emphasize the urgency further by having several types of watches and clocks, ticking more and more loudly, at different speeds. Finally, out of the rhythm of the train came the words "You're going to be late" repeated faster and faster, taken over by the kettle, etc., until the tension became unbearable.

"Local" Emphasis and Dramatic Curve

The "local" emphasis as well as the general dramatic curve can be either positive or negative; that is, either brought about by parallel movement or by counterpoint.

The "emphasis" is particularly important in certain types of comic cartoons, but just as indispensable in dramatic films. The approach in sound can be direct: in a film called *Cool Custom*, two troglodytes hit each other on the head, and the sound I used was that of two Chinese temple blocks, wooden and hollow, each with a different pitch. One of them is suddenly transformed into a block of ice: the sound used is a note on a Vibraphone, played with hard sticks.

But a comic effect can be obtained just as successfully by the use of a dramatic chord, out of context (negative emphasis).

The same applies equally to the dramatic curve. In *Fable of the Fabrics* a young shepherd plays a gay tune on a flute; the shadow of "old age" approaches and reaches him; the shepherd becomes old and bent: the tune on the flute slows down and gets lower and darker, is taken over by the bassoon until it stops completely.

240

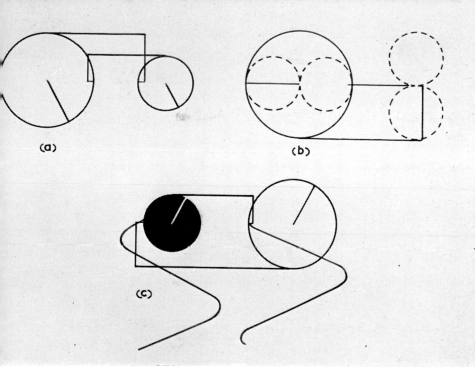

(a)   (b)

(c)

The Equation $\dot{x} + x = 0$ (Copyright Robert Fairthorne and Brian Salt; Great Britain).

INSTRUCTIONAL ANIMATION

Una Lezione in Geometria (Copyright Leonardo Sinisgalli; Italy).

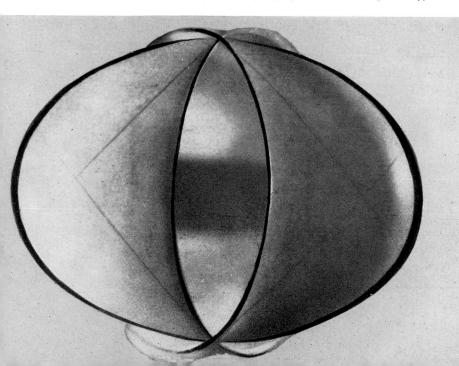

Light (Copyright Gaumont British Instructional; Great Britain).

Map Projection (Copyright G.B.I.; Great Britain).

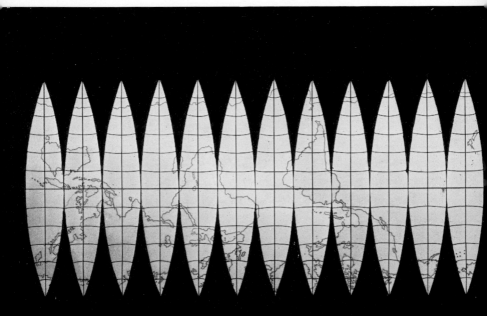

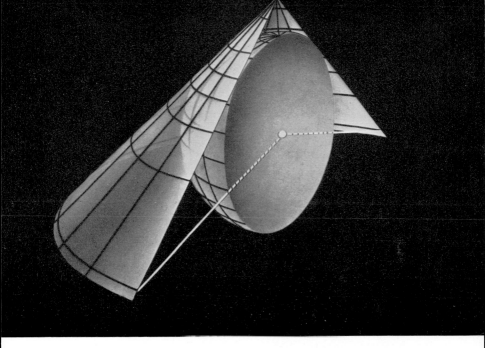

Map Projection (Copyright G.B.I.; Great Britain).

Digestion (Copyright G.B.I.; Great Britain).

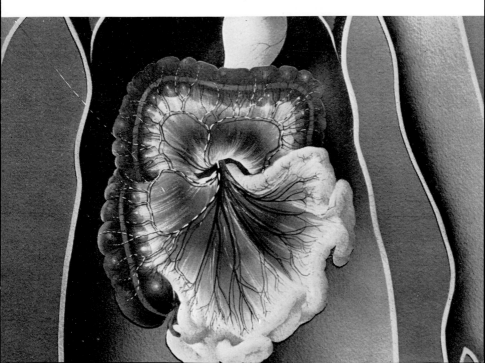

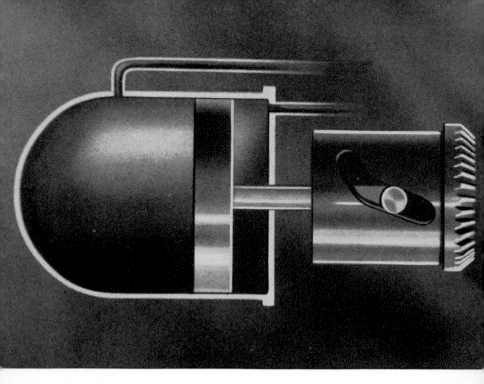

Airscrew (Copyright Shell Film Unit; Great Britain).

Malaria (Copyright Shell Film Unit; Great Britain).

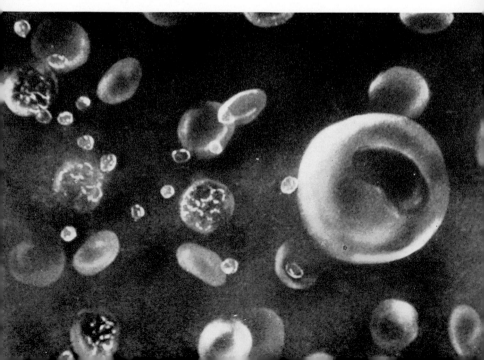

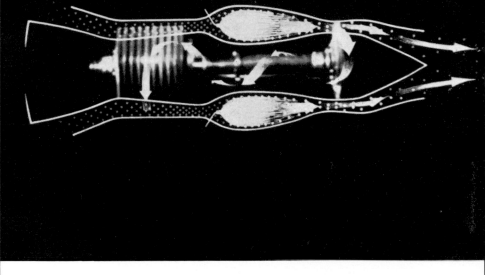

The Gas Turbine (Copyright Shell Film Unit; Great Britain).

The Search for Oil (Copyright Shell Film Unit; Great Britain).

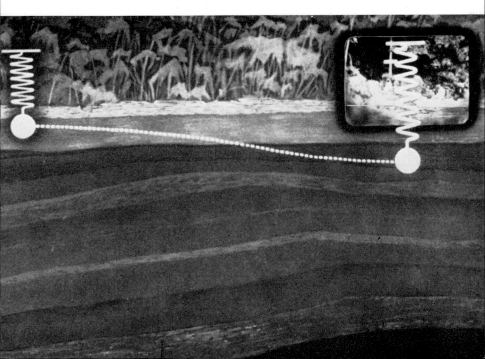

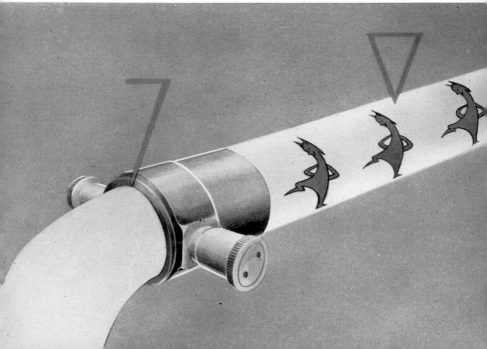

High Speed Flight (Copyright Shell Film Unit; Great Britain).

Water for Fire Fighting (Halas & Batchelor; Great Britain).

Handling Ships (Halas & Batchelor; Great Britain).

The World that Nature Forgot (Halas & Batchelor for M.P.O. and Monsanto Co.; Great Britain).

What on Earth is He? (Renzo Kinoshita; Japan).

Criticality (Larkins Productions for the Atomic Energy Authority; Great Britain).

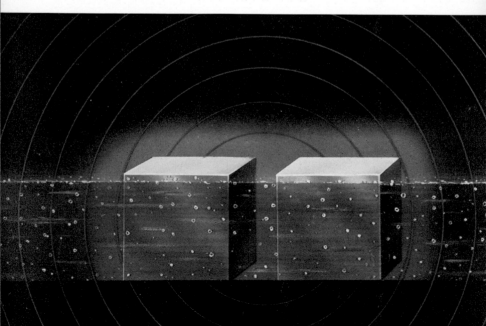

By contrast, in *Enterprise Part II*, the picture follows the text: "Let us now ... examine our own age, an age of hustle and bustle, huge nations, organizations, corporations, railway stations, docks, office blocks, aerodromes and ... a few homes." The music emphasizes not the immediate and direct meaning of the words, but their ultimate implication; it stands aside and surveys the scene in a contemplative mood, conveying not the "hustle and bustle" but the loneliness and resignation of those caught in it. After long discussions with the director, we agreed to use for this whole scene a 'cello solo, unaccompanied. This is much more an example of counterpoint than of actual contrast. The musical contribution is parallel, but at a different level.

Matyas Seiber writes:

There are two fundamentally different methods of procedure in relating music to animation. One is to have the music written and recorded first; the other, to write the music when the picture is ready. Both have their advantages and disadvantages.

First, the case of pre-composed and pre-recorded music.

Here, obviously, the composer has the advantage of greater freedom; he is not tied down so precisely to every fraction of a second as he is in the case of working for post-synchronization.

The first section of the film *The Magic Canvas* symbolizes something like "creation", with stars evolving. At a dramatic point, the shape of a human being develops. Then, after some movement of struggle, this shape breaks into two, one part flying away as a bird, the other remaining on the ground, enclosed behind bars. The rest of the film accompanies the flight of the bird. In the following sequence the bird flies through a terrifying storm which finally beats him down to the ground. Next, the storm abates, the sun comes out and everything revives; flowers blossom, the bird gathers new strength and flies up again. The bird flies out to the sea where it enjoys a playful ballet with waves and with white sails. It flies among clouds which gradually dissolve; then down again, earthwards, towards its other captive self. They unite, and together they fly up into the sky and disappear in the distance.

This film was an abstract project; consequently, I considered that a similarly "abstract" chamber music piece would be the most appropriate musical equivalent. I chose the rather odd combination of one flute, one horn and a string quartet. The form of the piece is that of a rather free "phantasy", consisting of several sections. A slow contrapuntal piece covers the first section. At the dramatic moment of the human shape breaking into two the horn enters for the first time. The speed increases, and at the moment when the bird breaks away the flute takes over. Now follows an "allegro" movement which covers the storm-sequence. The next section, the revival of nature, is expressed by a "pastorale" in the music. This is followed by a "scherzo", covering the play with the waves. Then a bridge section leads back to the recapitulation of the slow first movement, as the bird returns to the human shape. But the slow movement returns transformed: instead of the low-pitched, brooding mood as it appeared originally, it comes back now in a higher register, and a solo violin ends the piece, as the bird disappears in the distance.

I mention this film at some length because it was one of the rare cases when, within the framework of the story, it was possible to create an autonomous musical composition, a "Phantasy" consisting of a slow introduction, an Allegro, a Pastorale, a Scherzo and, finally, a Recapitulation of the slow Introduction.

Some of the synchronization of movements to music was not quite perfect in this film; but this, of course, depends largely on how much time and trouble is taken in planning the movements as close to the music as possible.

"FIGUREHEAD"

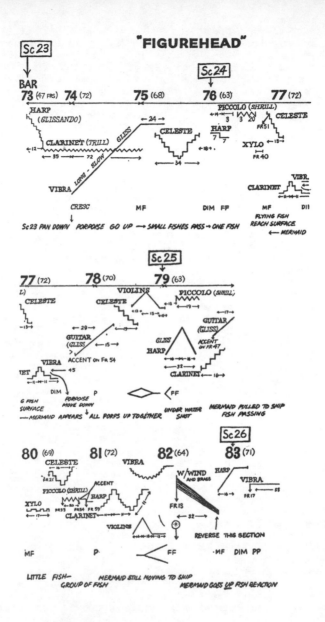

A visual digest from the pre-recorded sound track of an animated film can be of the greatest importance to the director and the key animator when music plays a vital part in the structure of the film. This helps them to achieve the maximum degree of accuracy in the synchronization of sound and vision. This chart from a sequence in *Figurehead* gives not only an analysis of the individual performance of each major instrument but also the timing in terms of individual frames.

250

How is this synchronization achieved? In the case of pre-recorded music, this is fairly simple: it depends on an exact analysis of the sound track. This is done on charts, such as that opposite, used for a film called *The Figurehead*.

Every note is measured by frame-lengths, the various instruments having their own line; dynamics are marked and bar-numbers of the score put in for reference. It is after studying these charts and listening to the music many times that the artists decide what shape their movement-composition should take.

Now let us deal with the other method; that is, when the music is written *after* the picture has been finished. This happens much more often.

It has the disadvantage for the musician that he cannot expand his music as he likes: he is absolutely tied to the details of the timing, and he has to keep precisely to the movements and gestures in the picture. On the other hand, it has the advantage that the composer can *see* the film before he starts composing. I find that seeing the movements and the background and being able to feel the mood of the finished picture give me much more inspiration and suggest more musical ideas than the mere description of the scene in script or storyboard. But the composer cannot, of course, work directly from the picture itself; he has to have on paper an exact analysis and timing of the visual track from which to work out his music. This is given him by the film-maker in the work book (see page 172).

The squares represent a fixed unit, a certain number of frames which have been agreed in advance between the animators and the composer. This means, of course, *tempo*. Every second consists of 24 frames on the film. Therefore the composer has to work with the utmost precision. There can be no question of working even half a second out, for this would mean that there are 12 drawings too many or too few for the animators. This would throw all their calculations of the movements out. If the agreed tempo is, say, 12 frames per musical beat, that means for the musician $M = 120$ (as there are 2 beats per second, or 24 frames). A chart of frame-numbers against metronome marks gives us the following values:

24 frames	M.60
22 ,,	M.65½
20 ,,	M.72
18 ,,	M.80
16 ,,	M.90
14 ,,	M.102.8
12 ,,	M.120
10 ,,	M.144
9 ,,	M.160
8 ,,	M.180 etc.

If, for instance, every square on that sheet represents 12 frames, that is to say, the composer works to a M.120 beat, then it is easy to locate—as long as he keeps exactly to that tempo—the precise musical place of every visual movement on the screen.

If it is desirable that certain movements—for example, tapping, or steps—should follow a certain rhythmic pattern, the composer might agree with the artists that this should be half-second beats.

That means for the animators that the impact of the movements must come on frames 1, 13, 25, 37, 49, 61, 67, 73.

Now how is it possible to achieve such mathematical exactitude in actual *playing*? A split second too early or too late and you are several frames out; the slightest fluctuation in tempo throws you right out of step with the picture. To follow a metronome is not exact enough: if you try to start two or more metronomes at the same time, you will see that after a short time they are normally out of step with each other.

This is not precise enough; the only device which is able to hold you (or the conductor) to frame-exact timing is the "click-track". This is made as follows: a strip of film is scratched every 12th frame if you want a 12-frame beat, or every 16th frame if it is a 16-frame beat, and so on. Then a loop is made of this film. This loop is run through a sound-channel during recording. It runs, of course, synchronized with the picture, that is at 24 frames per second, so that at every scratch it gives a loud click which is transmitted to the conductor through earphones. The poor fellow has to conduct the music with this devilish device clicking into his ears, keeping him tight to the tempo from which he cannot deviate a scrap, left or right!

Anyone who has ever tried to play to a metronome will remember the feeling he gets as if the metronome will suddenly start running away or falling back. It is, of course, not the metronome, but the player who is getting slower or faster, a fact he would probably never notice without his "conscience" ticking away mercilessly behind him. Conducting to a click-track is easy enough if the character of the music is merely dance-like or march-like; but as soon as some form of human expression creeps into the music, it becomes annoying and difficult to serve this tyrant of a timekeeper. Any kind of rubato is, of course, out of the question. But the click-track becomes an absolute necessity when frame-exact synchronization is required, or when the music is made up of several tracks which are finally "mixed" together, as it is so often the case. Then, of course, it is essential that every note on one track should correspond exactly to the respective note or notes on the other tracks.

The following is an example of this multiple-track technique. It occurs in a scene from the animated feature film *Animal Farm*, for which I composed the music.

The aged boar called Old Major summons the animals one night to the barn and tells them to revolt against Farmer Jones, the master who exploits them. At the end of the speech the animals, led by Old Major, burst into song, the animals' hymn.

Now this singing presented a specially tricky problem for me. The producers wanted the song to be without words, that is, to be sung with animal-like noises only. As we could not use any of the distorting devices, such as "Sonovox", I had first to find some actors who could, successfully, imitate animals and at the same time sing the notes in a recognizable musical pitch. When I knew more or less what I could expect from my singers, I planned out the exact score, specifying when the pigs would lead the singing, when the chickens, and so on. Under these single leading voices, however, I needed a solid background of sound, carrying the hymn right through, so I recorded the whole tune with a mixed chorus on one sound-band, an orchestral accompaniment on another, a special version for trombone and tuba on a third (to reinforce the pig-like noises as my pigs were not particularly strong)—so that at the final mixing any of these separate bands could be brought up or turned down. The solo animal voices were on still another track, and there was an additional track, too, with special effects such as the neighing of the horse and the "ee-aw" of the donkey. All this of course, had to be recorded at exactly the same speed. I selected for this particular section the *14-frame* tempo (cca. 103 metronome), and all the tracks were recorded to a 14-frame click-track.

The tracks were finally mixed together at a mixing session; we had sometimes as many as eight sound tracks running simultaneously in this film. As the tracks were all recorded to the same beat they were bound to be absolutely in synchronization. After many rehearsals the final balance of the tracks was agreed. This mixing was then re-recorded and became the final sound track. Here is an example of the mixing chart from which the sound-engineers work at the mixing sessions.

252

"ANIMAL FARM"   REEL 1B

TRACK	1	2	3	4	5	6	7
						15 CHEERS / 29	15 BACKGRD MUTTERING (ANIMALS)
	27 OLD MAJOR "BUT REMEMBER ARE EQUAL" 104					103 ANIMALS CHEERING	
	117 OLD MAJOR SINGING GASP 188	117 REV SONG BRASS 194	117 REV SONG F/ORCH 194	130 HORSE 140 DONKEY 188 GONG 194	125 PIGS 138 146 COWS 180	130	194
					202 DOG HOWL 206	204 DUCK 212	204 WAILING 235

A section of the mixing chart or *Animal Farm*, showing the dubbing plan for the mixing of seven separate sound tracks. This film in fact finally made use of twenty-one individual tracks for dubbing, and this necessitated a number of pre-mixing sessions to simplify the final task of the sound engineers.

20

COSTING THE PRODUCTION

IN all forms of animation a large proportion of the work is done by hand. Because of this, the costing of animated films becomes an highly individual matter for each studio and there is considerable variation in scale between the budgets of different kinds of studio.

This is not only a question of status, the fact that a studio with a high reputation can charge more for the work than one whose reputation has still to be made. It is also a question of the average working speed adopted by the studio and the rate of payment for the staff—whether the basic union rate is exceeded or not in the various grades of artists and technicians. In those countries where film production has been made a part of the state system, every technician is a state servant with a set scale of payment. Elsewhere, the rates of payment are the result of agreements reached between the appropriate trade unions and the employers. This is especially the case in Great Britain and the U.S.A.

In Britain the producer has to take into account four unions—his artists and technicians will belong to the Association of Cine Television and Allied Technicians (A.C.T.T.) and to the National Association of Theatrical and Kine Employees (N.A.T.K.E.), his actors (if any) to Equity and his musicians to the Musicians' Union.

In the U.S.A., Equity and the Musicians' Union operate similarly, but the situation becomes more complicated apart from these unions because the artists and technicians are organized regionally in the East and the West. Artists and technicians working in animation are separated from technicians concerned with live-action film production, and even further subdivided in Los Angeles, where a different union serves those working in television advertising films and those working for theatrical cartoons (the Screen Cartoonists' Guild and Screen Cartoonists' Union respectively). In New York the Screen Cartoonists' Union serves all artists and technicians concerned with animation.

254

Costing is naturally affected by the fact whether the studio pays the union minimum rate or over; it is further affected by the number of hours worked each week. Overtime is required in New York after a 35-hour week has been reached, in Los Angeles after a 40-hour week, in Britain after a 44-hour week. Overtime is $1\frac{1}{2}$ times normal rates in both the U.S.A. and Great Britain.

A further factor affecting costs is the sub-contracting of work to outside (or free-lance) artists, where different union rates obtain. Payment in this case is either on an hourly basis or at piece-work rates (e.g. in 1957 in the U.S.A. 42 cents per cell).

Rates of payment for artists and technicians on the studio staff are obviously a first consideration in costing a film. But another factor more difficult for the producer to assess and for the sponsor to appreciate is the manner in which the *texture* of the animation affects the price factor. The producer and his accountant must consider the number of drawings involved in the kind of film they are discussing. If a film is only lightly animated it may require as few as four drawings a foot; if the action is complex (involving several different characters all animated separately), then the degree of animation may be so high that a hundred drawings are required at certain stages for each foot of film. Labour costs must be measured accordingly—not only for the drawing but for checking and for rehearsing the photography when several layers of cells are involved. When the texture of the animation is complex, the labour of animating, inking and opaquing may reach a proportion equal to 60 per cent of the total cost of production. But if the texture of the animation is very nearly static (that is, when the bulk of the labour will in fact, through careful planning, be absorbed by the director, the designer and the background artist) the cost of animation, inking and opaquing could be as low as 10 per cent of the total.

The producer will require his production manager or his accountant to prepare a budget in the greatest detail before he can arrive at a firm price to quote to the sponsor. In addition to the labour costs (which, as we have seen, will be highly flexible according to the texture of the animation), the accountant will have to keep in mind certain fixed costs and overheads. The fixed costs can be listed as follows:

Composer's fee	Sound-film stock
Actors' fees	Picture stock
Studio hire	Artists' materials
Recording charges	Laboratory charges
Dubbing charges	Transport

The allowance for overheads in costing are the same as for any other business. Different kinds of studio premises and front office involve very differing kinds of rental and rates. Fine offices on Fifth Avenue or in Piccadilly add to the cost of a film; studios set in parks or gardens are similarly affected. In general, the larger the studio the higher in proportion are the overheads that creep through on to the budget. In these matters, the commonsense and the taste of the producer are in evidence. He must regard alike the comfort and happiness of his staff and the prestige of his own organization.

He is fortunate that the capital equipment involved in animation is relatively simple compared with other forms of film production. Animators, inkers and opaquers do not require elaborate equipment; their work is done on light-boxes. The camera and editing departments, however, do require certain specialized equipment which can be costly and consequently must be reflected in the studio overheads.

The producer is wise, however, to give his artists good surroundings with a workmanlike and pleasant, even a homely atmosphere of a kind likely to inspire efficiency and co-operation. The appearance of his own offices is equally important; here conferènces will be held at all hours as well as sponsors and other visitors received. Each producer must weigh these values against what he considers he can reasonably add to the budgets for his productions.

Since the advertising film for television has become the chief outlet of contemporary animation in Britain, France and the U.S.A., most of the studios that have grown up in response to this demand tend to be small. Because of the nature of the work they undertake (as large a number as possible of short commercials with a quick production turn-over against a tight schedule), the tendency is for the greater proportion of the work to fall on the planners (the producer, the director and the designer), and less on the animators, inkers and colourists.

In most of these small studios, the producer (normally himself an artist) does everything from planning the animation to keeping his company's books. If he is successful, however, he soon finds that he must employ assistants to deal with the innumerable details that arise out of administration and organization. As the work of the studio grows, it is both reasonable and economical for the staff to include a studio manager and production secretaries (the latter even for the animation directors and key animators).

Within the larger studios adaptations have been made to meet the needs of the new kinds of production. Studios formerly organized for the production of theatrical cartoons (where the bulk of the work has fallen on the animators) have found it necessary to make radical changes. Where there were formerly several animation teams at work there are now comparatively few, with a specialist in charge of each. Many animators with a flair for individual work have hived off from these studios to form their own small units employing very few highly-paid key animators while the rest of the more junior staff work for the normal union rates.

In contrast to all this concentrated, carefully budgeted work is the unhurried activity of the state studios in such countries as Russia and Czechoslovakia, on the one hand, or the National Film Board of Canada on the other. Here the labour costs are not the direct responsibility of the producers; producers, artists and technicians are alike employees. Animation texture in Russia is normally very rich in terms of man-hours; the work is undertaken with unhurried care. Inkers and colourists must be employed in considerable numbers in these studios, and the labour costs are likely to be very high. On the other hand, overheads for studio administration and equipment do not operate in the same way as they do for independent units working for profit.

The latter have to consider their status in their profession when making their final estimate for the costs of a future production. This is particularly true in the U.S.A. where a form of star system operates for the artists themselves, and it is worth both a producer's and a sponsor's while to pay extra for work of outstanding merit. Status derives from the average product of the unit just as much as from the work which receives public commendation or wins prizes at festivals. This average product will alternately be judged in commercial work on its ability to promote sales. It is on record, for example, that John Hubley's Maypo commercials, U.P.A.'s Piels Brothers commercials and the Halas & Batchelor Guardsman commercial for Murraymints in fact did help to sell their sponsors' products. Similarly, the goodwill that results very obviously from the best kind of public relations film sponsored, for example, by such an organization as Shell and B.P., will affect the attitude of other sponsors when they consider the appropriation they can set aside for further production.

The final price for a film is the subject for negotiation between the producer and the sponsor (or his agent). The producer (having determined his labour costs, his fixed charges, his overheads and the profit he feels to be reasonable in view of the status of his unit) puts forward his price. The sponsor might then be tempted to weigh this quotation against the possibilities of getting the work done more cheaply by a unit of less status employing (probably) less skilled talent and so producing less effective work. Whatever the status of the unit the minimum profit on which it can effectively operate is about 10 per cent of the actual cost of the film. Out of this profit must come the renewal or replacement of capital equipment from time to time.

Although, as we have said, a form of internal star system among animation artists operates in the United States, it does not reach the fantastic proportions familiar in the live-action studios for the stars and chief technicians. Directors and key animators seldom earn more in any country than the average salary for a live-action cameraman. Animation obviously works in a restricted market compared with that open to the live-action feature film, and the commercial values of animation are not yet high. It must also be remembered that the individual output of an animator can only be very small; even the most experienced and rapid worker can only produce the equivalent of some twenty to thirty feet of film a week. The average salary for an animator in the United States in 1975 was $400 per week; in Britain it was £70; and slightly more in Germany and France.

For longer or theatrical cartoons, the price averaged at £15 per foot in Britain and $150 in the United States; for the television commercial the equivalent price was £40 and $200. Very short commercials lasting from 7 to 20 seconds may be proportionately far higher in price if they include special sound tracks employing well-known personalities or vocal teams where agents demand large fees for a recording session.

Typical total cost in 1975 for television commercials with full-scale animation could be quoted as follows:

Duration	British Costs	U.S.A. Costs
20 second	£1,800	$10,000
30 second	£2,500	$15,000
60 second	£4,000	$24,000

A typical total cost in 1975 for a sponsored public relations film in Eastman Colour would have been £20 per foot in Britain and $120 in the United States.

In order to show how diverse the break-down of costs may prove to be for a short commercial film for television, we give here three different budgets in percentages, the first for a commercial where the animation carries the main emphasis, the second where the design is

258

the predominant feature and the animation less complex, and the third with minimum possible animation.

Finally, we include a further break-down of costs in percentages for a longer animated film in Eastman Colour, from one reel in length (ten minutes) or over, and with a total production time of not less than nine months.

PERCENTAGE COST BREAK-DOWN ON TELEVISION
ADVERTISING ANIMATED FILMS

	Complex Animation	Medium Animation	Slight Animation	Theatrical Film in Colour Complex Animation
	%	%	%	%
Direction	8	15	20	8
Labour	30	24	20	40
Sound	17	20	25	17
Materials and Processing	8	7	5	8
Overhead	27	24	20	27
Profit	10	10	10	—
	100%	100%	100%	100%

Profit is based on box office returns and cannot be budgeted

PART FOUR

OTHER FORMS OF ANIMATION

Apart from the recognized types of animation indicated here as fluid cell animation, the medium offers the artist an infinite variety of forms to challenge his
invention. As time goes on new techniques and branches of animation will be
opened up. Already there are many forms in actual practice, as shown here.

21

PUPPET AND OBJECT ANIMATION

THE puppet film, like the cartoon, is being extensively used to-day, very largely to meet the growing needs of the television commercial and of the theatre advertising film. This is especially true in the case of the animation of objects, such as advertisers' cartons, packs, cans and three-dimensional trade-marks and can even extend in certain circumstances to the animation of fluids and smoke. In this section we intend the generic term puppet film to include not only the animation of dolls but any solid objects. The principles involved in production remain the same.

The main development of the puppet-doll film has been in Czechoslovakia, Poland, Russia and Germany, all of those countries where there is a peasant tradition of craftsmanship in the carving and designing of puppets and dolls. As we have already established in the case of the drawn films from these countries, they are mainly interested in developing animation as a medium for subjects derived from folklore.

In the past puppets for films have been made mostly of wood on which both their features and their clothes are directly painted. For example, in the early puppet films of George Pal, the dolls sometimes had wooden heads and a certain proportion of accessories for their bodies made of cloth. This was also the case with Trnka's puppets. In Starevitch's films the figures were entirely clothed, and only the faces are seen to be of wood. Alexeieff and Pojar have taken to using plastics, among other contemporary materials.

Alexeieff and Ettien Raik have also specialized in object animation, which has given a new abstract quality to the medium.

The problem with all puppets is how to animate them as solid, three-dimensional objects by means of frame-by-frame photography. This is the inherent handicap of the puppet film in contrast to the free animation that is possible for the drawn figure. To animate the carved wooden face it was at one time considered necessary

263

to produce twenty-four models for each second of action, obviously a phenomenal task. The bodies could be made adjustable, using wire with rubber coating for the joints of the limbs, the position of which was fractionally changed for each frame of the shooting. Modifications of various sorts were introduced to lessen the labour of animating the face. Experiments were tried with faces made of flexible material, such as rubber, by Pal, Balein and Meyer. But even so, this yielded insufficient control over the face and the movable parts of the body in the complex process of frame-by-frame animation.

Modern animation methods for puppets involve the use of malleable plastics and even of magnetic control. Some of these methods have been developed as carefully guarded secrets. But none yet has achieved, or really can hope to achieve the complete freedom of the drawn film. The obligation of working in three dimensions instead of two is also onerous.

It is even more important than in the case of the cartoon to discover forms of puppetry that break free from any kind of naturalism, if only because a doll is so much more readily identifiable with a real human being or animal than is a drawing. But Alexeieff, for example, in such films as his Esso commercial and Ettien Raik in certain of his publicity films have been successful in getting away from realistic characters and action.

The most celebrated artist of the puppet film was the late Jiri Trnka, primarily a story-teller; his films were the patient reconstruction of legend through finely animated dolls whose appearance and movements are designed to reflect real life, and so inevitably must fall short of it. In the puppet film, as in all animation, there should never be any doubt that what is being achieved on the screen could only be achieved by this means. Better a live actor than a puppet emulating a live actor.

Trnka gave his views on the distinction of the puppet film from other forms of animation and from live-action fantasy.[1]

He had, he said, "an ambition to animate on the screen, where everything is possible, the three-dimensional figures of puppets, moving in contradistinction to the heroes of cartoons, not within their own plane but in space. From the beginning, I had my own conception of how puppets could be handled—each of them to have an individual but static facial expression, as compared with the puppets that by means of various technical devices, can change their mien in an attempt to achieve a more life-like aspect. In practice, of course, this has tended not to enhance the realism, but rather conduce to naturalism."

Later he added, "...in cartoons the different techniques of the many draughts-

[1] *In the Czech periodical,* Film, *Vol, VIII, No. 6.*

An early puppet film (Starevitch; France 1934).

THE PUPPET FILM

The New Gulliver (Ptushko; U.S.S.R. 1934).

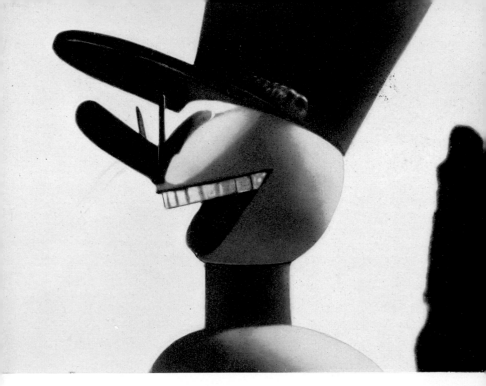

On Parade (George Pal; Holland).

The Story of the Bass-Cello, directed by Jiri Trnka (Copyright State Film; Czechoslovaki

Sfejbl on the Scent, directed by Jiri Trnka (Copyright State Film; Czechoslovakia).

The Song of the Prairie, directed by Jiri Trnka (Copyright State Film; Czechoslovakia).

Old Czech Legends, directed by Jiri Trnka (Copyright State Film; Czechoslovakia).

A Garland of Folk Songs, directed by Jiri Trnka (Copyright State Film; Czechoslovakia).

vention of Destruction, directed by Karel Zeman (Copyright State Film; Czechoslovakia).

Oni—The Demon (K. Kawamoto; Japan).

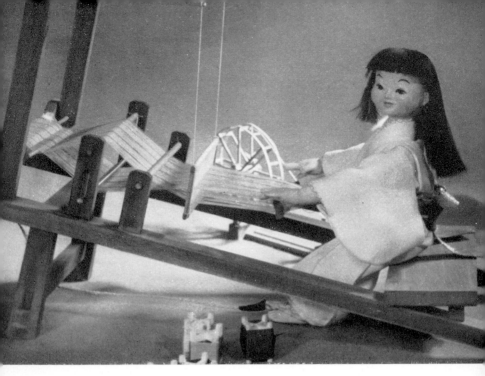

The Little Girl and the Naughty Fairy (Copyright Toho Film; Japan).

Figurehead (Copyright Halas & Batchelor; Great Britain).

Mr. Lookit (Copyright C.B.S. Lou Bunin; U.S.A.).

Little Frikk (Copyright Ivo Caprino; Norway).

Katarynka, directed by Wlodzimierz Haupe (Copyright Film Polski; Poland).

Jorinde and Joringel, directed by Himpel (Copyright Defa Studios; East Germany).

men participating in the actual piecing-together of the film obscure the character of the original drawing. Apart from this, the very nature of cartoon figures calls for continual motion; it is not possible to stop them, and neither is it possible to bring them into a state of contemplation. All this, of course, limits the creative possibilities of cartoons. After my experience with puppet films, I would definitely not like to return to cartoons, as I would feel considerably tied down in the originality of my designs.

"Puppet films stand on their own feet only when they are outside the scope of live-action films—when the stylization of the scenery, the artificially heroic look of the human actors, and the lyrical content of the theme might easily produce an effect both unconvincing and ludicrous or even painful."

Since the death of Trnka in 1969 his tradition of puppet animation continued practically without interruption in the studio named after him. His followers such as Bratislav Pojar and Václav Bedrich are maintaining the technical skills and tradition of puppetry, and in the meantime are able to express their own artistic individuality through their work.

22

THE PUPPET FILM: THE PRODUCTION PROCESS

THE preparation of a storyboard for a puppet film follows the same process as that for the drawn film, though allowances have to be made in plotting the action for the three-dimensional quality of the subject to be photographed. The puppet world is a solid one, with characters that move in space. However imaginative the settings and the characters, they have less freedom from the limitations of time and space than the wholly drawn creation which exists only as lines and paint on paper or celluloid. The action on the storyboard must therefore be timed rather differently for the less flexible medium of the puppet. The action must inevitably be slower, approximating to a more normal, more realistic conception of movement-in-time. Such considerations as the structure of model settings and their lighting plots will also be necessary at the storyboard stage.

Instead of the model-sheets that are required for the drawn character of cartoon, proportion sheets of even greater accuracy are needed for the individual puppets. These will become the blueprints to guide the craftsmen who make the advance models.

Like cartoon animation, the technique for stop-action puppet work must be worked out in terms of single motion-picture frames. This is in contrast to work involving mechanically propelled figures and objects, taken with a continuous-motion camera.

The basic requirements for stop action puppet animation is a studio of reasonable proportions to accommodate lighting equipment, scenic construction, camera tracks and dollies, together with a well-equipped workshop.

The camera should be equipped with a reliable trip gear having the smallest dimensions possible. This is to facilitate moving about in a confined space, such as through miniature doors or arches. The camera and trip gear are mounted on a slow-motion geared pan and tilt head absolutely free from shake in all directions, and this is mounted on a dolly running on a track.

274

The dolly and camera must run freely on the track, so that when tracking to or from an object the final picture on the screen will not appear to wobble or weave. A portable track will give the advantage that it can be used in different positions to get the right camera angle instead of moving the set.

One of the most important factors governing work with puppets is the size of the figures. If the studio is small and large sets are required, then the figures have to be made fairly small, otherwise there may be very little room left to accommodate the lighting equipment in addition to the sets and the camera. Also the puppets should not be too large for mechanical reasons.

If solid figures are being used and are intended to conform to either human or animal shapes, the basic parts of the puppet must be really solid. During animation the figure must retain its outward shape, and not be liable to compression or distortion in the course of manipulation. It is only too easy, for example, for clothing to become subject to uncontrolled movements. Every misplaced line is immediately obvious on the screen.

Next come the moving parts of the figure—such as the arms, neck, head and feet. It is unsatisfactory to joint the puppets like the human figure, for owing to the large number of times a joint has to be moved it becomes slack and this is fatal when it occurs in the middle of a scene. The joints or limbs when moved *must* remain in the exact position in which they have been placed for that frame during exposure. Often several parts of a figure are moving at the same time—as in walking—and the limbs must be capable of supporting their own weight.

The basic anatomical sections of the puppet are usually made of wood, and the limbs are best made of multistrand wire which must be soft and capable of being bent many times without fracturing. The head should be solid and so should the wig or the hair, since this lessens the tendency for unwanted movement when the figure is being handled. Support for the figure is best obtained by removable spikes or pegs. These are usually made of stout wire attached to the feet and made to fit into holes on the base of the floor of the set. Hands can be a problem, but to-day so many plastic materials lend themselves to animated hand construction. Hands should have a wire skeleton to help hold the position in which the fingers are placed.

A mobile puppet face can be achieved by using changeable masks which fit and register accurately to the basic head. The masks, of course, must be made in animated progression, that is phased from one expression to another.

Quality of surface finish on all miniature work should be of a high order, since the magnification employed is so great that the slightest blemish will be proportionately revealed.

The skills and techniques applied to puppet work are many. Among the most important is delicacy combined with firmness of touch.

Sets and décor, no matter how simple, must be made absolutely rigid so that when the objects or figures are animated the set will not shift from its original position. It should be strong enough to resist warping when under the heat of the lamps. Properties and miniature decoration should be of robust construction. Paper and other flimsy materials unless reinforced are unreliable; it is surprising how some materials twist and shrink under the dry heat of studio lights.

Lighting equipment can follow the usual motion picture studio practice—but on a smaller scale, unless large sets are to be lit. Small baby spot lights are very necessary as the small areas of the figures to be lit do not justify using normal spots. In any case the baby spot is more economical. A feature of model and puppet work is the lighting plot, and most of the principles here are the same as for live-action film-making.

As in cartoon animation, all camera and figure positions must be predetermined, but in the case of puppet work the camera has to pan and tilt as well as track. It is advisable to indicate for all pan and tilt movements a graduated scale or some form of division so that large or small increments of movement per frame can be calibrated and entered in the shooting script.

Track movements can be indicated for each shot by fixing temporary scales along the track with a suitable pointer on the dolly. Focus, too, needs a calibrated scale to be used in conjunction with the track scale. That is to say, if the camera has tracked to frame 50, the lens must be in a position to focus the object sharply at that frame. A frame counter on the camera is an essential piece of equipment and is the only indication of one's whereabouts in the shooting script.

All these positions can be predetermined in rehearsal. The movement of the figures on the set should match up with the camera movements, and the lighting must be pre-set to cover both these variables. The camera, when it is moved about, must not cast shadows over the set. Clumsy movement on the part of the operator can easily spoil a long and costly take.

Great care is necessary to avoid errors while shooting. In this work one can seldom get back in the middle of shooting to a definite position, as it is sometimes possible to do in drawn animation. An error usually means restarting the scene.

276

Much puppet animation is carried out visually, but many devices for checking the movements of the figures can be introduced, such as dividers, set-squares and improvised cardboard scales. The calculations during shooting are at times very complex, and great concentration is needed to avoid mistakes. If one imagines a scene involving a model set with as many as six puppets all in animation, with the camera tracking, panning and tilting for each frame exposed and, in addition, allowance being made for fades and dissolves, it is obvious that any distraction would prove disastrous to the final effect.

23

SILHOUETTE AND FLAT-FIGURE ANIMATION

THE silhouette film played a considerable part in the pioneer stages of animation. It had ancient lineage in the traditional shadow-theatres which became a minor art of some beauty.

In spite of the complex development of modern animation techniques, there are still a number of prominent film-makers producing silhouette films, such as the Ofuji Studio in Japan. Perhaps the most distinguished artist of all is Lotte Reiniger, who works now in Britain but is known all over the world for her silhouette films since she began her artistic career over thirty years ago in Germany. She made her first silhouette film in 1919, and completed a feature-length production in silhouette (*The Adventures of Prince Achmed*).

The Medium

There is a technical distinction to be made between silhouette and flat-figure animation. Both use jointed two-dimensional figures. The silhouette film uses these figures to cast shadows of varied definition by means of back lighting, whereas the flat-figure technique lights the figures from front and so permits them to be drawn and painted instead of remaining all-black silhouettes.

Both systems are economical as animation goes and allow for a considerable reduction in labour during the process of photography. The artist, too, is much nearer to the final film, which he can directly control himself with the help of very few assistants. Yet, compared with normal animation, the degree of expression possible through these two intermediate forms is strictly limited. The virtue of the figures is their flatness; they conjure no illusion of solidity or moulding. Their movements are restricted to one flat plane; they cannot give any illusion of movement in three-dimensional space.

Whereas the silhouette film creates a world of shadow-fantasy which can achieve great formal beauty, the world of flat-figure ani-

278

mation is one closer to puppetry. The jointing of the figures is usually an obvious factor in their movements and has to be exploited for its own sake since it cannot be avoided. Often the simple movement in the single two-dimensional plane becomes too obvious. The silhouette film, however, can suggest a certain degree of depth with the use of less defined grey or shadowy backgrounds.

But these very limitations may spur the ingenuity of the artists. In Japan the silhouette film stands out in front of all the forms of animation so far developed, possibly because normal Japanese animation technique is imitative of the West and not indigenous. In the silhouette film, however, Japanese animators have linked the new art with their old inheritance, and developed a national tradition.

Silhouette and flat-figure films, with their economical processes of production, are especially well adapted to the needs of the commercial short for television. In fact, in the briefest kinds of commercial, these bold and simple animation techniques can quite well prove to be more effective than more complex forms of animation.

Generally speaking, there is scope now for the fuller development of these intermediate forms of animation with all their attractive possibilities. Normal animation has gone in for complexity to meet the needs of the theatres; now that the simpler, more graphic forms are needed to make quick points on the small television screen, the initiative has to some extent been thrown back into the hands of artists whose talents have been most happily developed in these specialized branches of animation.

The Production Process

Lotte Reiniger and her husband Carl Koch are the best-known artists working in this special branch of animation. They have produced both silhouette and coloured flat-figure films of great artistic distinction for a variety of purposes, including theatrical entertainment, inserts in such films as G. W. Pabst's *Don Quixote* and Renoir's *La Marseillaise*, propaganda trailers (for example, for the General Post Office in Britain), children's entertainment on television and television commercials. We are grateful to them for giving us the following detailed description of their production procedure:

1. Once we have chosen our subject, which is frequently derived from some well-known opera or ballet, Lotte Reiniger starts drawing our first sketches. We explore imaginary scenes or situations conjured up by the general atmosphere of the characters and setting, as well as, of course, the music. These

279

drawings are key moments from any part of what we shall eventually develop into our story—groupings, backgrounds, characters in various postures, comic situations, figure shapes, anything that excites us initially.

2. Parallel with making these sketches, we begin discussing how we shall contract the original score down to the ten or fifteen minutes that we need for our film. We select those phases of the music that suit best the story treatment we are devising and contain the airs likely to be most familiar to our audience.

3. Next, with the music in mind, we prepare a written script of our story, which is largely of our own invention—a kind of "variation on the theme" of the full-length original.

4. After the script comes the preparation of the storyboard sketches, derived, of course, from our first scrap-book of initial sketches.

5. In collaboration with our director of music, who is responsible for arranging the contracted score, we record the music track for the film. The musical arrangement is normally scored for a very small orchestra, with the instruments chosen to suit the mood of the film as we have conceived it. The music must interact with our story and our characters.

6. Next we analyse every bar of the music track on a music chart, showing the exact length of the track in terms of bars of music and frames of animation. This chart acts as our guide to the detailed movement of the figures, since each beat of music is now measured for us in the chart in terms of the given number of frames required on the picture track.

7. All this time we are also getting our principal characters ready. They emerge gradually from a multiplicity of sketches. As soon as we feel they are ready for experiment we draw them on thin card, and cut them out and joint them. What we are looking for now is movements of face and body which begin to take on an inner life of their own that appeals to us. They must have postures and movements which reveal at once the distinctive, dramatic characterization that belongs naturally to this particular kind of flat, mobile figure. Our particular style of figure design is asserting itself, emphasizing flatness with a stylization very like that of the ancient Egyptian figures, their faces seen always in profile (in the case of our principal characters), but with their bodies turned frontwards.

8. The proportions of each character are determined at the sketching and storyboard stages, though naturally we need to have each individual character designed and cut-out in many different sizes and versions according to the nature of the shots—long shot, medium shot or close-up—and the expressions required in each scene. The basic sizes are, roughly speaking, five in number, varying from about 24 inches to as little as one inch. We also need segments of the figures for certain close-ups, for example a head or a hand, all elaborately jointed for detailed movement. The figures, cut out from thin card, are dressed by means of various kinds of paper—translucent, filigree or opaque—and by other thin materials.

In addition to size, we have to allow for the different kinds of posture that our figures must assume in individual scenes—sitting, running, and so on. For each standard size of figure it is usually necessary to make a large range of different hands, feet and faces (with movable eyes and mouths). If the film is in flat-figure animation (as distinct from silhouette), then the outlines and colours on the figures themselves become an added factor in their design. But the actual method of making the figures mobile through jointing remains, of course, the same for both the silhouette and flat-figure animation.

The kind of life we are trying to achieve through these figures is, of course, an artificial one of its own; we are creating a special sort of world of character

280

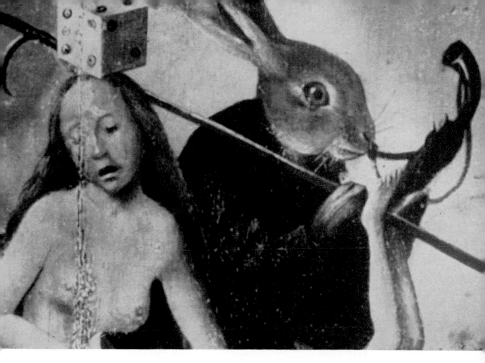

Il Paradiso Perduto (Luciano Emmer; Italy).

FILMS OF STILL PAINTINGS AND DRAWINGS

Painter and Poet series (Halas & Batchelor; Great Britain).

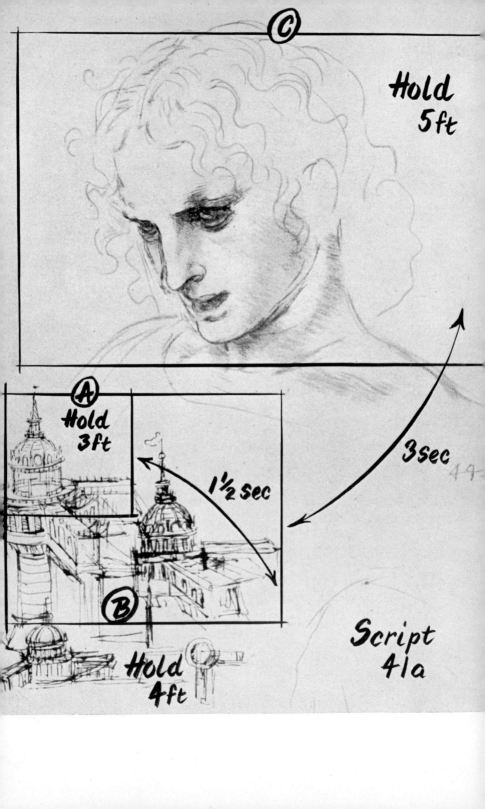

Ⓒ

Hold
5ft

3 sec

1½ sec

Ⓐ
Hold
3 ft

Ⓑ
Hold
4ft

Script
41a

Hook the Hawk (Copyright C.B.S. Hazard Durfee and Ab. Liss; U.S.A.).

pposite: *Drawings of Leonardo da Vinci* (Basil Wright and Adrian de Potier; Great Britain).

A Short Vision (Copyright Joan and Peter Foldes; Great Britain).

A Short Vision, original sketch by Peter Foldes with poem.

A Short Vision (Copyright Joan and Peter Foldes; Great Britain).

A sequence of action sketches by Lotte Reiniger for one of her early silhouette films made in Germany, *The Magic Flute*. The frame-by-frame movements of the puppets are graded in the sketches.

and setting and action. Our figures move within their own simplified limits, freed from the restrictions of actuality. They are the timeless creatures of fantasy with their own laws of movement and action—their own style or stylization, in fact.

9. Parallel with this work of designing and cutting out the figures comes the design of the sets. Like the performing figures these, too, are cut-outs. We use no painted backgrounds on sheets of paper as in normal animation. The sets are cut out in sections, and the figures can move in and out of these sections with the controlled timing necessary for the action. Some of our settings are made of translucent materials (in particular, coloured gelatines) which lie on top of each other and give various coloured densities of light.

The lighting of silhouette films comes exclusively from beneath the table on which the sets or figures are manipulated beneath the camera; the silhouette film registers its pictures in terms of various shades from black to white.

The lighting of the coloured cut-out films comes both from behind and in front; the rear lighting gives a high degree of luminosity to the transparent or translucent elements in our settings (such as skies and clouds) and the frontal lighting accentuates the colour design of the characters and of the opaque elements in the sets. Also light from this double, and opposite, source eliminates any small unwanted shadows cast by the characters. The sense of distance, too, in this essentially flat world can be suggested in many ways through both the design and the make-up of the sets—including slight spacing of the various layers. For example, a moving sea can be suggested with a multiplicity of variable shadows if light sources placed at different angles behind a gelatine sheet are interrupted by a system of spirals made of either translucent or opaque materials. The different spirals are then turned individually with a

285

timing which differs according to the impression of receding distance that we want to create.

10. The shooting stage is first reached when all the preparations are complete for photographing whatever sequence in the film we happen to have chosen with which to initiate ourselves into the subject. We like to ease our way into a film in this manner, chosing the particular sequence which we think will act as the best guide to our work on the rest of the film. It becomes a kind of test sequence.

For silhouette or flat figure animation there are the following main layers of material between the camera and the light source beneath the table:

(i) a clear plate of crystal glass which acts as the translucent surface on which the work is manipulated;

(ii) the transparent coloured backgrounds (such as sky, clouds, waves, and certain elements of landscape);

(iii) a sheet of translucent, non-slip plastic;

(iv) the non-transparent elements in the settings (houses, walls, furniture, etc.);

(v) the figures themselves which are always in the forefront when they have to move.

This is the basic lay-out, but there are certain additional effects which may be required and are installed between the crystal glass plate and the light source—such as mobile waves, mists, clouds, shadows and certain kinds of supernatural effects. Other forms of effect can be obtained in a different way, by means of mounted objects placed between the set-up and the camera—rain or fore-ground mist, for example, or supernatural forms.

We complete our shooting frame by frame, recording each exposure in a shooting book. The action is controlled by means of the original music chart, which acts as a guide to each frame-by-frame phase of the movements. We are thinking in terms of so many frames to each beat of music, and we adjust the limbs and the expressions of our characters in such a way that they respond to the music as subtly as we can make them.

This for us is the crucial part of the work in our medium, at once the root and the climax of its artistry. It is so because we have to be able to sense intuitively how we may create a living action in terms of our particular characters in the time dictated to us by the needs of the music. We rehearse the movements in sketch form as well as by manipulating the figures themselves. But the final result depends on our intuitive understanding of what our flat, jointed cut-out characters can perform most expressively. That for us is our art.

24

THE ANIMATION OF STILL PICTURES

THE nature of film is action developed in time. Even the photography of completely still pictures can be given a certain rhythm by the calculated timing of their successive appearance on the screen. If the pictures are also chosen to sustain a certain dramatic development of subject, then the barest form of animation is achieved. To this is added the movement of the picture in front of the camera, or the camera in front of the picture, and the dynamic possibilities of editing.

What has been said applies alike to the filming of well-known paintings and the presentation of drawings created specially for this kind of production. Examples are the film "treatment" given by Luciano Emmer and Enrico Gras to the paintings of Bosch and Giotto, and by John Halas in the film *John Gilpin* made from the series of drawings done by Ronald Searle for the camera.

This kind of work can only be done successfully if a very careful plan is made of the various elements in the pictures which must be brought together in the successive phases of the film. It is essential that the pictures themselves should contain absorbing pictorial interest, so that every static shot should have a visual quality and vitality that compensates the audience for the lack of motion. By vitality we do not necessarily mean the suggestion of violent action, such as some of the close-ups of elements in Bosch's work obviously have when they are suddenly displayed with all the giant magnification of the cinema screen; the vitality may be implicit in the composition of the painting, striking because of its formal beauty, which was the case with Giotto's compositions as they were seen in Emmer's film *The Drama of the Son of Man*. Both Giotto's frescoes with their formal stillness and Searle's very active drawings for *John Gilpin* had a story to tell as picture followed picture in a chain that progressed forward with the narrative.

The sound track has a particularly important function in these films which animate still pictures. It must bring a dynamic forward-moving quality through the use of music and narration.[1] It must link closely to the camera presentation and editing. Camera-movement, editing and sound can between them superimpose a rhythm on the pictures. An example of this is Emmer's film of Goya's pictures with music played by Segovia. This dynamic treatment was used by Paul Haessaerts in his film *Rubens*, though here an effect representing flashes of lightning superimposed on Ruben's painting of the Crucifixion was surely illegitimate in this kind of film-making.

The convention demands, in our view, no form of tampering with the pictures, which should never in themselves seem to become animated, even if only by using tricks of artificial lighting. On the contrary, the photography should be made to serve the textures, the tones, the brushwork of the great artists—to bring the qualities of their painting close to the eye of the audience and to underline these qualities through the suggestive power of music, as was done in a recent series of Italian films on certain painters of the Renaissance. In addition, the particular art of the film, which all the time reinforces the fuller view of a picture with some telling close-shot of a detail, can analyse the dramatic content of a painting and emphasize its drama through the dynamic continuity of editing.

Film-makers who present the work of great artists through the medium of the cinema must approach the task with a special sensitivity. It is only too easy to become carried away by the application of motion picture technique to the presentation of still pictures. Technique must be used, but it must be used sparingly and with restraint. For the dynamic quality of the film can quickly overweigh or push aside the textures of painting. Unique qualities of appreciation are needed in the film-maker to achieve the right balance between his medium and that of the artist. If he is a painter himself, like Peter Foldes, he may well bring a special understanding to the task of filming still paintings.

These films are not, of course, specifically the animator's province —they have been made alike by film-makers normally concerned with live-action photography, by specialists in art, as well as by animators. Their technique, however, is in one sense a branch of animation, because the technique of the film is applied to the presentation of graphic material. The whole relation of painting to film-making is a comparatively new study, and links directly with the "live" presentation of the art of painting, a field that has caught

[1] *See the analysis of the music composed by Roman Vlad for "Paradiso Perduto" in* The Technique of Film Music, *p. 162.*

the imagination, among others, of Picasso, who developed the experiment of painting-in-time in the film *Le Mystère Picasso*, which he made with H. G. Clouzot. In some sequences of *Le Mystère Picasso* paintings were created in their natural time on a translucent screen without the hand of the painter being visible; in other sequences pictures taking a longer time to evolve were shown in quick-time evolution of two or three minutes' duration.

Television, which constantly demands large quantities of film material, is making use of the capability of the mobile camera. Many programmes specially designed for children's entertainment are produced by means of this technique. A series of illustrations, approximately 100 to 120 in number, are used in this form, with the camera providing sufficient movement over the pictures to maintain a limited interest. The voice of a narrator telling the story contributes further to the interest of this form.

25

THE WORK OF NORMAN McLAREN

THE technique of Norman McLaren's films has been the subject of many articles.[1] He has been fortunate in finding sponsorship more or less continuously during the past twenty years for the research and experimental work which is the basis of his achievement. His chief sponsor has been the National Film Board of Canada, for which he has worked since 1941.

McLaren is a highly individual artist and regards himself as a research worker in film techniques. When asked by us what decided the subjects for his films, he said that they came about in various ways.

Some suggest themselves purely as the result of certain technical investigations McLaren has been carrying out—for example, *Dots* and *Loops*, his wholly abstract films made without a camera and with hand-drawn synthetic sound.

Subjects for other films have formed in his mind as the result of a particular kind of music with which he wanted to associate his work —for example, *Begone Dull Care*, another cameraless abstract film made for the most part as a continuously flowing, hand-coloured image on the celluloid strip without frame divisions and cued to the vigour and bounce of music played by Oscar Peterson's jazz trio.

Again, Canadian folk-songs have led to specific film treatments— *C'est l'Aviron*, for example, experimented with conventional animation but introduced a "zoom" technique which allowed drawing after drawing to overlap in a continuous series flowing towards the camera as the boat rocked forward through space.

Other subjects have resulted from propaganda directives—such as *Hen Hop*, which was a cameraless animation publicizing War Savings with a country-dance accompaniment.

---

[1] *The most comprehensive is probably "Norman McLaren; his career and techniques"*, *by William E. Jordan in the* Hollywood Quarterly of Film, Radio and Television, *Vol. VII, 1953, No. 1.*

More recently McLaren has made *Neighbours*; this technique of experimenting in the animation of the movements of live actors (called sometimes "pixilation") accompanied by synthetic music and sound effects, linked after a while in McLaren's mind with a subject he had for some time wanted to develop in a film. But it was the technical experiment that precipitated the subject, rather than the subject the technique.

On being asked what decided the part to be played by the sound track, and what relationship the track bore to the visuals, McLaren claimed that for him the sound was normally the starting point for the visuals. This was true of films such as *Begone Dull Care*, *Fiddle-de-dee* and *Blinkety-Blank* and *Le Merle* as well as the films which have folk music or songs as their basis. On the other hand, *A Phantasy*, *Chairy Tale* and *Neighbours* had their sound track added after the visuals were made, though *Neighbours* was shot in metrically even lengths with a future music score in mind. As a matter of principle, McLaren never introduces words (apart from films derived from folk songs) into his sound tracks; for one reason, it would restrict the distribution of his films which he wants to appeal equally all over the world. His research is always directed towards the entirely wordless film, the film that springs from pantomime and dance. The abstract film, he claims, may appear abstract in form, but the fact that it moves puts a wealth of human implication (of suggestion, as it were, "on the side") into the mobile shapes.

A very close mechanical relation is worked out between track and image, whichever comes first. McLaren is, however, against using mere parallelism of sound and image. He prefers each to work together along different lines, making a distinct contribution to the final effect. Music can often state a point which it may be difficult to establish through a picture alone, and vice versa.

When asked if there were any implications or principles behind his use of colour, McLaren claimed that for most of his films movement, not colour, was the prime factor. Many of his colour films were originally worked out in black-and-white, including *Dots*, *Loops*, *Hen Hop*, *Hoppity-Pop*, and the stereoscopic film *Now is the Time*. Colour was then introduced at a later stage to heighten the emotional effect. Colour plays an integral part in certain other films. *Le Poulette Grise* showed through a series of dissolves the building up of a pastel drawing. It was intended to put the emphasis on the growth of a picture, its evolution through the artist's hand and eye, rather than on the finished work. In *Around is Around* the basic colour was changed for each sequence phase in the moving pattern,

291

and in *Begone Dull Care* colour was used both to paragraph the general movement of the film and to reflect the mood of certain movements in the musical phrasing.

The Production Process of Norman McLaren's Films

WE are grateful to Norman McLaren and the National Film Board of Canada for contributing the following account of the way in which films using the linear technique are made:

McLaren dispenses with the use of a camera completely, by drawing and painting directly on to standard 35 mm. motion picture film.

To make a five-minute cartoon, he takes a roll of clear, transparent celluloid, about 500 feet long and 1¼ inches wide, on which he draws a succession of miniature pictures, each ¾ inch high by ⅝ inch wide. Each picture differs slightly from the one previous and there are over 7,000 of them for a five-minute work.

In other words, the clear celluloid, is, as it were, his virgin canvas, on which he draws and paints, with little more mechanical aid than the average painter. The media he uses are inks and colour dyes, which are applied by various types of pens, ranging from the finest croquille, through ordinary writing nibs, to large speedballs. On occasions, brush work is used, but only for special effects such as fluctuating textures, because the texture and density of images, when applied by brush, are not sufficiently constant from picture to picture.

The animated drawing is done entirely by the one artist, and in almost every respect it is the only precise equivalent, in filmic terms, of the painter and his canvas, more especially the miniaturist painter. Because of this fact, there are two essential differences that distinguish McLaren's work from most other cartoon animation and although they are differences in method of production, they have a very direct bearing on the artistic quality of the work.

First, as has been pointed out, the drawing from start to finish is the work of one person. This is totally unlike regular cartoon procedure, where the drawing is done by a hierarchy of artists on a conveyor-belt principle, which makes for a standardized style of drawing and painting devoid of personal quality and treatment. This is particularly noticeable, after seeing McLaren's work, which has a purely personal style of penmanship and drawing as distinct from the impersonal commercial slickness of a Disney.

Second, the animation is built up, frame by frame, in natural chronological succession, unlike the normal commercial procedure in which widely separated key points in the action are drawn in by one set of artists subsequently filling in points in the action between these key drawings. Then "in-betweeners" do the remaining intermediate drawings. This means that all movement has to be very carefully conceived and plotted out *before* actually being drawn.

McLaren's technique, on the other hand, permits of the creation of final, detailed action, in natural sequence at the moment of its drawing; and this provides an opportunity for *improvisation* of movement, quite unobtainable when animators, break-downers and in-betweeners come in between the original conception and the finished product.

This is, of course, unlike the usual method of cartoon animation where each drawing is done on a scale about 11 inches by 14 inches and then photographed in succession on to motion picture film.

McLaren has taken full advantage of the chance to improvise movement. His films are full of a spontaneity not seen in most other cartoons, except perhaps those of Len Lyre, who to our knowledge is the only other artist who has dispensed with a camera and resorted to direct drawings on the film.

Brahms' Hungarian Dance (Copyright Oscar Fischinger; Germany).

SPECIALIZED FORMS OF ANIMATION

Tusalava (Len Lye; Great Britain).

Prince Achmed (Copyright Lotte Reiniger; Germany).

Juno (Copyright Lotte Reiniger; Great Britain).

L'Idée (Copyright Berthold Bartosch; France).

Night on a Bare Mountain (Copyright Alex Alexeieff and Claire Parker; France).

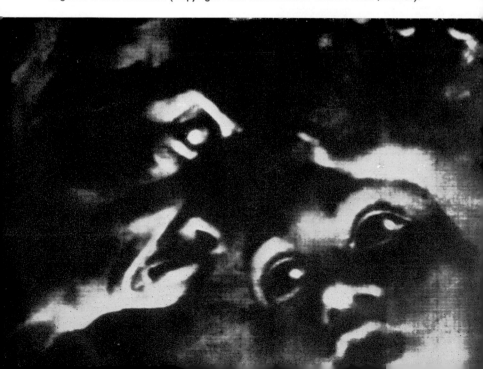

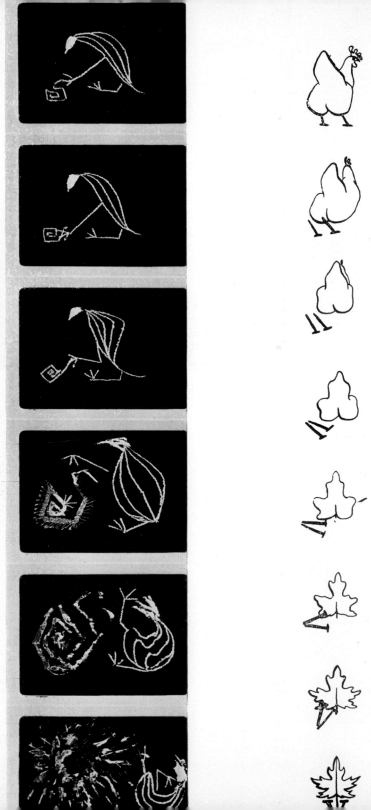

La Sève de la Terre (A. Alexeieff; France).

Opposite: *Blinkety-Blank* (Copyright National Film Board of Canada).

The Bathrcom (Kuri Jikken Manga Kobo; Japan).

Magic Canvas (Copyright Halas & Batchelor; Great Britain).

Ars Gratia Artis (Dušan Vukotic. Copyright Zagreb Film; Yugoslavia).

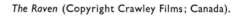

Theatre de Monsieur et Madame Kabal (Walerian Borowczyk; France).

The Raven (Copyright Crawley Films; Canada).

The Birth of Destruction (Copyright State Film; Czechoslovakia).

nspiration (Copyright State Film; Czechoslovakia).

To achieve this direct contact with his medium, McLaren has had to sacrifice many elements that are normally thought to be an essential part of movie cartoons.

Complex scenes with many characters and much detail obviously cannot be drawn on a minute area ¾ inch by ⅝ inch. Animated characters have, therefore, to be pared down to their utmost visual simplicity, and expressed in purely linear and calligraphic terms. Characters like the dollars in *Dollar Dance* or the little man in *Victory Trailer* are not given "character" by being endowed with a human face, eyes, mouth, arms, a costume, etc. Each remains its simple geometric form; its "character" is put across *entirely* by its movement.

The reliance on pure movement is one of the most noticeable characteristics of McLaren's films.

There are other characteristics, however, which should be mentioned as they seldom, if ever, appear in the regular run of cartoons to-day. They represent an out-and-out return to the methods of the primitives with their non-naturalistic approach.

One of these characteristics is the absence of anything corresponding to editing by "shots", i.e. cutting or fading from one scene to another. A typical McLaren film consists of one long shot from beginning to end. The action is carried by a continuous and steadily changing point of interest within the frame.

A change of scene is generally effected by another noticeable characteristic of his style—metamorphosis. Metamorphosis is the changing of one form into another.

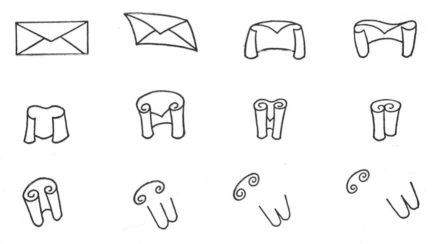

Metamorphosing imagery in animation is nothing new. One of the very first cartoons, *Drame Chez les Fantoches* (1907), made a brilliant and very natural use of it. Its linear images disintegrated and reformed at will, to meet the needs of the story.

Unfortunately, this approach to imagery was never followed up by the early cartoon makers, who were already tending towards naturalism. Consequently, a whole field of animated imagery lay unexplored, until quite recently when McLaren approached the subject with a new production technique and a new creative attitude.

Metamorphosis is used in many ways: sometimes as a quick transition from one object to another of quite dissimilar visual or mental association. This would normally replace a cut or dissolve. A good example of this is the "bread-bicycle-hat-beef" sequence in *Dollar Dance*.

Another use of metamorphosis is the development of a sequence through purely visual association of shapes.

At other times, metamorphosis is used in a surrealist way, a stream of mental associations closely akin to a dream-like flow of subconscious thoughts.

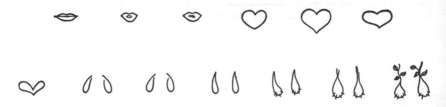

Another of McLaren's characteristic uses of metamorphosis is the sudden break-down of the contour of a three-dimensional object into its two-dimensional, linear components, and vice versa. This is a mobile and filmic equivalent of what the abstract painter does to natural forms on his canvas; in McLaren's films it causes a dislocation of the literary meaning of a sequence, and its use is consequently restricted to passages of pure dance, where the development of the mobile symbolism is temporarily arrested.

The following outline shows the technical process through which McLaren's hand-drawn films pass:

1. Music recorded first.

2. Music track run on a movieola and each note, phrase and sentence marked with grease pencil.

3. Track put on a frame counter and the notes measured cumulatively from zero at start.

4. Measurements are put against the notes on a dope sheet, which is usually a simplified musical score, and by substraction the length of each note in terms of frames is written in.

5. The grease pencilled sound track is run through a two-way winder, along with a roll of clear machine leader, called a dummy. The notes are copied and identified with indian ink on the dummy.

6. The final drawing is done with the aid of an apparatus whose purpose is to hold the film in place, move it on from frame to frame and provide a means of registration from frame to frame. It is actually an adapted camera gate with

302

claw mechanism and optical system that reflects the image of the frame just drawn on to the frame about to be drawn.

7. The dummy is threaded through this apparatus. On top of it and riding along with it is threaded another track of clear machine leader for doing the final drawing on. With a bottle of ink, pen and dope sheet at hand drawing can begin.

8. All drawing is done in natural sequence, starting at the first frame of the film and working straight through to the last.

9. When finished, the drawn track goes into the lab. for a couple of prints; one for a checking print to synchronize up with the sound track, the other for a master for release printing.

10. If colour release is desired, various kinds of dupes are made from this master and assembled in parallel to act as the separation negatives for the particular colour process used.

26

SPECIALIZED FORMS OF ANIMATION

Alexander Alexeieff and Claire Parker have for the past thirty years been pioneers in the development of specialized forms of animation using three dimensional objects. They have provided us with the following descriptions of their three main processes.

Pin Screen Animation (from 1931)

The apparatus consists of a white plate, 125 × 100 × 2.5 centimetres, perforated at right angles to its surfaces with one million holes, 0.5 mm. in diameter, in which slide as many steel rods, 0.45 mm. in diameter, 3 cms. long, and pointed at one end. The plate is held upright in a frame allowing access to both the front and the rear surfaces. The rods, longer than the thickness of the plate they transpierce, protrude beyond one or the other of its surfaces. Their points are all turned towards the camera, which faces the front surface. When all the rods are pushed to their extreme forward position, (i.e. flush with the rear surface) the front surface, bristling with the mass of protruding points, appears black, if lighted obliquely. (This black tone results from the overlapping multitude of fine black shadows cast by the rods which prevent the light from reaching the white surface.) When, on the contrary, the rods are flush with the front surface, there are no shadows and it appears white. By pushing the rods to positions between these two extremes, all the grey tones are obtainable.

The face of the screen is modelled with small rollers into the whites, greys, and blacks of the picture which constitutes the first phase. When this phase has been recorded by the camera, the picture is remodelled for the following phase, recorded on the next frame, and so on.

The pin screen is designed for black-and-white films. It corresponds to the most refined engraving techniques and is thus especially suited to lyric works. Easy as charcoal or pastel, it is more precise in tone values and ideally clean. It gives the artist complete autonomy over his work. Its texture is analogous to that of the half-tone print and permits shading, which is impracticable in the animated cartoon technique.

Three-Dimensional Animation

The objects to be animated are *motionless during the exposure* of each frame. After the first phase has been recorded on the first frame of the film, the aspect of the objects is modified by the animation team while the shutter is closed. This second aspect (or phase) is then recorded on the second frame, and so on.

304

The frame-by-frame changes in the aspect of the objects can be made in the following ways:

(1) Modification of lighting and exposure.
(2) Shifting the position of the camera or the objects.
(3) Movement of articulated objects.
(4) Substitution of objects. (This last is the most difficult, the costliest, and the most versatile of the four.)

In every case, strict rigidity of the objects during exposure and high precision of their movements is indispensable. The articulations of objects and machinery should have no recoil. We use micrometric controls. Our wire suspensions are extremely taut and attached to a control key with dialled levers for each dimension. The phases of movement are calculated and numbered in advance on a "score", test negatives made and screened for rhythm control, and, if necessary, the "score" modified before the final shooting, which takes much less time than its preparation.

This process requires a team of from three to seven persons. It is costlier than the animated cartoon. It can be used for black-and-white or colour animation.

It excels in advertising films because of the emotional or lyrical effects it can produce. It outclasses the animated cartoon in the movements specific to the cinema: zooms, the rotation of real volumes in space, and lighting effects. However, it lends itself less readily than the animated cartoon to rational explanations and literary or comic ideas.

Totalized Animation (from 1951)

The objects to be animated are *in motion during the exposure* of each frame. We call these objects "generators". The light rays emanating from a generator while in movement trace the path of this movement on the motionless film frame in the camera. We call this tracing an "illusory solid".

The generators are moved by compound pendulums. The parameters of the pendulums and of the camera shutter are controlled by an electric timing system. The launching points of the pendulums are set by machinery which is withdrawn from sight during exposure.

When the parameters and the launching points are unchanged during a sequence of frames, the path of the generator is identical on each frame, and the sequence is seen as a "still" of the illusory solid. To animate the illusory solid, we change the parameters of the timing system, the positions of the launching points, and the shape of the generator between exposures. The sequence which results is then either a metamorphosis or a movement. An exposure can vary from a few seconds to a minute or more. If the exposures are made through a stroboscope, the sequence shows a multitude of generators moving in space.

This process is economical in man-power—a team of three is sufficient—but requires costly precision machinery. It can be used for black and white or colour, and is suited to the animation of forms similar to shells, flowers, rings (smoke), waves, fireworks, and abstract forms. These illusory solids have an aesthetic quality based upon the laws governing vibrations, and are thus highly novel illustrations of the correspondence between the plastic arts and instrumental music. Totalized animation may be considered as a step toward a valid cybernetic solution of the animation problem.

27

ANIMATION FOR THE WIDE
AND MULTI-SCREENS

WITH the change in the shape and impact of cinema screens, the animator must be prepared to adapt his technique and his artistry to new forms of motion picture. The old cartoon technique with its various simplifications no longer operates for very large screens.

In Cinemascope the animator needs obviously to change his field-sizes, but not his production process, since the camera itself, with its special anamorphic lens, completes the work by the same means as a camera with a normal lens. Most wide screen work is carried out on 70 mm. size today combining the previous system of using 3 × 35 mm. film. This naturally makes the system easier to operate for both the cameraman and the projectionist since only one camera and one projectionist are involved. However, the animator must by now be aware that the larger the screen becomes in relation to the field of vision of each member of the audience, the greater the wealth of detail and complexity of perspective that must be incorporated with the design.

The following account was written for the British Film Academy Journal by one of the authors, John Halas, shortly after the completion in 1954 of the first experimental animation in this system undertaken by himself and Joy Batchelor for Louis de Rochemont's production *Cinerama Holiday:*

Cinerama makes use of a deeply curved screen with an aspect ratio of approximately 1: 2.85. The composite picture produced by three combined 35 mm. picture-tracks projected simultaneously side by side constructs the greater part of a complete half-cylinder 146 degrees wide and 55 degrees high; a pair of human eyes covers together about 180 degrees by 90 degrees. The frame on each of the individual picture-tracks is one-and-a-half times the standard height. A fourth 35 mm. film-strip carries seven separate magnetic sound-tracks, side by side. These are fed to seven speakers—five located behind the screen and two placed one on each side of the audience, so that the sound can be made to travel round the theatre. The problem of matching along the two joining edges of the three separate sections of the picture is met by using "gigolos", tiny steel combs, whose saw-toothed prongs move rapidly in the projector at the edges of the picture-tracks, "fuzzing" the joins slightly where they overlap.

306

From the point of view of the animator, a new camera craftsmanship had to be developed. And, beyond the technical problems themselves, the physical powers and physical limitations of a new medium in motion pictures had to be discovered.

We constructed a miniature Cinerama screen in our London studio and started experiments with new plastic materials. My object was to achieve depth with the aid of light and create designs in this form. Covering the huge 51 foot Cinerama screen with drawings and animation alone would have taken us longer than the time we were allowed. The idea of drawing and painting with light had been tried out by my colleague Allan Crick in our film *Figurehead*. This was a technique based on the use of transparent celluloids, polaroid screens, and filters. By the adjustment of polaroid filters the colours of transparent celluloids could be automatically changed. These light effects suited the subject well; it was a fantasy about Neptune's daughter who falls in love with a handsome but unresponsive wooden figurehead and takes him down with her to the sea bed.

We convinced de Rochemont that this technique would be a good one to develop further for the inserts in *Cinerama Holiday*. Our aim was to create a series of artists' impressions of the people and places shown in the Cinerama film, all executed in the style of a mural but lit like a stained-glass window. First, we set up a sheet of transparent curved plastic about six feet wide and four feet high, framed in wood. In front of this plastic sheet the Cinerama camera was to be stationed; to the rear of the plastic sheet and on a level with its upper edge were extended wooden slats supporting tight wires on which could be clamped our coloured plastic cut-outs in any position we wanted. Cloud effects were achieved on a second panel placed behind the main panel; on this scouring powder was applied and rubbed clear when the appearance of cloud was needed.

The photography was carried out with the normal Cinerama live-action camera, but with a reduced exposure to ensure the faithful reproduction of colour values.

In the course of composing pictures for Cinerama, certain rules and limitations became apparent, depending on whether one is dealing in terms of normal live-action shooting or transparent paintings. As far as the range of vision is concerned, the Cinerama camera lenses are the nearest approximation to the human eye that exists in motion pictures. If the position of the lenses is correct, the audience should automatically feel themselves to be in the picture, but if the camera is not used expertly the shots easily become unreal, and therefore unconvincing. As a result, certain essential rules of shooting were formulated— some based purely on optical necessities and others to allow for the overlap of the match lines between the three separate pictures. Suddenly to move the horizon up and down in normal shots, or to place the horizon too high or too low in the shots, or to move vertical objects across the screen with a speed greater than the eyes can comfortably follow, were equally undesirable.

Shots with too light a colour tended to show up the match lines between what we call the A, B and C sections of the picture, and so light colours had to be avoided. Too many horizontal shapes are just as dangerous and so had to be broken up. However, such practical limitations as these could be turned into aesthetic advantages, as happens in other artistic media. Other essential rules were formed, as a result of our experience: for example, the need to keep the camera on the move both in and out (but preferably in) became a regular rule.

The famous Roller Coaster sequence in *This is Cinerama* or the bob sledge and the roundabout section in the New Hampshire State Fair sequence in *Cinerama Holiday* were based on this concept. The framing of the picture with large foreground objects proved a great help in emphasizing distance. It is a characteristic of the medium to make objects look larger than they really are,

307

and to provide an accentuated perspective in exteriors. The half-cylindrical curved screen naturally draws the eye inwards. This factor is one of the main assets of Cinerama.

The exploitation of a wide curved screen of such dimensions with such cameras for actuality subjects is natural, but with drawings and paintings these effects had to be recreated by human hands. It was necessary to compose 16 separate painted scene-shots, and we learned to adjust our technique of design to the huge, concave, cylindrical screen. We had, in fact, to create distortions in the design to exploit to the full the immense advantages to the artist of having such a screen at his disposal.

Magic Lantern, which was first demonstrated in Prague, and later *Living Screen,* which was shown first in Brighton, England, and in New York had also an historic place in the development of animated film. Animation and normal live action film had each in turn to match meticulously a living subject performing on the stage. This close relationship entailed a total departure from fixed projection, since the projection source sometimes had to be placed at the side or back of the theatre to match the action. Timing between the live actors' appearances and the film had to be precise to the extent of 1/12th of a second or the equivalent of two film frames, otherwise both the motion and the sound would appear to be out of sync. Such accuracy was natural for a computerised time device, but gave the animator a new challenge in technical accuracy, through which he could nevertheless achieve unusual effects, especially when the task was to create an illusion of space travel.

The multiscreen system, of which there are numerous types according to its application, came into its own through international world exhibitions. Animation is used only to a limited extent because the constantly changing images on multi-screens, which are often projected from several sources, automatically maintain enough interest for the public. Nevertheless the potentiality of creating an unusual effect by using a selected part of the screen only and drawing attention to another, as well as the flexibility of various projection directions is still waiting to be exploited by the animator.

28

FUTURE ANIMATION TECHNIQUES

DURING the last decade various new developments have taken place in animation techniques.

First of all, the elimination of hard outlines round cartoon characters, with the result that the characters become an integral part of the total pictorial composition, instead of isolated forms. This style of approach has shifted the emphasis from the old convention of the comic strip to graphic qualities which are entirely pictorial. The development crystallized in John Hubley's films *Tender Game, Moon Bird* and *The Hole*, George Dunning's *Flying Man*, and Murakami and Wolf's *Box* and *The Breath*. The stylistic influence of these cartoons has been sufficiently marked to make this technique universally accepted throughout the world, and the approach is applied nowadays in forms like TV commercials and feature-film titles.

Secondly, there has been a strong movement towards introducing a much greater adult content in modern cartoons. Cartoons today are no longer a medium entirely angled towards the young or the adolescent, although obviously many cartoons of this type are still being produced. The horizon has been greatly extended. The majority of subjects from Europe, a considerable number from the States and many from Japan contain ideas requiring intellectual penetration; these cartoons make philosophical statements and even present complex arguments. Cartoons may have become a platform for universal world consciousness in such films as the Yugoslav cartoons *The Wall* and *The Tamer of Wild Horses*, the Czech *Hand* and *Deserter*, the English *Automania 2000* and *The Question*, the Japanese *Egg*, the Rumanian *Homo Sapiens*, the Hungarian *Duel*, the American *Stars* and *Man*, and the Yugoslav *Diary*, among many other examples.

Thirdly, the universal search for short-cuts in the technical process of animation has intensified, and many new systems have been introduced which claim to simplify or automate some aspect of production. A short description of several is given below. Most of these processes have some degree of merit. In many cases years of research and considerable expense have been involved in the development of a new technical system, even if the adoption of it has not been as general as the inventor may desire.

Animascope

Developed by Leon H. Maurer and Harry Wuest, this system transfers normally photographed live actors, dressed to resemble cartoon characters, directly on to 35-mm. film by means of simple laboratory printing and processing.

An automatic travelling matte is used to combine these images with the backgrounds. This process of production for the most part resembles a normal live-action one, with the result that the cartoon characters appear to move, act and behave like live characters.

The inventors believed that their method promoted the production of cartoon films involving the most complex action and the most detailed characterization at a considerable saving in both cost and time. The process makes use of only conventional and readily available equipment, and permits virtually unlimited production values at a level of costs which would have been completely impossible in the past.

Although a fully animated film is currently very expensive, it is debatable whether this system helps the development of animation as an art, especially if it is accepted that the art of animation starts at the point where it leaves attempts at realism aside and becomes creative in a field where live-action photography is impossible.

The system is securely patented throughout the world, and users are advised to employ the system only with the assistance of the inventors.

Technamation

Another new animation system, Technamation, utilizes the photosensitive resistance of light-polarized film. In light-polarizing film or filtering, the molecules are oriented in a given direction or axis. When the light, polarized in this manner, enters a second light-polarizing filter whose polarizing axis is parallel to that of the original filter it is transmitted freely by the second filter. However, if the polarizing axis of the second filter is at right angles to that of the first the polarizing axes are crossed, and practically no light will pass through the second filter. The amount of light which can pass through the two polarizing filters is therefore dependent on the angular relation of their polarizing axes.

Each motion area is associated with a light-polarizing area having several different directions or axes of polarization. By varying the polarizing axis of an incident beam of light (i.e., by constantly turning a light-polarizing filter in front of a light source), the relation of its axis to those of the polarizing areas is continually and progressively changed. One area after another appears to change progressively in density, and the illusion of movement is created.

The Traceur d'Ectoplasmes

This is a mechanical adaptation by Arcady of the cathode-ray oscillograph. The advantage of this system is that the animator can achieve a completely controllable form of fluid motion. This has enabled Arcady to combine special lighting effects with his static backgrounds, which are sometimes fantastic landscapes, designed either in a single plane or in a series of planes set up in depth—the so-called multiplane system.

The lighting effects originate from a coloured luminous spot which is broken up and projected on to an oscillating mirror, which reflects the rays on a translucent screen, where they become integrated with the static backgrounds. The cyclic movements of the lighting effects are filmed phase by phase using a stop-motion camera technique, which creates an evolving animation in the total image.

A rich accumulation of textures is achieved in Arcady's films by interposing in the trajectory of the light-source screens and masks, which are themselves subject to controlled motion. The total flow of movement remains highly flexible and can be combined with other visual elements, such as paintings, kaleidoscopic images and drawn animation.

The Animograph

Invented by J. Dejoux of France, this machine is the result of co-operation between the Société Française d'Optique et de Mécanique and the Service de la Recherche de la Radio-Télévision Française. One of the advantages provided by it is that the animator can see the production of a film take place under his eyes and can make immediate corrections if he is not satisfied with the result.

The work is carried out on a special Kodatrace film, in punched bands 70 mm. wide, made out of tri-acetate or frosted cellulose. Two gates are involved. The cartoonist draws his first image on the 70-mm. film, which is directed through a rotating Polaroid mirror placed at an angle of 45° between the two gates and registered instantly. The rotating Polaroid mirror lets through only one image at a time, and the subsequent images are slowly mixed together by means of a Polaroid disc set at a pre-determined speed by the operator, who can advance or reverse the controls at will.

For one second of action the animator needs to draw only three or four images instead of the customary twelve to twenty-four. This obviously saves considerable time, although, according to reports, the work cannot be developed in the same precision and detail as normal cell cartoon animation. At this stage the equipment is more suitable for television entertainment than cinema or TV commercials, since there can be no saving when detailed dialogue animation is required, because in this case the animator has to follow every single syllable of the spoken words.

The motives behind the considerable research into these various automatic systems is an attempt to save labour and ease the task of the artist. Both these objects are essential; the animation industry is undoubtedly expanding in many different directions, but at the same time one finds that animation skills are being acquired by fewer and fewer artists. Consequently, there is bound to be a shortage of animation artists, and the increasing demand will have to be met by means of up-to-date mechanical processes operated by a new type of artist technician who must not only be capable of creating formal drawings and characters but also understanding the elementary mathematical codes needed to translate these in terms of the machine's language. This relationship is rather different to the conventional approach of the Disney or UPA periods, which, unfortunately perhaps, are out of date in the 1970s.

Stimulus of World Fairs

The fourth development stems from World Fairs like the 1964/5 New York Exhibition, the Lausanne National Exhibition in Switzerland or the Montreal Expo in 1967, which have produced an interesting technical stimulus for animation as well as for normal film production.

The initial design for Cinerama, the curved screen, developed into many interesting varieties. Saul Bass's *The Searching Eye*, made for Kodak, was designed for a tri-screen proportion and is a good

312

example of this. The picture was projected on to a triplicate screen, and was arranged in such a way that one part of the screen could be visually counterpointed with the other parts. This convention, which was used in the 1964 New York Fair, emerged once again very dramatically at the Montreal Expo in 1967, for example in the Canadian, Ontario, Canadian Railways, Japanese and British Pavilions. These multi-screen presentations were a combination of live action, animation and special effects, in most cases demonstrating the highest technical skill.

The most imaginative system of this kind so far is the Czechoslovakian invention of Polivision by Josef Svoboda, which consists of a montage of 8000 slides, eight films and thirty-six screens. Some of the films are projected on mobile cubes and spring wires, giving a pulsating flicker and providing a most exciting visual experience. The effect is further reinforced with specially placed mirrors and rotating coloured lights. The visual elements are made up of animation, still drawings and live photography. This provides an example of how a projection system can free itself from static screens, and provide a special new experience. Abstract animation has been complemented by a highly imaginative technological invention.

Josef Svoboda has also developed his Diapolyecran system, which was displayed for the first time at Montreal. It uses 112 independent screens, creating a total screen of 32 ft. by 20 ft. The screens are three-dimensional cubes, each 2 ft. square, and housing inside two Kodak slide projectors; 15,000 slides are projected on these screens, and the drawings dissolve smoothly into each other, giving the illusion of movement with dramatic impact. The cubes can themselves move to and fro, providing an unexpected three-dimensional effect. Here, indeed, is a system with a future.

Computer Animation

The fifth development makes use of the computer to assist animation. This is by far the most significant development during our decade, and will affect the whole future of animation fundamentally. At present, however, the system presents many difficult technical problems.

Computer animation belongs to the department of computer graphics. It forms a very small part of the whole spectrum of computer technology, and too few people are at present involved in its development. One of the basic problems is the animator's

313

inability to talk the computer language. The artist may find his relationship to the computer too impersonal. In any case, this relationship has to be established through a mathematician or, more precisely, a computer programmer, who is capable of translating the visual requirements for animation into the necessary mathematical formulae.

However, there is the simpler type of on-line graphical system, such as the Elliot 4100. The computer has a display attachment, and the designer can use a light pen for input to the computer, which is then displayed pictorially with the appropriate annotation. These images can be instantly revised or changed by the designer using the light pen. An electrical engineer could also see where a circuit has gone wrong. The display could be photographed from the tube for permanent reference by a digital plotter and a film created from the record. While this system is useful, it is not an ideal one for animators.

It is the sixth development of the 1960s that is most interesting in this field. Dr. Zajac and Dr. Knowlton, both from Bell Telephone Laboratories, have been developing systems which appear to be far more effective than anything seen before. Both scientists have their own approach, and both have produced some excellent examples of animation.

Dr. Knowlton's achievement is mostly in the area of abstract and texturized patterns. His system may suit the conventional artist better, because in his language, the artist can figure out frame by frame developments and see what the picture will look like as the animation progresses. Dr. Knowlton has also overcome the problem of producing half-tone effects, even if these effects are only optical illusions. Computer displays could until now only produce drawings composed of dots and thin lines. Colour is added by the movie laboratories, conventionally by means of optical printers or by the use of colour filters with the motion-picture camera while photographing the display tube. To achieve a more sophisticated pattern of shading and to solve the problem of colour will be the next stage of development, among others.

To work on these, and to exploit further possibilities, a special department for computer animation was created at the Polytechnic Institute of Brooklyn, New York, in 1967. Several professional film animators have joined Dr. Zajac's team. We reproduce below with Dr. Zajac's kind permission his article explaining his method.

Suppose you are teaching a course in celestial mechanics. You want to show the satellite orbits that would result if Newton's universal law of gravitation were other than an inverse square law. On a piece of paper you write:

DELT = 1·0
TFIN = 1000
EXP = −3
CALL ORBIT (DELT, TFIN, EXP).

Then you take the paper to the computation centre. After a few hours, you return to pick up a movie, which you then show to the class.

In the movie the positions of the satellite and parent bodies are drawn on a frame of film every minute of their orbits (DELT = 1·0) for the first 1000 minutes (TFIN = 1000). The satellite and parent body, obeying an inverse cube gravitational law (EXP = −3), start out in circular orbits. However, as you have shown in class mathematically, circular orbits for an inverse third power gravitational law are unstable. The 1000-frame (42-second) movie drives home the point; the students see the initial, almost perfectly circular orbits disintegrate, with the satellite making ever-closer swings about the parent body until the two bodies collide (Figure 1).

To those who have tried to make an animated scientific film by conventional means, this account may sound Utopian. Hand animation for a movie of this sort first requires the computation of the coordinates of the satellite for each frame of film. Then comes the tedious task of drawing and properly positioning the satellite 1000 times on celluloid "cels". Finally, the cels have to be individually photographed.

Yet, at the Bell Telephone Laboratories, I can today write the programme I have shown and obtain 16 mm. film, ready for viewing, withing three or four hours. At present, there is only a handful of installations in the world where this procedure is possible. But within a few years, I suspect it will be available at most major universities and industrial laboratories in the United States and Western Europe.

The cost of making the film, including computer time and processing, but not including my labour, would be about $30. However, this cost and the above description are deceiving, for they do not take into account the work of my colleague, F. W. Sinden, who constructed the "sub-programme" called ORBIT which computes the orbit and produces the film. To have a more balanced view, we have to consider how computer pictures are drawn and how sub-programmes such as ORBIT work.

The Computer-driven Cathode Ray Tube

Figures 2 and 3 are themselves computer drawn, to illustrate the picture-making process. The instructions or programme for the picture are fed into the computer, usually on punched cards (Figure 2). The computer then calculates numbers that specify the picture and the commands for film advances. These are read on to magnetic tape, shown in the bottom right of Figure 2. Next, the tape is rewound; it is then connected to a cathode ray tube and the film-advance mechanism of a camera (upper right, Figure 3). As the tape is run from its beginning, the numbers on the tape are translated into electron beam commands for the cathode ray tube; the picture appears on the face of the tube and is recorded on the camera film (the shutter is always open). When a frame is completed, a command from the tape to the camera causes the film to advance to the next frame. All this happens at electronic speeds, so that a film such as the celestial mechanics film described earlier might be made at the rate of 5 to 10 frames per second, or about one quarter of the rate of standard movie projection.

315

Programming of Computer Animation

The cathode ray tube performs only two basic tasks: (1) it "types" a small font of standard-sized letters and (2) it sweeps a straight line segment between two specified points. (The description here pertains specifically to the SC-4020, a computer-driven cathode ray tube manufactured by the General Dynamics Corporation. However, other computer-driven cathode ray tubes work in a similar manner.)

Although these tasks are performed with high precision and reliability, they are in principle extremely simple. The advantages of computer animation do not lie with an elaborately versatile cathode ray tube. Rather, they lie with the power of a high-speed digital computer. Indeed, the special virtue of computer animation is that it brings the power of computing to the film medium.

To illustrate this power, let us consider how one builds a programme for an animated film, starting with the line-drawing ability of the cathode ray tube. An example of the basic line drawing command is:

CALL LINE $(-5, 3, 15, 22)$

This command causes the electron beam to connect the point with horizontal coordinate $X = -5$ and vertical coordinate $Y = 3$ to the point with coordinates $X = 15$, $Y = 22$. The plotting area of the cathode ray tube is a square with X and Y ranging between -512 and $+512$, giving more than one million reference points.

The above instruction is written in a standard scientific programming language called Fortran, although Fortran users will note that in the interest of clarity, I have taken certain liberties with standard Fortran. A Fortran programme is actually executed in two passes through the computer. On the first pass, the symbolic Fortran instructions are translated into the basic numerical code of the computer; the output is a set of punched cards or a magnetic tape. In the second pass, this numerical code is read from the cards or tape and executed; the result is the final numerical output of the computer.

Fortran was written to allow symbol manipulation, akin to ordinary algebra (Fortran stands for "FORmula TRANslator"). For example, the two commands

Y = 5
CALL LINE $(-15, Y, 30, Y)$

will cause a horizontal line to be drawn from the point $X = -15$, $Y = 5$ to $X = 30$, $Y = 5$. Symbolic specification is convenient in the writing of "loops", for example

DO THRU*, I = 1, 100
Y = I
*CALL LINE $(-15, Y, 30, Y)$

The first instruction signals the formation of the loop. It commands the computer to execute 100 times the instructions following, up to and including the instruction marked by the asterisk. Each time through the loop, the Y coordinate of the line is given the value of the counter, I. So on the 29th pass through the loop $Y = 29$, on the 30th pass $Y = 30$, and so on. In this example, 100 horizontal lines, spaced vertically one unit apart and lying between $Y = 1$ and $Y = 100$ would be drawn on a single frame of film.

Computer loops are tailor-made for animation. To illustrate, first introduce the instruction CALL FRAME. Fortran translates this into a command to the camera to advance the film by one frame. Insertion of CALL FRAME into the loop gives:

DO THRU* 1 = 1, 100
Y = I
CALL LINE $(-15, Y, 30, Y)$
*CALL FRAME

316

The result is animation. We get 100 frames of a movie showing the steady upward motion of a single horizontal line.

Even this simple four-instruction programme illustrates several points. First of all, note that a computer loop is not the same as a film loop. A film loop repeats the same sequence of *events* over and over. A computer loop repeats the same sequence of *commands* over and over. A command, such as $Y = I$, may call for a change from the previous passage through the loop. Thus, the event produced in each passage through the loop generally *differs in a systematic way* from the event produced in the previous passage.

Secondly, note the ease with which we can change the programme to produce a new animated sequence. Suppose we want the action to go only one-half as fast. We simply replace the command $Y = I$ by $Y = I/2$, and the command DO THRU* I = 1,100 by DO THRU* I = 1,200. Or, we might decide that the line should extend from $X = -5$ to $X = 50$. This requires only that we change the LINE call to CALL LINE $(-5, Y, 50, Y)$.

In fact we could allow for all of these changes at once by using symbols. The addition of an instruction, READ, allows us to specify particular values at the time of running. The complete programme then looks like this:

```
READ, SPEED, X1, X2
DO THRU* I = 1, 100 × SPEED
Y = I/SPEED
CALL LINE (X1, Y, X2, Y)
*CALL FRAME
STOP
3, 10, 72
```

The READ instruction says to the computer, "When the card containing STOP has been reached, all instructions in this programme will have been loaded in. Look for numbers on the next card. Set SPEED equal to the first number, X1 to the second number, and X2 to the third number. Then execute the programme."

For each particular set of values of SPEED, X1, X2, we get a different film. This illustrates another point of great importance; a successful programme generates more than a single film; it makes possible a whole *family* of films. The family is a function of several variables just as in mathematics a family of curves can be a function of several variables. For each particular choice of values, a new film results. Different choices may give films that do not even resemble each other. Thus, in the celestial mechanics example, a single programme using the Newtonian law of gravitational force yields movies of circular, elliptical, parabolic and hyperbolic orbits, depending on the initial conditions.

Modern computing allows still another freedom. We can make our programme into a subprogramme. First, we decide on a name. In Fortran, we are limited to names of six symbols. We pick HRZLIN (standing for horizontal line). Then we modify the previous programme as follows:

```
SUBROUTINE HRZLIN (SPEED, X1, X2)
DO THRU* I = 1,100 × SPEED
Y = I/SPEED
CALL LINE (X1, Y, Xw2, Y)
*CALL FRAME
```

This programme is stored in the computer or on cards once and for all. If in some film in the future, we decide we want to show an ascending horizontal line, we would write:

```
READ, SPEED, X1, X2
CALL HRZLIN (SPEED, X1, X2)
STOP
2, 5, 50
```

317

If we did not want to experiment with several different SPEEDs, X1s and X2s, but rather knew that these variables should have the values 2, 5, and 50, the programme would be shorter still:

CALL HRZLIN (2, 5, 50)

This illustrates the powerful "naming" or subroutine capability of programming. By this means we can build up a library of programmes as we go along. This library differs markedly from the usual film library. Each entry represents a family of films rather than a single film. Each entry probably embodies loops. But these are computer loops, not film loops.

The reader can now perhaps understand the celestial mechanics example given at the outset. Having F. W. Sinden's general programme, ORBIT, for producing a family of orbit films as a function of the relevant variables, it is simply a matter of writing the instruction CALL ORBIT and specifying values to obtain the particular orbit film desired.

Applications of Computer Animation

Computer results usually emerge in the form of numbers printed on paper, sometimes hundreds of thousands of numbers per sheet on hundreds of thousands of sheets of paper. With computer animation one can translate the numbers into a series of pictures which can be scanned in succession as a movie. Figure 4 is a frame from such a movie.

Instructions for the desired movie enter the computer as a deck of punched cards.

In this new method of animation, both film motion and display on the tube can be controlled automatically by information on a magnetic tape.

In this case, I was studying, by digital computer simulation, the orientation control of a satellite. At first, I had the computer print out numbers giving the satellite orientation at successive instants of time. The problem of visualizing the satellite motions from the printed numbers was formidable. So I wrote a sub-programme which took the numbers that would normally be printed out and used them to compute a perspective drawing of a box representing a satellite. Figure 5 shows the superposition of every fifth frame of the movie for the first satellite orbit (in the movie itself the Earth turns). An orbital clock in the upper right-hand corner counts off orbits.

In the programme it is easy to change the point of view of the perspective. In Figure 6, also taken from the movie, the viewer is travelling in orbit with the satellite.

Most of the applications of computer animation so far have been of this sort—usually short sequences visually displaying the results of a scientific computation. Examples are:

A movie of successive iterates of an iteration procedure for solving an optimization problem (Bell Telephone Laboratories; Sandia Corporation).

Flow of a viscous fluid, including the formation of a von Karman vortex street (Los Alamos).

Propagation of shock waves in a solid (Los Alamos; Lawrence Radiation Laboratory, Livermore, California).

Lines of constant pressure, temperature, precipitation, etc., in a dynamic meteorological model of the Earth's weather (Lawrence Radiation Laboratory).

Vibration of an aircraft (Boeing Aircraft).

Simulation of an aircraft carrier landing (Boeing Aircraft).

Most of the animation has been in black and white; however, the movies produced at the Lawrence Radiation Laboratory have been in colour.

The possibilities of the use of computer animation in this way as an output means for standard computing are limitless. Indeed, one can argue that

318

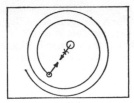

Figure 1 Two massive bodies interact according to an inverse cube law of force. The bodies either spiral in and collide, as shown, or spiral ever outward. From *Force, Mass and Motion*.

Figure 2 A programme on punched cards for a picture is fed into the computer. The computer writes the numbers representing the computed picture on to magnetic tape. From *A Computer Technique for the Production of Animated Movies*.

Figure 3 The computed picture is read from magnetic tape to drive a cathode ray tube and camera film advance mechanism. From *A Computer Technique for the Production of Animated Movies*.

Figure 4 Box representing a satellite changes attitude according to a mathematical model of the Earth's gravity. Clock counts off orbits. From *Simulation of a Two-Gyro, Gravity-Gradient Attitude Control System*.

Figure 5 Superposition of every fifth frame during one orbit from *Simulation of a Two-Gyro, Gravity-Gradient Attitude Control System*.

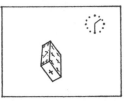

Figure 6 Satellite as seen in an orbiting reference frame. From *Simulation of a Two-Gyro, Gravity-Gradient Attitude Control System*.

Figure 7 Orbits of bodies with inverse square law interaction. The plus sign is the moving centre of mass. From *Force, Mass and Motion*.

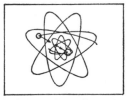

Figure 8 Orbits of two bodies with a direct cube force law of interaction. From *Force, Mass and Motion*.

319

graphical output is "natural," and the usual numerical computer output is woefully inefficient. The human eye has great pattern recognition ability; for this very reason the usual first step in handling scientific data is to plot it. The human eye also quickly picks out a moving object from a static background. Movies allow one to take advantage of this ability by adding the dimension of time to the familiar spatial dimensions in studying computer output.

Moreover, many of the calculations done on a computer are of essentially dynamic phenomena. One wants to see the unfolding or evolution of a process either as a function of time or of some other variable. Motion pictures are the obvious way of accomplishing this.

Finally, as the sample frames of Figures 4–6 show, it is easy to make perspective views of solid objects. It is likewise easy to make two perspectives side by side, that is, to make stereographic movies. This line of research has been pursued by A. M. Noll of the Bell Telephone Laboratories. Among other things, he has made a movie of a four-dimensional cube rotating about one of its axes, as seen when projected into three dimensions.

Educational Use of Computer Animation

The use of computer animation for the display of the results of scientific computations is a form of education—one scientist passing information to another. It suggests the use of computer animation for the classroom.

One immediately thinks of a whole host of phenomena and concepts that uniquely lend themselves to illustration by computer movies. The idea of a "limit" in the calculus, for example, is essentially a dynamic one, as the standard terminology suggests—"f(X) *approaches* f(X$_a$) as X-X$_a$ *approaches* zero." Other examples are Newton's laws of motion, kinetic theory in physics and chemistry, fluid flow in engineering—in fact, one can argue that a good deal of the instruction in the physical sciences is in terms of "movies" of mathematical models of nature—except that the student does not normally see the movies; he only hears verbal descriptions of them.

Perhaps more important is the opportunity computer animation gives to the scientist and engineer to make his own movies. As our examples have shown, the user programmes computer animation in the language of mathematics, a language in which the physical scientist or engineer is proficient. Moreover, the

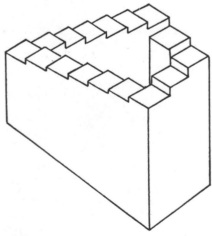

Figure 9 Illusion of the enclosed winding staircase that seems to go ever upwards. From *A Pair of Paradoxes*.

320

scientist can make films with a minimum of dependence on directors, producers, and animators. Much as in writing a book, where one submits a manuscript and receives back a proof in print ready for reading, so can one now submit a programme and receive back a proof film, ready for viewing. The scientist can be master of his own house; if he wishes, he can maintain complete creative control over the films he makes.

One might expect the professional science film-maker to feel threatened by this development. Paradoxically, the opposite has been the case with the few film-makers who have had a chance to try computer animation and to appreciate its flexibility and power. One professional animator told me that he has always been envious of composers. All a composer needed was a piano to try out his latest creation. The animator on the other hand could only with great labour try out his ideas. For example, if the action were too fast, cels would have to be redrawn and the scene laboriously rephotographed. In computer animation, such things as speed can be left as a variable. The film-maker has much more freedom to experiment. He is free to bring his full artistic abilities to bear in his partnership with scientists in film-making.

One of the few purely educational computer animated films is *Force, Mass and Motion*, by F. W. Sinden of the Bell Telephone Laboratories. The film illustrates Newton's laws in two dimensions. Orbits are shown of two massive bodies under central force action for various laws, such as inverse cube, direct cube, etc., as well as for the familiar inverse square law. Figure 1 and Figures 7 and 8 are frames from Sinden's movie.

Another educational movie by Roger N. Shepard and the author is entitled *A Pair of Paradoxes*. It combines two psychological phenomena discovered recently. One, due to L. S. and R. Penrose of the University of London, is a winding staircase that seems to go ever upward while at the same time closing upon itself after each circuit. The other, due to Shepard, is a tone that seems to go ever upward while at the same time remaining near the middle of the scale. Figure 9 is a frame from this movie.

The Future

It is now several years since films were first animated by computer (some computer films are known to have been made on the Whirlwind computer at MIT in 1951). However, they have made relatively little impact, especially in science education where their prospects are perhaps brightest. Probably the reason is the lack of a suitable champion. As I have indicated above, most of the development has been in industrial laboratories, where the interest has been in straightforward technical applications as a computer output device. Very little work has been done at universities, and that which has been done has also been aimed at scientific rather than educational research.

To exploit the full educational potential of computer animation will require the partnership of three specialities: computing, film-making, and the subject-matter science or technology about which a film is to be made. A central facility where these skills could come together would give the educational uses of computers a great push forward. So far no such facility exists.

Another need is for higher-level computer languages. We have already seen an example of a computer language in Fortran, which allowed us to write formulas to programme in terms of symbols rather than numbers, and to name sequences of instructions as subprogrammes.

Recently, a great deal of activity has gone into improving on Fortran, especially in the mechanism for naming. In particular, computer languages in certain specialities have been written. These contain, built into the language, names for the concepts and operations peculiar to that speciality. Such a language for movie-making would be very useful. It would contain convenient ways of specifying and moving objects mathematically and ways of projecting the object into a picture plane; it would allow the programmer to imagine himself as a cameraman with commands for panning, zooming in or out, dissolving, fading, etc.

A big first step in the direction of a universal movie language has already been made. K. C. Knowlton of the Bell Telephone Laboratories has written a language for movie making called BEFLIX which allows one to do many of the things mentioned. Figures 2 and 3 illustrating computer animation are taken from a 17-minute movie made in BEFLIX entitled *A Computer Technique for the Production of Animated Movies.*

The instructions in BEFLIX look quite different from those in Fortran. An example is:

PAINT, A, B, WRITE, 2

which says: "Paint the rectangular area specified by the opposite diagonal points A and B. First erase what is now in this area and then write in 2s". By filling rectangular areas of the screen with various alphabetical and numerical characters, Knowlton generates the different textures of grey shown in Figures 2 and 3. Unlike the satellite and orbit examples of Figure 1 and Figures 4–6, each frame of which was a line drawing, a frame of a film in BEFLIX is completely filled with varying shades of grey. Thus, BEFLIX is more akin to the scanning technique of television. BEFLIX can be easily learned in a few weeks by persons with no knowledge of mathematics or computing.

Special-purpose computer languages are attempts to make easier the specification of image inputs to the computer. Another recent development in this direction is the light pen, the stylus-like device that allows one to draw computer-recognizable pictures on the face of a cathode ray tube. The combination of the light pen and special-purpose languages is perhaps the ultimate in a graphical man-machine communication system—one which is still in its infancy.

The future for computer animation is, in my opinion, very bright. It is, however, too early to tell exactly what its impact will be, especially in science education. Here, the computer does best the animation that is couched in mathematics—precisely the animation that is hardest to do by hand. So hard, in fact, that only a few examples of it have been tried in the classroom. We therefore have little experience with which to predict the future.

But all those who have tried computer animation so far are excited by its possibilities. I think their expectations will be more than fulfilled.

Since then, as expected, especially during the early 1970's, there was a rapid expansion of computerised animation technology on both sides of the Atlantic. With the aid of grants from the British Science Research Council a great deal of work has been carried out by the computer department of the University of Edinburgh and the Atlas computer unit at Harwell, England. We follow Dr. Zajac's article with Stan Hayward's description of some recent development carried out at the Imperial College of Science and Technology in London during the years of 1974–1975.

Stan Hayward, film director, scriptwriter and animation consultant, has given his views on the computer animation scene:

There are two ways the computer can animate. For geometrical shapes with regular movements such as a cube spinning in space, the shape and movement may be generated by numbers. Freehand shapes like cartoons may also be

322

moved in two dimensions and go from one shape to another providing the movement can be translated mathematically such as zooming or rotating, but if a movement like a walk cycle is required then it is more convenient to actually digitise (convert the drawings to numbers) each drawing of the cycle and store these, then call them up in sequence, and effectively do it as an animator would, but with the added advantage that each drawing need only be drawn once; the computer will do all the other routines of scaling, moving, duplicating, etc.

Problems

Computers can draw just about anything a human can draw, but unlike a human they are limited to the devices that actually display the line or make the mark, and these have severe limitations of style; and to a lesser extent the means of putting drawings into the computer do not allow the range of style and touch that an artist would have. Except for the scientific purposes, the computer output has to be upgraded by film or video techniques to make it cinematically acceptable. There are several ways of doing this:

16 MM. MICROFILM, WHITE ON BLACK NEGATIVE. Standard computer microfilm output. Both line and characters unsuitable for normal film use, but extremely good for producing a fast line-test of a shape or movement. Good positives may also be produced for diagrammatic work.

16 MM. MICROFILM OPTICALLY COLOURED. As above, but coloured in labs. It is possible to get a range of line grades that may be given different colours.

It is fast, and ideal where flat artwork is required with block filling. It becomes increasingly expensive with every added colour, and this soon becomes a limitation.

Currently the most usual method of producing "computer animation" for artists. It is also increasingly being used to make teaching films of technical character.

16 MM. MICROFILM ELECTRONICALLY COLOURED. Similar to above except the colour synthesiser is used. Putting the film on tape allows video effects to be added, and also live action superimposition. This will certainly be the fastest growing use of computer animation as digital computers become more and more compatible with analog hardware, but at present the problem of going to film from tape cheaply and with good resolution has not been solved adequately.

16 MM. MICROFILM ROTOSCOPED. By projecting the microfilm and tracing off the image, it can be painted or cut out as in normal animation methods.

This is the most suitable way to merge computer artwork with normal artwork, but is slow by other methods.

GRAPH-PLOTTING. The computer operates a plotter which draws out the image to any size required (up to about 3′ sq.).

It is most useful when only a few drawings are required, or the drawings have to be modified or cut out. It can draw directly onto animation cel if these have to be overlaid on photo backgrounds.

ANALOG DEVICES. Character generators allow numerous typefaces to be typed directly onto the computer screen. Pattern generators produce a whole range of Lissajous figures and geometric shapes that are very good for special effects. These may also be plotted out.

The Future

The overall trend in computer/video/film techniques is to get the 'instant image' with full colour and sound. The ways of achieving this end are varied; in computers there is a move towards coloured displays; but these are expensive and limited in colour range. In video there is a move towards digital TV, which would solve most of the computer-video problems for animation, but at the moment this is too expensive. In film there is a move towards the instant movie, comparable to Polaroids still photography; but this is still in the future. The immediate future is likely to continue with hybrid techniques, although these may in themselves be combined to make a new system. Two such ideas are currently being researched at Imperial College.

THE VIDEO ROSTRUM CAMERA. The rostrum camera has a table moving on the XY axis and the camera on the Z axis. It is very similar to numerically controlled machine tools that are operated by punched tape. It is a fairly straightforward job to control a rostrum by tape, but is only economical if there is a high throughput. If the camera was video, then the cameraman could see his field on a TV monitor, and having shot a scene play it back immediately for the animator. If correct, then have it transferred to film on a laser beam recorder of the type now becoming available.

COMPUTERISED STUDIO. The second idea now in an advanced stage of development, takes the use of the computer close to its logical conclusion.

If you are going to use a computer at all, it is better to use it as fully as possible rather than for individual jobs.

There are four stages in the production of an animated film:

1. *Information Retrieval*. Checking and listing of personnel, services, and equipment available for production. Comparison with previous films of similar type. Storing and referencing key artwork.
This could be done in the computer and on microfilm.

2. *Management*. Costing, scheduling, planning. The day to day running of a studio using the computer to optimise resources, predict bottlenecks, and make cost comparisons with previous films using the same resources. A "studio profile" would be built up that would allow accurate estimates to be made on any job.

3. *Creative*. Simulation of animation by line testing. Storing of commonly used designs and animation cycles. Matching of soundtracks to simulation display. Electronic colouring. Production of artwork.

4. *Technical*. Numerical control of cameras, editors, plotters, displays, sound and colour synthesis, printouts of dopesheets and soundtracks.
The Imperial College system now under development consists of a minicomputer with digitiser, graph plotter, and 16 mm. camera.
A special facility of the system is the "Menu". This allows the storing of drawings and animation routines which include: Interpolation, rotation in 2D and 3D, squashing, stretching, scaling, editing, merging, exploding, wrapping, duplicating, block filling, and matrix transformation.

The user digitises the drawings needed and then stores them. These are then displayed on the screen and given the correct position and field size, they are then manipulated by the required routine in a given number of frames and shot from the screen a frame at a time. An example of animation would be to digitise a map of the world and have this wrapped onto a sphere and rotated by increments of 10; this would give 36 increments for a complete cycle, and result in the sphere going round in one and a half seconds.

The menu also contains a list of symbols that are commonly used such as squares, circles, dotted lines, etc. The animator may create symbols of his own, and for a particular animation cycle might use arms, legs, eyes, etc. in a permanent store.

The system has not been created specifically for the animation industry, but as an extension of the rapidly developing field of computer aided design (CAD) which is used in engineering and architecture. The films being made at the college are by engineers and architects who can put more information into a moving blueprint than a still one.

It is probable that the next generation of animators will consist largely of science orientated users rather than arts. There are already more hours of microfilm made at the Imperial College and London University every week than the entire output of animated film by the animation industry here every month. The management science department has had several PhD's on systems in television, and the engineering department does constant development on numerical control. The combined experience of these departments has shown that film making may be considered as a system just as much as car production.

The future of computer animation will be very broad based, and touch upon anything that requires the simulation of events to be visualised. A James Bond film might simulate a car chase on the computer screen, with very accurate results being shown by putting into the computer the type, weight, speed, etc. of the cars. This would be quicker, cheaper, and a great deal safer than actually rehearsing it a few times.

In conclusion, I suggest that, after sound and colour, the computer is the next stage in film making, and that within the next two years the computer will play the most significant role in rationalising the film and TV industry.

The position, therefore, at present is that the scientist and the animator can now create drawings that can move in three or four dimensions, drawings which can rotate in space, and drawings involving great mathematical precision representing a complex mathematical factor or scientific principle. The process takes a fraction of the time for a production of a conventional cartoon, a condition every animator has wished for ever since the invention of cinematography. What may now be needed is an artist of Klee's talent who could invent a new convention for creating shapes and forms. The tools are there, and the next ten years will surely lead to the development of exciting visual discoveries.

CONCLUSION

THE most important factor in all animation is the one that cannot be explained in a technical work such as this, or in any book for that matter. It is the factor of talent and inspiration, which lies at the root of all fully creative work.

The inspiration of the animator must be tough, enduring and resilient. It must increase with wear and tear during the long and often wearying process of preparation and realization, which for the shortest film may take perhaps one month and for the longest perhaps three years. Whereas a painter has direct personal contact with his canvas and works in the comparative privacy of his studio, the animator must have enough inspiration to spare to excite his sponsor and to guide his staff during the long period of work that lies ahead on each production. The animator must learn to share his artistry with others, and to achieve his work through them.

The animator, in fact, soon learns that he cannot work solely in an artistic vacuum to please himself. He must work to please others, and he is fortunate indeed if his talent becomes so recognized and established that he can please others in the way that really pleases himself.

In order to acquire the money to make a film that he can fully regard as his own creation he may only too often find that he has to lend his technical skill to the realization of films in which it is difficult for him to be more than mildly interested. To maintain a studio and its staff he must have continuity of work, and this means he must undertake commissions from as many sources as possible. Only the lone worker existing on the borderline of professional and amateur status can keep his talents in reserve in order to make the occasional film that suits him. This basic financial problem for the full-time professional animator is, of course, due to the fact that animation implies the application of the graphic and allied arts to celluloid, with the consequent production costs that are involved the

326

moment we enter the film studio. Animation is, in fact, the most expensive form of art, commercial or otherwise, that there is! And it is also in many respects the most exciting, because it is alive and moves!

Every established art has its critics, part of whose function it is to attempt to evaluate what each new work has accomplished in the light of their knowledge of contemporary achievement in the same field and the traditions that have been built up in the past. The live-action film is still a very young art, but an international tradition of film criticism has grown up during the past thirty years which, even though the good critics themselves are few enough in number, their judgment is well informed, and therefore of the greatest value to the creative artist, even if he disagrees entirely with what they say about his work.

But animation, the art within an art, has no such tradition of informed criticism. For the true critic of animation must be both an art critic and a film critic combined. The artistic development of animation would have gained a great deal if its output could have been as consistent as that of the live-action film, and if knowledge-able critics had been able to specialize (at least to some extent) in the continuous consideration of the values involved in this new form of graphic art. The criticism of animation as such has so far gone by default.

It is difficult to look far ahead in this astonishing medium. It is struggling as free as it can from an economic and artistic strait-jacket, confined mostly to the production of fairy stories on the one hand and the *grotesqueries* of the comic strip on the other. We have tried to show that it is an art of great potentialities, which have been spasmodically revealed in the films of a few perceptive artists working, when they can, for perceptive sponsors. We have shown the direct link that animation has with the limitless world of the graphic arts, to which it has brought the great gift of motion and, in consequence of this, the extra dimension of time. The static picture moves into action and assumes the pattern of a drama. And, because it is also a film, it inherits the technical and artistic qualities of film, in particular the dynamic qualities that come from editing and the close synchronization with sound.

We are convinced that in the next few years we shall see an astonishing growth in the scope of this new art, that is if the sponsors and the public are wise enough and enlightened enough to give the good animator as free a passage and as wide a field of operations as they give to the painter, the writer and the composer.

327

APPENDIX

OPINIONS ABOUT THE FUTURE

THE following questions were put to a representative number of highly experienced British and American producers and directors in animation—Gene Deitch, Joy Batchelor, Stephen Bosustow, Geoffrey Sumner, John Hubley, Adrian Woolery and Philip Stapp.

(1) *Do you think that the use of the cartoon film is expanding? If so, in what directions?*

GENE DEITCH: The largest new use, in my experience, is the animated children's series for television. Daily and weekly cartoon serials are being prepared by many producers. The future may even see cartoon features produced as TV "spectaculars". And, of course, great advances are being made in educational, public information, commercial, sales promotion, training, experimental and entertainment cinema, etc.

JOY BATCHELOR: The use of the cartoon film is expanding in some directions and contracting in others. Cartoon film for future entertainment, both full length and shorts, has virtually ceased in Europe and America owing to rising costs of production, diminishing box-office returns and the changing habits and tastes of the public. Commercial television brought about an unprecedented increase in the use of animation, first in America, then in Great Britain and currently in Western Europe, at the same time stimulating theatrical advertising films in the medium in those countries where they were already accepted. Use of animation for commercial television is already lessening in America and this trend is forseeable in the United Kingdom also. In Western Europe where the process is only at the beginning one can expect considerable expansion. The use of animation for informational or prestige purposes continues steadily. A small but significant growth in animation is as an individual form of expression—a by-product of the TV "boom" in animation which has created greater numbers of people with a knowledge of the medium and with sufficient leisure and energy to experiment.

ADRIAN WOOLERY: Yes, particularly in light of our expanding technology and the requirements to explain complicated mechanical and scientific subjects. Animation lends itself well to this task. It is also expanding in subjective ways in the development of the cartoon commercial. Aside from new techniques, it is being psychologically perfected to attain new and more effective results, and economically, through cost control.

STEPHEN BOSUSTOW: There is no doubt that the use of the cartoon film is expanding. New cartoon studios are starting up in key cities all over the world and colleges are beginning to include animation courses in their film departments. As of this writing, the greatest expansion is in the field of TV spot commercials. However, the use of animation is also growing in the TV programming field and in feature length pictures for theatres.

JOHN HUBLEY: Yes, at a modest rate—mainly in the direction of instructional and educational film, and, of course, commercials for television.

(2) *Do you think animation is in a general state of stagnation as regards its style and presentation? How would you like to see it develop artistically?*

GENE DEITCH: Too many studios rely on the work of one or two designers, many of whom are imitative of each other, to characterize their entire output. I believe that animation studios should open their doors to the great graphic artists and cartoonists of the world to create variety and a fit style for each film.

JOY BATCHELOR: The general effect of commercial television animation is to produce a stereotype. Far too high a percentage of the total footage produced is uniform in thinking, which *is* stagnation. Fortunately, any large volume of output rarely fails to contain a small percentage of bright and fresh ideas.

STEPHEN BOSUSTOW: Not at all. The animated film is a young medium and, although there has been a tendency in certain studios to revert to formula in the style of animation, there are many new and exciting films being made every year. These films are a constant source of inspiration for the aggressive film-makers and serve as the basis for the artistic development of the medium. In our feature film *Magoo's Arabian Nights*, we are employing a new type of effect by composing the scenes in terms of design, without regard to the rules of perspective or dimension. This novel use of line and colour, in which objects will be depicted according to their importance to the story rather than to their true size and position, will, we hope, increase the visual appeal of the film and help preserve its story-book quality.

JOHN HUBLEY: There is a tendency toward clichés of design in a traditional sense, and even the so-called modern style. (The large profile nose, hair line, arms and legs, black dot eyes, etc.) But more disturbing are the clichés of action (stylized flutter-lip action—sandpiper-like leg motion for walks and runs, multiple image jitters for fright, and many others). The trend toward more rapid timing of actions and reactions is reducing the human characteristics portrayed in the animated image. I would like to see the development of animation which is capable of deeper emotional expression; the portrayal of characters that are more profound and human. This will require stories dealing with ideas and relationships beyond the usual cat and mouse chase or "cute" children's tale.

ADRIAN WOOLERY: Animation will never reach a state of stagnation as long as we have the human factor of imagination. As long as new thinking and enthusiasm is brought into the industry it will continue to develop and prosper. We have barely scratched the surface of the medium,

329

artistically. I have no particular ideas on how it should develop, other than it should remain flexible and current, incorporating the latest art forms when appropriate.

(3) *Is the old gag technique dating?*

GENE DEITCH: The basic comedy sight-gag is still potentially wonderful. But the generally practised reduction of this principle to physical injury and endless retaliation, as seen in most theatre cartoons, is dated and wearing. There is nothing wrong with visual comedy and perhaps the animated cartoon is the last refuge of the tradition of pantomime, tasteful slapstick and wildly improbable fun.

JOY BATCHELOR: The old "gag technique" *does* date—it is a good index of the age of a cartoon film. There are, however, a number of situations which have remained funny for a great many years and will presumably continue to do so and the art will lie, as it always has, in inventing a fresh approach.

ADRIAN WOOLERY: With respect to violence and mayhem in earlier cartoons, yes. However, any basic philosophy is the belief that the visual or audio gag "is the thing". Of course, there is a technical point of how it is integrated in the over-all film, but aside from this problem, the gag is probably our most distinguishable and identifiable characteristic. You might say that to-day the gag is becoming more sophisticated.

STEPHEN BOSUSTOW: There will always be comedy and a solid use of the old gag technique. However, in the development and expansion of the animated cartoon film business, there are more and more dramatic and commercial films being made that do not require gags or a situation comedy approach.

GEOFFREY SUMNER: The "gag" is as its name suggests the reappearance of the music hall performers' "business". A piece of pointed mime. In fact the performance of an action in a certain way. What way? To illustrate character. To carry the story on. To cover a gap. To introduce a new element. Ideally a gag should have its beginning in the last gag and introduce the next one. This is the sort of thing achieved by the masters of comedy in silent films—Chaplin and Keaton, for example. Thus the style of the gag is the style or manner of the picture. The gag should fit the kind of picture it is. The gag in cartoon has all the resources of un-limited dimension, complete and controllable timing and complicated reaction. Apart from entertainment films, the gag technique is what animation has as an advantage over simple blackboard or lantern slide demonstration in the expressing of complicated technical information. The objects once drawn can move, grow, recede, transpose or even disappear.

(4) *Do you believe in small or large creative units?*

GENE DEITCH: There are advantages to both. The ideal for me has been a group of small units within a large and flexible organization. Story groups of three or four seem to be a practical maximum for talk-idea sessions. Some story men prefer to work alone and then receive criticism

330

or help, others produce best in the stimulation of group enthusiasm. A production unit consisting of a director, designer and two or three animators seems ideal for small projects such as TV commercials.

JOY BATCHELOR: In general, a small creative unit is to be preferred every time. The communication of ideas is easier when small numbers of people are involved. Where the volume and complexity of the task is enormous (i.e. in a feature film) then there is a great deal to be said in favour of a large creative unit if only to provide sufficient stamina.

ADRIAN WOOLERY: Both. I believe only in creative units, whether large or small. The main problem is to acquire a top-notch creative unit and it is almost impossible to build a large one. To-day the trend would seem to be toward the smaller units, partly due to cost control.

STEPHEN BOSUSTOW: There will always be a place for both small and large creative units. There are advantages in both systems.

JOHN HUBLEY: I believe small creative units help to enable individual artists to develop their abilities, become more expressive, and obtain greater control over their medium.

Do you think cartoon is capable of handling realistic subjects, especially involving the human figure?

GENE DEITCH: There are new techniques which make it possible, but why bother? If there is a creative end to be gained, or if the essence of the animation film can be applied it might be worth exploring, but for the mere imitation of live photography, no.

JOY BATCHELOR: The representation of the human figure is something far better left to live action and the same may be said for realistic subjects.

ADRIAN WOOLERY: I believe it capable, but not effective and I do not subscribe to the principle. Animation is most successful and effective when used in a broad and exaggerated manner in the realm of fantasy and caricature. It should be divorced from any attempt to simulate live action. Animation is a separate medium, and although it may be used to augment or supplement live-action film handling realistic subjects or the human figure, it should not attempt to imitate it.

STEPHEN BOSUSTOW: The cartoon medium is no doubt capable of handling realistic subjects. However, it would be much too expensive and there is really no reason for it as the live-action camera can do it better. A better use of the cartoon film is a caricature, to emphasize or exaggerate the problem or characters in an imaginative way that would be impossible for a live-action camera.

JOHN HUBLEY: Yes, provided animators master fundamentals of drawing form and volume, and then combine this with fresh, personal expressions of human action. The mechanics of moving the human figure cannot be isolated from the motivational drives and dramatic meaning of any action, without rendering it empty and useless. It is primarily the emotional content of an action that is of interest to an audience, and the goal

331

of animators must be to express this in graphic motion; not merely to move arms, legs, and bodies around in space. At this point it will become possible to deal with "realistic subjects" and make them exciting and believable.

(6) *To what extent to you think a storyboard should be developed prior to production?*

GENE DEITCH: I believe in complete scene and shot breakdown in storyboard or a thumbnail board form before production begins. I use a thumbnail storyboard as a sort of bar-sheet, indicating all effects, dialogue and music cues, scene transitions, etc. Great savings in cost, and an overall perspective of the film in advance are to be gained.

JOY BATCHELOR: As fully as possible without detriment to the following phases of production.

STEHPEN BOSUSTOW: If time and money allow, the storyboard should include as many details as possible, particularly if it is to be assigned to a large production unit. However, if only a few people are to be working on the picture, the storyboard can be quite sketchy, with the details being developed during production by the key people who have an overall feeling for and knowledge of the story.

ADRIAN WOOLERY: The storyboard is the first step, after the idea. Every problem must be solved and the story completely resolved on the board prior to consideration of any production.

JOHN HUBLEY: It has been my experience that the more detailed a storyboard and the more carefully it is designed to reflect the appearance of the finished production, the more successful the film.

(7) *Do you believe in post- or pre-recording of music?*

GENE DEITCH: There are advantages to both methods and it depends entirely on the nature of the project involved. The most practical and commercial method is pre-scoring. I frequently go a lot further, and have developed the live-mix procedure to the point where I can get a completely pre-mixed track, complete with all dialogue, music and sound effects, and final, split-second editing, all in advance of production, and still be protected for post-production adjustment!

JOY BATCHELOR: For many years I believed strongly in pre-recording of music thinking this would give greater unity to the track, enable the composer to contribute in a more positive way to the film and give more accurate synchronization. I now consider that there are many advantages to be gained from having the music post-recorded, chief among them being general improvement gained in timing and adjusting the picture in the cutting room instead of editing at storyboard or direction stage.

ADRIAN WOOLERY: Either method is equally successful. However, the choice of post- or pre-recording is determined by a breakdown of the practical and necessary production procedure of the individual studio and the type of film. I have used both methods.

STEPHEN BOSUSTOW: Very often it is extremely helpful to bring the composer in early in the storyboard development as music contributes a great deal to the success of a picture and, sometimes, is a good basis for timing the picture as well as for putting over mood and story points. However, pictures relying more on dialogue or narration do not require the composer's services until the picture is pretty well complete. On some low budget pictures, even canned music added after the film is complete may be adequate.

JOHN HUBLEY: I prefer pre-recording, but don't believe that rigid procedures in any phase of production are desirable.

(8) *What stage in the planning of a subject by the sponsor should the animator be consulted?*

GENE DEITCH: When he first entertains the notion that he might want an animated film.

JOY BATCHELOR: What is needed at the inception of any animated film is someone with a knowledge of the medium—its limitations as well as its possibilities—who thinks in visual, dramatic and filmic terms. This person may well be an animator, a storyboard man or a director, or all three. But to exclude this kind of thinking from the early stages of planning nearly always produces a literary or text book result.

ADRIAN WOOLERY: As early as possible but in any event no later than the final storyboard development.

STEPHEN BOSUSTOW: Naturally, a film-maker who is used to making a film from concept to completion likes to be called in by the sponsor as early as possible in order to participate in every phase of development. However, as the animated film business expands, and in order to control content and cost, many sponsors and advertising agencies either have writers on their own staff or retain writers to develop stories before calling in animation companies to bid on the picture. There are successful films being made both ways, although I believe better films result when the producer is called in to help develop the initial concept.

GEOFFREY SUMNER: The storyboard, or breakdown of the film, has as many different forms as there are ways of putting actions in relation to one another.

The classic storyboard is the set of working drawings of the sequence of a film used in large studios on the Disney model where numbers of subsidiary workers must conform to a total pattern they can almost never see.

It is used in conjunction with model sheets. It could be called the "model sheet" of the sequence of the film.

It is strictly for use within a studio and should not be shown to dangerous people like sponsors.

An earlier stage is the treatment, which can be specifically directed at sponsors. If the basic idea of the film is simple, the treatment need be no more than half a dozen drawings and a brief synopsis to convey a ten minute film.

A storyboard must necessarily be constructed after the music has been done. The musician and the director can work together from a stage following the treatment. From the finished recorded track the storyboard is made.

333

JOHN HUBLEY: The earliest possible.

PHILIP STAPP *preferred to express his opinions on these questions in the form of a simple, composite answer.*

The term "cartoon film" seems to me an unfortunate one. It suggests, I'm afraid, the cute antics of little flat figures drawn either in facile sentimentalized curves or in stylized geometric simplification. I think that audiences who have been surfeited with these cute cartoons (at least in the areas with which I am familiar, Western Europe and the U.S.A.) are becoming increasingly bored with the tired imitations of each other's work. On the other hand there will always be an audience for those animated films made with a fresh imaginative approach.

The growth of the medium as an art will depend not only on the creative ability of the film-maker but on his economic problems in the society in which he works. There are many traps and pitfalls. If he is coerced by any sponsor into compromises, either commercial or political, he will probably continue to grind out run of the mill exercises. Or, success may force him, in our industrialized and specialized age, into a position where he is more business man than artist, becoming administrator and director of groups of craftsmen who in turn become cogs in a long assembly line of animators, tracers, painters, lay-out men, etc. I submit that this system may produce passable entertainment but cannot produce a work of art, even a minor work of art.

Nevertheless, in spite of these hurdles, the medium has a powerful fascination for the artist. He can develop his visual ideas within the element of time, in counterpoint to controlled sound. The medium is also capable of producing powerful concentrated emotional reactions. Serious subjects can be dealt with in small doses. Information which may seem dull can be transformed by imagination into a lively intellectual experience for the spectator. Ideas can be made to dance. Many techniques are still unexplored. We need, in all countries, situations where mature artists of tested ability can make researches without any kind of coercion. Such centres exist for scientists. Why not for the artist?

GEOFFREY SUMNER *adds this further comment to the general approach to making sponsored cartoons:*

If a thing moves, it does something. If it does something, it performs an action. But "performs" also has meaning of "performer" or "performance". That is representation or demonstration either for entertainment or instruction; or a kind of half-way stage which can be generally called "information". In other words films are a show, either a public show, like any play, circus, concert performance, or busking act, or a private show directed at some part of the public, which may or may not be special in some way. If special they require a specialist film. However, the audience for specialist films is still a member of the public (so certain general rules apply to both sorts of film), he is after that a specialist, and therefore entertains certain opinions, and last of all he is (apart from the human failing of idleness) likely to apply more than the normal degree of attention to a film, because he has been brought to it for a purpose.

In regard to the making of films, therefore, the prime consideration is audience. And in sponsored films the word "client" is pretty well synonymous with the word "audience". This is the ideal position but not always the case. Too often a film is bent by a manufacturer, a publicity committee or a technical adviser, away from the shape most suitable for the audience involved. However, the efforts of the maker of the film and the agent of the sponsor (advertising agent, public relations officer, technical adviser) should all be devoted to giving the audience involved the best possible service. The process can be broken down into "What is to be shown?" "How is it to be shown?" "Whom is it being shown to?"

As far as public entertainment films are concerned the resolution of all these problems lies in the hands of the film-maker when he acts as his own producer. If he is employed by an independent producer the "What is to be shown?" will probably be decided between the producer and the film-maker, although the producer has the initiative. He may also fix the market (To whom?) and will certainly control the finance and the exploitation of the finished film. Gradually going down the scale from the freedom of public entertainment to the limitations of specialized technical instruction, the film-maker has less and less independence in "What is to be shown?" and "Whom is it being shown to?" He should, however, keep sovereign control over "How is it to be shown?" the style and manner. He is also the expert on audiences simply as audiences and can judge reactions, etc. In the success of the method of conveying the right matter to the right people lies the success of the film.

FILM MEASUREMENT TABLES

Reproduced by permission of the Shell Film Unit, London.

Time mins.	secs.	35 mm. feet	metres	16 mm. feet	metres	Time mins.	secs.	35 mm. feet	metres	16 mm. feet	metres
0	0.6	1	0.30	0.4	0.12	0	24.0	36	10.97	14.4	4.39
0	1.3	2	0.61	0.8	0.24	0	24.6	37	11.28	14.8	4.51
0	2.0	3	0.91	1.2	0.37	0	25.3	38	11.58	15.2	4.63
0	2.6	4	1.22	1.6	0.49	0	26.0	39	11.89	15.6	4.75
0	3.3	5	1.52	2.0	0.61	0	26.6	40	12.19	16.0	4.88
0	4.0	6	1.83	2.4	0.73	0	27.3	41	12.50	16.4	5.00
0	4.6	7	2.13	2.8	0.85	0	28.0	42	12.80	16.8	5.12
0	5.3	8	2.44	3.2	0.98	0	28.6	43	13.11	17.2	5.24
0	6.0	9	2.74	3.6	1.10	0	29.3	44	13.41	17.6	5.36
0	6.6	10	3.05	4.0	1.22	0	30.0	45	13.72	18.0	5.49
0	7.3	11	3.35	4.4	1.34	0	30.6	46	14.02	18.4	5.61
0	8.0	12	3.66	4.8	1.46	0	31.3	47	14.33	18.8	5.73
0	8.6	13	3.96	5.2	1.58	0	32.0	48	14.63	19.2	5.85
0	9.3	14	4.27	5.6	1.71	0	32.6	49	14.94	19.6	5.97
0	10.0	15	4.57	6.0	1.83	0	33.3	50	15.24	20.0	6.10
0	10.6	16	4.88	6.4	1.95	0	34.0	51	15.54	20.4	6.22
0	11.3	17	5.18	6.8	2.07	0	34.6	52	15.85	20.8	6.34
0	12.0	18	5.49	7.2	2.19	0	35.3	53	16.15	21.2	6.46
0	12.6	19	5.79	7.6	2.32	0	36.0	54	16.46	21.6	6.58
0	13.3	20	6.10	8.0	2.44	0	36.6	55	16.76	22.0	6.71
0	14.0	21	6.40	8.4	2.56	0	37.3	56	17.07	22.4	6.83
0	14.6	22	6.71	8.8	2.68	0	38.0	57	17.37	22.8	6.95
0	15.3	23	7.01	9.2	2.80	0	38.6	58	17.68	23.2	7.07
0	16.0	24	7.32	9.6	2.93	0	39.3	59	17.98	23.6	7.19
0	16.6	25	7.62	10.0	3.05	0	40.0	60	18.29	24.0	7.32
0	17.3	26	7.92	10.4	3.17	0	40.6	61	18.59	24.4	7.44
0	18.0	27	8.23	10.8	3.29	0	41.3	62	18.90	24.8	7.56
0	18.6	28	8.53	11.2	3.41	0	42.0	63	19.20	25.2	7.68
0	19.3	29	8.84	11.6	3.54	0	42.6	64	19.51	25.6	7.80
0	20.0	30	9.14	12.0	3.66	0	43.3	65	19.81	26.0	7.92
0	20.6	31	9.45	12.4	3.78	0	44.0	66	20.12	26.4	8.05
0	21.3	32	9.75	12.8	3.90	0	44.6	67	20.42	26.8	8.17
0	22.0	33	10.06	13.2	4.02	0	45.3	68	20.73	27.2	8.29
0	22.6	34	10.36	13.6	4.15	0	46.0	69	21.03	27.6	8.41
0	23.3	35	10.67	14.0	4.27	0	46.6	70	21.34	28.0	8.53

Time mins.	secs.	35 mm. feet	metres	16 mm. feet	metres
0	47.3	71	21.64	28.4	8.66
0	48.0	72	21.95	28.8	8.78
0	48.6	73	22.25	29.2	8.90
0	49.3	74	22.56	29.6	9.02
0	50.0	75	22.86	30.0	9.14
0	50.6	76	23.16	30.4	9.27
0	51.3	77	23.47	30.8	9.29
0	52.0	78	23.77	31.2	9.51
0	52.6	79	24.08	31.6	9.63
0	53.3	80	24.38	32.0	9.75
0	54.0	81	24.69	32.4	9.88
0	54.6	82	24.99	32.8	10.00
0	55.3	83	25.30	33.2	10.12
0	56.0	84	25.60	33.6	10.24
0	56.6	85	25.91	34.0	10.36
0	57.3	86	26.21	34.4	10.49
0	58.0	87	26.62	34.8	10.61
0	58.6	88	26.82	35.2	10.73
0	59.3	89	27.13	35.6	10.85
1	0.0	90	27.43	36.0	10.97
1	0.6	91	27.74	36.4	11.09
1	1.3	92	28.04	36.8	11.22
1	2.0	93	28.35	37.2	11.34
1	2.6	94	28.65	37.6	11.46
1	3.3	95	28.96	38.0	11.58
1	4.0	96	29.26	38.4	11.70
1	4.6	97	29.57	38.8	11.83
1	5.3	98	29.87	39.2	11.95
1	6.0	99	30.18	39.6	12.07
1	6.6	100	30.48	40.0	12.19
1	7.3	101	30.78	40.4	12.31
1	8.0	102	31.09	40.8	12.44
1	8.6	103	31.39	41.2	12.56
1	9.3	104	31.70	41.6	12.68
1	10.0	105	32.00	42.0	12.80
1	10.6	106	32.31	42.4	12.92
1	11.3	107	32.61	42.8	13.05
1	12.0	108	32.92	43.2	13.17
1	12.6	109	33.22	43.6	13.29
1	13.3	110	33.53	44.0	13.41
1	14.0	111	33.83	44.4	13.53
1	14.6	112	34.14	44.8	13.66
1	15.3	113	34.44	45.2	13.78
1	16.0	114	34.75	45.6	13.90
1	16.6	115	35.05	46.0	14.02
1	17.3	116	35.36	46.4	14.14
1	18.0	117	35.66	46.8	14.26
1	18.6	118	36.97	47.2	14.39
1	19.3	119	36.27	47.6	14.51
1	20.0	120	36.58	48.0	14.63
1	20.6	121	36.88	48.4	14.75
1	21.3	122	37.19	48.8	14.87
1	22.0	123	37.49	49.2	15.00
1	22.6	124	37.80	49.6	15.12
1	23.3	125	38.10	50.0	15.24
1	24.0	126	38.40	50.4	15.36
1	24.6	127	38.71	50.8	15.48
1	25.3	128	39.01	51.2	15.61
1	26.0	129	39.32	51.6	15.73
1	26.6	130	39.62	52.0	15.85
1	27.3	131	39.93	52.4	15.97
1	28.0	132	40.23	52.8	16.09
1	28.6	133	40.54	53.2	16.22
1	29.3	134	40.84	53.6	16.34
1	30.0	135	41.15	54.0	16.46
1	30.6	136	41.45	54.4	16.58
1	31.3	137	41.76	54.8	16.70
1	32.0	138	42.06	55.2	16.82
1	32.6	139	42.37	55.6	16.95
1	33.3	140	42.67	56.0	17.07
1	34.0	141	42.98	56.4	17.19
1	34.6	142	43.28	56.8	17.31
1	35.3	143	43.59	57.2	17.43
1	36.0	144	43.89	57.6	17.56
1	36.6	145	44.20	58.0	17.68
1	37.3	146	44.50	58.4	17.80
1	38.0	147	44.81	58.8	17.92
1	38.6	148	45.11	59.2	18.04
1	39.3	149	45.42	59.6	18.17
1	40.0	150	45.72	60.0	18.29
1	40.6	151	46.02	60.4	18.41
1	41.3	152	46.33	60.8	18.53
1	42.0	153	46.63	61.2	18.65
1	42.6	154	46.94	61.6	18.78
1	43.3	155	47.24	62.0	18.90
1	44.0	156	47.55	62.4	19.02
1	44.6	157	47.85	62.8	19.14
1	45.3	158	48.16	63.2	19.26
1	46.0	159	48.46	63.6	19.39
1	46.6	160	48.77	64.0	19.51

PRINCIPAL FILMS REFERRED TO IN THIS BOOK

A FOR ATOM (U.S.A.; John Sutherland).
ADVENTURES OF PRINCE ACHMED, THE (Germany; Lotte Reiniger).
ALL LIT UP (Britain; Halas and Batchelor).
ANIMAL FARM (Britain; Halas and Batchelor).
AROUND IS AROUND (National Film Board of Canada; Norman McLaren).
ARS GRATIA ARTIS (Yugoslavia; Dusan Vukotic, Copyright Zagreb Film).
AS OLD AS THE HILLS (Britain; Halas and Batchelor).
BALANCE 50 (Britain; Larkins Studio).
BAMBI (U.S.A.; Walt Disney).
BATHROOM, THE (Japan; Kuri Jikken Manga Kobo).
BATTLE AT KERZSENCE (U.S.S.R.; I. Ivanov Vano and J. Norstein).
BEGONE DULL CARE (National Film Board of Canada; Norman McLaren).
BERGÈRE ET LE RAMONEUR, LA (France; Les Gemeaux).
BLINKETY BLANK (National Film Board of Canada; Norman McLaren).
BROTHER ELECTRON ORGAN (Japan; Renzo Kinoshita).
BROTHERHOOD OF MAN, THE (U.S.A.; U.P.A.).
BUTTERFLY BALL, THE (Britain; Lee Mishkin/Halas and Batchelor).
CATALYSIS (Britain; Halas and Batchelor).
C'EST L'AVIRON (National Film Board of Canada; Norman McLaren).
CHAIRY TALE, THE (National Film Board of Canada; Norman McLaren).
CHARLEY SERIES (Britain; Halas and Batchelor).
CINERAMA HOLIDAY (U.S.A.; animation inserts by Halas and Batchelor).
CLOCK CLEANERS, THE (U.S.A.; Walt Disney).
COLONEL HEEZALIAR (U.S.A.; John R. Bray).
COLOUR BOX (Britain; Len Lye).
CRITICALITY (Britain; Larkins Studio).
CURRICULUMACHINE (Japan; Renzo Kinoshita).
DIAGRAM (Poland; Daniel Szczechura).
DIARY (Yugoslavia; Nedeljko Dragic, Zagreb Film).
DIGESTION (Britain; G. B. Animation).
DISGUSTED BINCHESTER (England; Nicholas Spargo).
DOTS (National Film Board of Canada; Norman McLaren).
DRAMA OF THE SON OF MAN, THE (Italy; Luciano Emmer and Enrico Gras).
DRAME CHEZ LES FANTOCHES (France; Emile Cohl).
DUNDERKLUMPEN (Sweden; Per Ahlin for GK Films).
DUSTBIN PARADE (Britain; Halas and Batchelor).
FANTASMATIC (Switzerland; Copyright G. and E. Ansorge).
FELIX THE CAT (U.S.A.; Pat Sullivan).
FIDDLE-DE-DEE (National Film Board of Canada; Norman McLaren).
FIGUREHEAD, THE (Britain; Halas and Batchelor).
FLOWERS AND TREES (U.S.A.; Walt Disney).
FLY ABOUT THE HOUSE (Britain; Halas and Batchelor).
FOX HUNT, THE (Britain; Hoppin and Gross).

FROM RENOIR TO PICASSO (Belgium; Paul Haessaerts).
FUJI FILM CASSETTE TAPE (Japan; Taku Furukawa).
GAS TURBINE, THE (Britain; Shell Film Unit).
GERALD MCBOING-BOING (U.S.A.; U.P.A.).
GERTIE THE TRAINED DINOSAUR (U.S.A.; Winsor McCay).
GOLDEN ANTELOPE, THE (U.S.S.R.; Lev Atamanov).
GRAIN DE BON SENS, UN (France; Jean Image).
GUARDSMAN, THE (Britain; Halas and Batchelor).
HAPPINESS FOR TWO (Yugoslavia; Zlatko Grgic, Boris Kolar, Ante Zaninovic, Zagreb Films).
HEN HOP (National Film Board of Canada; Norman McLaren).
HIGH SPEED FLIGHT—APPROACHING THE SPEED OF SOUND (Britain; Shell Film Unit).
HOOK THE HAWK (U.S.A.; Abe Liss).
HOPPITY POP (National Film Board of Canada; Norman McLaren).
INVITATION TO THE DANCE (U.S.A.; M.G.M.).
IS IT ALWAYS RIGHT TO BE RIGHT (U.S.A.; Lee Michkin/Steve Bosustow Production).
JASPER'S CLOSE SHAVE (U.S.A.; George Pal).
JOHN GILPIN (Britain; Halas and Batchelor with Ronald Searle).
JOHN THE HERO (Hungary; Marcell Jankowitcs, Pannonia Films).
JOIE DE VIVRE (France; Hoppin and Gross).
KOKO THE CLOWN (see OUT OF THE INKWELL).
KRAZY KAT (U.S.A.; Ben Harrison and Manny Gould).
L'IDEE (France; Berthold Bartosch).
LITTLE RED RIDING HOOD (U.S.A.; Walt Disney).
LONGITUDE AND LATITUDE (Britain; GB Animation).
LOOPS (National Film Board of Canada; Norman McLaren).
MADE IN JAPAN (Japan; Renzo Kinoshita).
MADELEINE (U.S.A.; U.P.A.).
MAGIC CANVAS, THE (Britain; Halas and Batchelor).
MALARIA (Britain; Shell Film Unit).
MAN IN SPACE (U.S.A., Walt Disney).
MARATHON (U.S.A.; Commercial by Samuel Magdoff).
MASCOT, THE (France; L. Starevitch).
MEN WHO DID SOMETHING FIRST (Japan; Renzo Kinoshita).
MERLE, LE (National Film Board of Canada; Norman McLaren).
MICKEY'S MOVING DAY (U.S.A.; Walt Disney).
MISTER MAGOO (U.S.A.; U.P.A.).
    MISTER RAGTIME BEAR (first Magoo film).
    MISTER TROUBLE INDEMNITY (first of Mago series).
MYSTERE PICASSO, LE (France; H. G. Clouzot).
NATIONAL COLOUR TELEVISION (Japan; Shinichi Suzuki).
NEIGHBOURS (National Film Board of Canada; Norman McLaren).
NERVINE (U.S.A.; Jack Tinker and Partners Production, Samuel Magdoff).
NEW GULLIVER, THE (U.S.S.R.; A. Ptushko).
NIGHT ON A BARE MOUNTAIN (France; Alexandre Alexeieff and Claire Parker).
NINE LIVES OF FRITZ THE CAT, THE (U.S.A.; Robert Taylor and Steve Krantz).
NOW IS THE TIME (National Film Board of Canada; Norman McLaren).
OF MEN AND DEMONS (U.S.A.; John and Faith Hubley, Copyright IBM).
ONI—THE DEMON (Japan; K. Kawamoto).
OUT OF THE OLD MAN'S HAT (Sweden; Per Ahlin and Gurmar Karlson).
OUT OF THE INKWELL—KOKO THE CLOWN (U.S.A.; Max Fleischer).
PARADISE PERDUTO (Italy; Luciano Emmer and Enrico Gras).
PHANTASY, A (National Film Board of Canada; Norman McLaren).
PIRROT (Takchiko Kamei with Amina; Japan).

POPEYE (U.S.A.; Max Fleischer).
PRAISE BE TO SMALL ILLS (Japan; Copyright EKO Co. Ltd., Tadanariokamoto).
QUARTET, THE (Poland; Copyright Film Polski).
RAINBOW DANCE (Britain; Len Lye).
REASON AND EMOTION (U.S.A.; Walt Disney).
ROMANCE OF TRANSPORTATION (National Film Board of Canada).
ROOTY-TOOT-TOOT (U.S.A.; U.P.A.).
RUBENS (Belgium; Paul Haessaerts and Henri Storck).
RUDDIGORE (Britain; Halas and Batchelor).
SCREAMING YELLOW ZONKERS (U.S.A.; Hurvis, Binzer, Churchill Production, Samuel Magdoff).
SEARCH FOR OIL, THE (Britain; Shell Film Unit).
SHORT VISION, A (Britain; Joan and Peter Foldes).
SISYPHUS (Hungary; Marcell Jankovics, Hungarofilm).
SNOW QUEEN, THE (U.S.S.R.; Lev Artamanov).
SNOW WHITE AND THE SEVEN DWARFS (U.S.A.; Walt Disney).
SPRING-HEELED JACK (Czechoslovakia; Jiri Trnka).
TELL-TALE HEART, THE (U.S.A.; U.P.A.).
THEATRE DE MONSIEUR ET MADAME KABAL (France; Walerian Borowczfk).
TO YOUR HEALTH (Anglo-American; Stapp, Halas and Batchelor).
TRADE TATTOO (Britain; Len Lye).
TRIUMPH (Yugoslavia; Borislav Sajtinac, Neoplanta Film).
TYRANNIE (France; Phillippe Fausten).
UNICORN IN THE GARDEN, THE (U.S.A.; U.P.A.).
UNUSUAL MATCH, THE (U.S.S.R.; M. Pashchenko).
VAIN BEAR, THE (U.S.S.R.; Alexander Ivanov).
VICTORY THROUGH AIRPOWER (U.S.A.; Walt Disney).
WATER FOR FIREFIGHTING (Britain; Halas and Batchelor).
WHAT ON EARTH IS HE? (Japan; Renzo Kinoshita).
WITHOUT FEAR (Britain; Larkins Studio).
WORLD THAT NATURE FORGOT, THE (Anglo-American; M.P.O. and Halas and Batchelor).

GLOSSARY OF ANIMATION TERMS

A ACTION. Movement of characters and objects in order to tell the story.
ACTION SKETCH. Rough drawing indicating a stage, or series of stages, of an action.
AIR BRUSH EFFECTS. Softening the outlines of shapes and forms by means of graduated tones.
ANAMORPHIC LENS. The lens producing the special "squeezed" image necessary for widescreen productions such as Cinemascope.
ANGLE. (a) The assumed viewpoint of the observer (i.e. an imaginary camera) which determines the perspective in laying out a scene. For variety of continuity a different angle is often used in long shots, medium shots and close-ups of the same subject.
(b) Of lens. The angle at the back node of the lens subtended by the width of the gate.
ANIMATION. The art of giving apparent movement to inanimate objects. The word is also used for the sequence of drawings made to create the movement, and for the movement itself when seen on the screen.
ANIMATION BOARD. Adjustable board on the camera rostrum on which the pressure pad, register pegs, panning slides and glass frame are fitted.
ANIMATION CYCLE. Repetition of the same series of animated drawings.
ANSWER PRINT. The finished film offered by the laboratory to the producer for his final acceptance.
APERTURE. The size of the opening in the iris or shutter of the camera, controlling the amount of light reaching the film.
ATMOSPHERE SKETCH. The artist's impression of a location to be developed later for background.

B BACKGROUND. (a) The setting against which action takes place. It may be drawn or painted on paper, with the animation cells placed over it, or drawn on the cell, and placed over the animation paper.
(b) Objects or characters appearing far away from the observer.
(c) Action or sound subsidiary to the main action or sound.
BACK LIGHTING. Back lighting is used on the rostrum camera beneath either a drawing or a celluloid to give a silhouette or a transparent effect.
BACK PROJECTION. An image thrown from the rear to achieve a shot which is amalgamated with a picture in the foreground.
BACKWARD TAKE. Photographing a scene with the camera running in reverse. Frequently used to make a line grow (or "run out") from a

341

point. The line is painted on cell and part of it scraped off for each exposure. When the film is projected forwards, the line will appear to grow. Footprints, trails from aircraft and many other effects can easily be obtained by this method.

BLANK. Cell without a drawing used in photography to keep the number of cell levels constant throughout a scene, to avoid changes of tone.

BUMP IN OR OUT. Causing an object to appear or disappear in one frame of film. A very economical, but often interesting effect, especially if accompanied by a sound.

C CALIBRATIONS. Markings to indicate the movement of a background in panning shots, the movement of the camera in tracking shots, or as a guide to the position of in-between drawings.

CAMERA EXPOSURE OR INSTRUCTION CHART. Frame-by-frame instructions to the cameraman as to the cell levels, background movement and camera movement. Also serves as a guide to other departments.

CAMERA TRACK. Movement of the camera towards, alongside or away from an object.

CELL FLASH. Bright patch on film caused by reflection of light from uneven surface of cell into the lens.

CELL LENGTHS. Celluloid sheets especially prepared in a specific, non-standard size required for a shot.

CELLS. Transparent sheets on which animation drawings are traced. Short for celluloid, but this material is not recommended, as it is highly inflammable. Cellulose acetate or other colourless plastic is usually used.

CHARACTER. Representation of a personality, as distinct from an object (q.v.).

CHARACTER SKETCHES. Drawings defining features, proportions, clothes, etc., of a character, and specifying his type expressions, and reactions.

CHARTS. Camera: frame-by-frame instructions to cameraman as to cell levels, background movement, etc.
Music/Speech: frame-by-frame analysis of sound track, so that animation will synchronize with it.

CHECKING. A rehearsal of the camera exposure instructions with the actual cells and backgrounds prior to photography.

CLEAN-UP. Making finished drawings from roughs (q.v.)
Removing surplus ink, paint, finger-prints and dust from cells before photography. A very important procedure.

CLICK TRACK. A system of rhythmic measurement audible on a sound track for the guidance of the music conductor.

COLOUR KEY. A specimen cell of each character or object painted in colours or tones as a guide to the painting of the whole scene. Designed together with the background.

COLOUR TEMPERATURE. The number of foot candles necessary for colour photography.

CONCERTINA MOVEMENT. Movement transferred from one character or object, or one of their parts, to another.

CONTINUITY. The smooth unfolding of the story of a film, by means of progressive changes of scene.

CUT. (a) Direct change of scene in successive frames.
(b) Removal of frames from the film.

CUT-BACK. Correction of a mistake in photography. A label is photographed stating the number of frames on which the mistake occurs (cut back so many frames) and these frames are shot again. The mistake is then cut out of the print before projection.

CUT-OUTS. (*a*) Things which do not change in outline during movement can be animated by hand as a cut-out drawing. A guide showing the portion of the cut-out for each frame is drawn on cell, and placed on the pegs. The cut-out is put in position, under the guide. The guide is removed and the exposure made. Simple animation can be made with jointed figures in this way.

(*b*) The foreground of a scene which goes over the animation can be drawn on paper and cut out to save an additional cell level.

CUTTING COPY. The complete film made up of separate scenes joined together. It is not usually possible to photograph the film straight through from beginning to end, with all scenes in the correct order. After final adjustments are made to the cutting copy, the negatives are cut and assembled to match it, and a print made without joins.

D DIRECTOR. The person who takes responsibility for what appears on the screen and the methods by which the result is achieved.

DISSOLVE. See MIX.

DOLLY. A movable carriage on which the motion-picture camera is fixed.

DOPE SHEET. (See CAMERA EXPOSURE CHART.)

DOUBLE EXPOSURE. Two different images blended by superimposition.

DOUBLE FRAME. One animation drawing photographed for two frames instead of one. Either halves the speed of a movement or the number of drawings required for an action of a certain time. Triple and quadruple frame animation is possible for very slow movement. In certain circumstances, this technique is more likely to cause optical jitter (q.v.) than single frame.

DOUBLE HEAD PROJECTION. Running picture and sound in synch.

DRY BRUSH EFFECTS. A blurring effect achieved by painting directly on to the celluloid. Used mainly for representing speed.

DUBBING. The mixing of various sound tracks into a single track.

DUBBING SESSION. The merging of mixing at a recording session of separate sound tracks.

E EFFECTS. Sound: sounds accompanying movements to give particular emphasis. Not necessarily natural sounds.

Animation: use of special effects, such as rain, fire, water, in animation.

ELECTRO-PHOTOGRAPHIC TRANSFER. The photographic recording of pictures projected electrically, as through the cathode ray tube of television.

F FADE-IN. The scene gradually appears from black.

FADE-OUT. The scene gradually darkens to black.

FIELD. The area which a lens will include as an image on the film.

FLOW. A term used to describe the smoothness of animation.

FOCAL LENGTH. The focal length of a lens is the distance from the back node of the lens to that point on the optical axis at which parallel rays of light, passing through the lens, converge.

FRAME. (*a*) One image or picture on the film.

(*b*) The background, cell levels, cut-outs, and foreground which are assembled on the pegs under the camera to be photographed so that they will appear on a frame of film.

FRAME GLASS. Sheet of glass used to press down upon the cells under the camera to keep them flat. (PLATEN).

FRAME MASK. Space within which scenes and movement are designed. Its dimensions are the same as the field covered by the lens at a given distance. Registered to the pegs in the same way as animation drawings.

G GATE. Apparatus in camera and projector to hold each frame momentarily still behind the lens.

GUIDE-LINES. (See CALIBRATIONS, CUT-OUTS.)

H HOLD. Photographing one drawing on several frames, so that it appears still on the screen.

HOT-SPOT. Part of the field which is over-illuminated. Appears as an over-exposed patch on the film.

I IN-BETWEENS. Drawings between two key positions (q.v.).

INERTIA. Tendency of a body to preserve its state of rest or motion in a straight line, until that state is changed by external force.

INKING. The tracing of the outlines from the animated drawings on to the cells.

IRIS. A circular opening, which can be made to expand or contract:
(*a*) in the lens, to control exposure; or
(*b*) over the animation, to change the scene.

J JITTER. Uncontrolled movement on the screen caused by faulty animation, tracing or camera work. (See STROBING.)

JITTER, OPTICAL. Flicker on the screen caused by animation which is not sympathetic to the eye. Objects in strong tonal contrast with the background, whose shape does not harmonize with the line of movement, are the worst offenders. Their successive images are retained by the eye longer than normal, which causes an apparent double image. (See STROBING.)

K KEY ANIMATOR. (See KEYS.)

KEYS. Animation drawing of the principal positions in a movement. Keys are made of positions where any part of a figure or object stops, starts, or changes direction.

L LAY-OUT. Design of a scene, including background, characters in correct relative size, colours, cell levels and camera movement.

LAY-OUT SKETCH. The initial composition of the visual content of a shot.

LENGTH OF CELL. Variable sizes of celluloid sheet used throughout the production of animated films.

LIGHT BOX. Animation desk with registration pegs and glass drawing surface illuminated from below.

LINE-TEST. Sequence of pencil animation drawings photographed and projected, usually in negative, to check quality of animation before proceeding with tracing on to cells.

M MARRIED PRINT. The print of a film in which sound and vision are printed together.

MASTER NEGATIVE OR POSITIVE. The final negative or positive print of a film which acts as standard for subsequent prints.

MATCH-LINE. The indication on the lay-out and backgrounds where one object crosses another.

MIX. One scene fades out, at the same time as another is fading in, so that the two scenes are superimposed for a short period.

MODEL SHEET. The specifications concerning the proportions of the characters.

MOMENTUM. The degree of motion in a body, the product of its mass and velocity. Used loosely to describe the tendency of a moving body to remain moving. (See INERTIA.)

MONTAGE. The interrelation of motion-pictures through editing.

MOVIEOLA. An editing machine for the purpose of assembling picture and sound.

MULTI-HEAD PROJECTION. Simultaneous projection on separate projectors of the picture and the sound tracks.

MULTIPLANE. Elaboration of camera rostrum. The animation board has a plate-glass base. A number of glass layers are placed beneath the camera lens at varying distances. These layers are lit and operated independently, and an increased sense of perspective developed.

MULTIPLE HEAD PROJECTION. Projection of sound and visuals from separate machines.

MUSIC CHART. Information given to the animator of the detailed accentuation of the music.

N   N.G. TAKES. Takes which are "no good".

O   OBJECT-ANIMATION. All animation not containing human or animal figures.

OPAQUING. Filling in the tones and colours on the cells.

OPTICAL AXIS. Line passing through the optical centre and the focal point of a lens.

OPTICALS. Mixes, Fades, Wipes, etc., which are made by the processing laboratories on an optical printing machine after the scenes have been photographed, instead of in the camera during photography. Entails making duplicate negatives.

P   PAN. Contraction of *panorama*. In live action, the camera pivots and sweeps round an arc for an horizontal pan, and tilts up or down for a vertical pan. This effect is reproduced in animation by a background sliding past the camera.

PANNING GEAR. The mechanism which moves the camera E-W or N-S, or alternatively the animation board carrying with it the peg-bars.

PARALLAX. The difference between the image seen through the viewfinder and the image recorded by the lens, due to the lens and viewfinder being in different positions. Increases as the subject is brought nearer to the camera. Can be remedied to a certain extent by tilting the viewfinder so that its axis and the optical axis of the lens coincide at the position of the subject.

PEG-BAR. (See REGISTER PEGS.)

PENCIL-TEST. (See Line-Test). PLATEN. (See FRAME GLASS.)

PRE-RECORDING. Recording of sound tracks prior to animation.

PRESSURE PLATE/PAD. A device to enable background and cells to be photographed flat at an overall even pressure. It consists of a sheet of

345

plate-glass in a wood or metal frame hinged to the animation board. Beneath it is a pad of felt or several thicknesses of cloth, blotting paper, or sponge rubber. (See also FRAME GLASS.)

PUNCH. Used to punch holes in animation paper and cells for the purpose of registration.

R REFLECTIONS. Parts of the rostrum, the camera, or their surroundings reflected in the pressure-glass and photographed. Can be remedied by carefully painting all parts with matt black, shielding the lens and the lights and using polaroid screens. Are more troublesome with darker backgrounds and larger fields.

REGISTRATION. To ensure correct position of animated drawings and cells, in their relation to one another, to the background and the camera.

REGISTER HOLES. Holes punched in animation paper and cell corresponding to register pegs.

REGISTER PEGS. Device in the camera-gate to ensure that each frame of film is in exactly the same position as the preceding and following frames.

RE-TAKE. Shooting a scene again.

ROSTRUM. Rigid support for the camera and the animation board, so that they do not alter position relative to each other in an uncontrolled way.

ROSTRUM CAMERA. Apparatus for producing an image on cine-film. Its minimum requirements for animation work are that it must be capable of exposing one frame or film at a time as required.

ROSTRUM CAMERAMAN. The operator of the camera. His duties, apart from photography, usually include changing cells, animating cut-outs by hand and operating the rostrum.

ROSTRUM CAMERA REPORT. A detailed description of a scene, its footage, stock used, processing required, etc., which may accompany the exposed film to the laboratory.

ROTASCOPE. A piece of equipment for transferring a live-action shot to animated drawings.

ROUGH ANIMATION. The first sketches towards the achievement of animation.

ROUGH CUT. The initial edited version of the film.

RUN OUT. In animation: Cause a line or shape to develop from a point. In photography: Exhaust the supply of film in the magazine. This usually occurs in the middle of a scene and means re-taking, so it is advisable to keep an accurate record of all film used from a roll.

RUSHES. The first positive prints from the negative material of the film.

S SCRIPTS. (a) Illustrated: The rough idea of the story, with "thumb-nail" sketches.

(b) Timed, or Shooting: A detailed specification, showing the time of each action, divided into scenes.

SEQUENCE. Any number of consecutive scenes which together express a situation.

SET-UP. Term used for the field covered by the camera at a given distance from the drawings on the animation board.

SET-UP KEY. A controlled drawing to indicate the position of one or more set-ups for the guidance of the rostrum cameraman.

SHOOTING. Photographing.

SHOT. A single picture-unit in a sequence of action.

SHOW PRINT. The final print.

346

SINGLE FRAME. Each animation drawing photographed for one frame only.

SONOVOX. An electronic device for modulating one sound source by another—the most usual application being the modulation of musical tones by voice frequencies.

SOUND CHART. The detailed analysis of the characteristics of the sound.

SPEECH CHART. Information given to the animator of the detailed speech to which the characters must conform with their lip movements.

SPEED LINES. An added impression of speed given by means of lines symbolizing quick movement.

SPROCKET HOLES. The holes on cine-film by which the film is guided through the camera, and held still in the gate. Of exactly the same dimensions, and an equal distance apart. Placed along the edges of 35 mm., 16 mm., and 8 mm. film and between the frames in the centre on 9.5 film.

SQUASH. Distortion of animated forms.

STROBING. The alteration of the speed of an object due to a succession of exactly similar objects being viewed or photographed intermittently. JITTER and JITTER, OPTICAL.)

STROBOSCOPE. An instrument for viewing stroboscopically.

STORYBOARD. Board to display in sequence the action and lay-out sketches of an animated film.

SYMPATHETIC MOVEMENT. Movement on the screen which the eye will readily accept as continuous. (See JITTER, OPTICAL.)

SYNCHRONIZATION. (*a*) Animating so that an action will occur at the same time as its accompanying sound.

(*b*) Matching the cutting copy to the sound track so that a married print can be made with sound on the same reel of film as the picture.

T   **TAKE.** The photography of a scene. Each new take of the same scene is numbered (T.1, T.2, etc.).

TAKE-BOARD. Label photographed at the start of each scene, for identification purposes. States the title of film, number of scene and number of take.

TEST CAMERA. Camera and rostrum (usually of a simple type) used solely for line-testing.

TESTING. Avoiding subsequent problems by making sure of exposure, lighting, focus, before shooting begins.

TILT. The upward or downward pivoting movement of the camera across the screen.

TIMING. Determining speed of action and sound.

TRACKING. The approach to or movement away from the combination of cells and background made by the camera.

TRACK-LAYING. Editing of the sound to the picture.

TREATMENT. Preliminary stage to writing script. Assembling ideas and situations for the film in hand.

TRIP GEAR. Apparatus used in photography which enables single frames of film, or a succession of single frames, to be exposed at constant speed by means of a clutch and an electric motor.

W   **WIPE.** One scene appears to slide over the preceding scene. The dividing line between the scenes can take any desired form.

WORK BOOK. The analysis in advance of the timing and action of the film.

SELECTED BOOK LIST

THE ART OF WALT DISNEY, Robert O. Field (Collins, London 1944).

LE DESSIN ANIME, L. Duca (Prisma, Paris 1948).

ANIMATION, Preston Blair (Walter T. Forster, U.S.A. 1949).

HOW TO CARTOON FOR AMATEUR FILMS, John Halas and Bob Privett (Focal Press, London and New York 1951).

L'ESTHETIQUE DU DESSIN ANIME, Marie-Thérèse Poncet (Libraire Mizet 1952).

THE ANIMATED FILM, Roger Manvell (Sylvan Press, London 1954). (With pictures from the film *Animal Farm* by Halas and Batchelor.)

THE TELEVISION COMMERCIAL, Harry Wayne McMahan (Hastings House, New York 1954). (Revised and enlarged edition 1957.)

HOW TO ANIMATE CUT-OUTS, C. H. Barton (Focal Press, London and New York 1955).

DESSIN ANIME: ART MONDIAL, Marie-Thérèse Poncet (Le Cercle du Livre 1956).

LE CINEMA D'ANIMATION DANS LE MONDE, (Institut des Hautes Études Cinematographique, Paris 1956).

IL CINEMA DI ANIMAZIONE, Walter Alberti (Edizioni Radio Italiana 1958).

STORIA DEL CARTONE ANIMATO, Enrico Gianeri (Editrice Omnia, Milan).

DESIGN IN MOTION, John Halas and Roger Manvell (Studio, London, 1962).

FILM AND TV GRAPHICS, John Halas and Walter Herdeg (Graphis Press, Zurich; Studio Vista, London, 1967).

ANIMATION IN THE CINEMA, Ralph Stevenson (Zwemmer, London; Barnes, New York, 1967). Revised edition.

INDEX